The Beginnin___
of the Danc___

The Bennington School of the Dance

A History in Writings and Interviews

Compiled and Edited by
ELIZABETH MCPHERSON

Foreword by Charles Reinhart

McFarland & Company, Inc., Publishers
Jefferson, North Carolina, and London

LIBRARY OF CONGRESS CATALOGUING-IN-PUBLICATION DATA

McPherson, Elizabeth.
  The Bennington school of the dance : a history in writings
and interviews / compiled and edited by Elizabeth McPherson ;
foreword by Charles Reinhart.
     p.   cm.
  Includes bibliographical references and index.

  ISBN 978-0-7864-7417-2
  softcover : acid free paper ∞

  1. Bennington School of Dance (Bennington, Vt.) — History —
20th century.   2. Dance schools — Vermont — Bennington —
History — 20th century.   3. Dance teachers — Vermont —
Bennington — History — 20th century.   4. Dance — Study and
teaching — Vermont — Bennington — History — 20th century.
5. Bennington (Vt.) — Social life and customs — 20th century.
I. Title.
  GV1587.4.M38 2013
  792.80710743'8 — dc23   2013014206

BRITISH LIBRARY CATALOGUING DATA ARE AVAILABLE

On the cover: Doris Humphrey at the Bennington School of
the Dance, 1941 (courtesy of Charles Woodford)

Manufactured in the United States of America

*McFarland & Company, Inc., Publishers
  Box 611, Jefferson, North Carolina 28640
  www.mcfarlandpub.com*

To my parents,
Clifton and Patricia McPherson

Acknowledgments

There are many people I wish to thank, without whom this book would not have made it to completion. First and foremost, my husband Joel Cadman, who helped process photographs and read through various versions of the book. Secondly, my colleagues Neil Baldwin, Tina Curran, Yaël Lewin, and Carl Paris, who read drafts at different points in my progress. Their advice and edits were insightful, detailed, and helped me shape the book into its final form. Charles Humphrey Woodford also made careful and important edits to an early draft. Dawn Lille graciously interviewed May O'Donnell on my behalf for an earlier project, then allowed use of the interview for this project. Librarians Jeni Dahmus of Juilliard, Joe Tucker of Bennington College, Nancy Cricco of New York University, Dean Jeffries of American Dance Festival, Nova Seals of Connecticut College, Janice Braun of Mills College, Sara Harrington of Ohio University, and Carolyn Parsons of Mary Washington University located documents and photographs and answered many research questions. Work-study students Joshua Boucher, Lydia Chrisman, and Sara Green at Bennington College (sponsored by the college) provided needed support in terms of scanning documents and photos and other essential tasks. Various individuals at Bennington College including Susan Sgorbati (Dance Department) and Nicole Arrington (Communications Office) assisted me in obtaining rights. Many thanks go to the Morrison-Shearer Foundation, Barbara Morgan's Estate, Ann Vachon of the Limón Institute, the O'Donnell Green Foundation, Jeanne Roosevelt, and Lucy Venable, who verified information and/or provided me with the rights to publish information and photos. Grants I received from the American Association of University Women and from Montclair State University were greatly beneficial in the final stages of writing, allowing me to work full-time on the book in the summer of 2011. Finally my thanks to my two daughters Delia and Cora Cadman for their patience, love and support through my absorption with this book.

Table of Contents

Table of Contents

Foreword
by Charles Reinhart

Without the support system for modern dance, established those many years ago in Bennington, Vermont, would modern dance be as successful as it is today? It's an interesting question to ponder.

Modern dance was born during the late nineteenth and early twentieth centuries, as the Victorian age began to wane. In this period when societal restrictions for women were many, four women challenged mores on dance, arts and gender. These four pioneers who gave birth to this American indigenous art form were Loie Fuller, Maude Allan, Ruth St. Denis and Isadora Duncan. At that time, Europe was considered the last word on art, fashion, and sophistication. Thus our four pioneers eventually set sail independently, and ultimately achieved from Europeans the notice and acclaim they sought.

Only one, Ruth St. Denis, became a pathway to modern dance's second generation. Miss Ruth teamed up with Ted Shawn and formed Denishawn, a team effort that produced Martha Graham, Doris Humphrey, and Charles Weidman. From Germany came Hanya Holm and the four became the founding choreographers at the Bennington School of the Dance. (The fifth, second generation choreographer, Helen Tamiris, was not included in the mix.)

Bennington featured some very compelling attractions. You could teach, choreograph and even be paid (sometimes only expenses) as well as escape the grueling summer heat of pre–air-conditioned New York City. The coming of World War II ended the main festival at Bennington in 1942, though workshops continued to exist through 1946, and continued at Connecticut College, New London, through 1947. In 1948 the full festival resumed and remained there till 1977. The festival moved to Duke University in Durham, North Carolina, in time to open the 1978 season, and it continues there currently.

1

In 1934, there were 103 students. Today we have 445 from 19 countries taking American Dance Festival (ADF) classes. There were great dancers then and now, but today we have more of them. Some years ago when told of a new modern dance group, the question was raised as to the quality of the dancers, but today we know they are wonderful.

ADF, whether at Bennington, New London, or Durham has kept its original purpose and philosophy over the years — that is to serve the gifted choreographer through performances, commissions of new work, and restoring past masterpieces. Today, ADF continues to train dancers, provide residencies for companies, inform the public, and encourage the art form's growth and recognition both nationally and internationally. Elizabeth McPherson's book given us many splendid views of the Bennington years, where ADF all began. Our wonderfully rich history is illuminated through personal narratives in the following pages.

Charles L. Reinhart is the former director (1968–2011) of the American Dance Festival, and currently the president of the board and director emeritus.

Preface

In 2008, while working in the Juilliard Archives, assisting archivist Jeni Dahmus in organizing and processing Martha Hill's papers, I discovered a large number of folders of work by Hill and Mary Josephine Shelly on their own Bennington book that was never published. This was for many reasons, including the death of Shelly in 1976 and that another book on the Bennington School of the Dance was published in 1981. In speaking to some of Hill's friends and colleagues, they told me how deeply disappointed Hill was that her and Shelly's book was never completed or published. She seemed to find the task of pulling it all together on her own too daunting with her immense responsibilities directing the Juilliard Dance Division. I began reading through the writing (mostly Shelly's) and was completely captivated. Her writing is descriptive, colorful, and detailed. It seemed imperative that these writings be shared with a larger audience. Shelly's writing makes up the core of this book.

I searched for people who might have been at the Bennington School of the Dance in order to interview them. Finding these individuals was mostly by word of mouth. I interviewed these former participants at the Bennington School of the Dance and turned the interviews into first person narratives. After reading an article I wrote, a representative from the Morrison-Shearer Foundation contacted me to suggest I read Sybil Shearer's autobiography — that there might be material in it that would be useful for my book. One contact led to another, and I located Norman and Ruth Lloyd's son David, who found writing his mother had done on Bennington. I also spent hours at the Jerome Robbins Dance Division of the New York Public Library listening to interviews and pouring over documents. I read through more than seventy transcripts on the Bennington School of the Dance that reside in the Columbia Center for Oral History Collection of Columbia University. These were conducted for the Bennington School

3

of the Dance book that was never published. I made visits to Barbara Morgan's Archives, Bennington College, Mills College, and Duke University (home to the American Dance Festival) to survey their collections of documents and photos from the Bennington School of the Dance. I was contacted by Suzanne Brewer whose aunt Edith Vail had been a student at the Bennington School of the Dance and had taken numerous photos while there. Brewer is overjoyed to have the photos shared with a broad audience.

Little by little, I put the pieces of the book together. I compiled the "Facts and Figures" sections primarily from the advance bulletins and yearly follow-up reports on the school. The narratives that I developed from interviews, along with some extant writings, follow each of Mary Josephine Shelly's write-ups to give a second voice/reflection on the events of each summer. A humorous and insightful group discussion with several key Bennington School of the Dance faculty members (found in Chapter 12) summarizes some significant aspects of the school and follows the chapter on the last summer of 1942. The "Recollections and Anecdotes" in Chapter 13, I drew primarily from the interviews conducted by Theresa Bowers of Columbia University's Columbia Center for Oral History Collection. The interviews were with a broad spectrum of people, from Bennington College faculty to modern dance company members to faculty from universities across the country—very much reflecting the diverse population that participated in the school. Because most of the people interviewed through Columbia University have passed away, there could be few follow-up queries, and the interviews, by arrangement with Columbia, cannot be printed in full. I organized the excerpts or short stories by theme to enhance cohesiveness. My commentary introduces each chapter, and I have also added bracketed asides throughout the book to provide further detail and/or explanation. I sorted, and culled through the more than 200 photographs I collected from Bennington College, Mills College, the Barbara Morgan Archive, Suzanne Brewer, and Juilliard. When I began putting the photographs together with the stories, it was thrilling when by chance a photograph would exactly illustrate a story. All of these pieces, in a mosaic form, have brought the school to life for me, which I trust will hold true for other readers.

Introduction

Since my earliest studies of dance history, the Bennington School of the Dance has held a mythical quality for me, something like Camelot, often described so fantastically as to seem unreal. One of my major goals with this book was to bring the school down to earth by letting participants at the school (faculty, staff, and students) tell the story themselves. The Bennington School of the Dance was early in the history of modern dance. As you read the participants' stories, they reveal that it cemented the foundation of modern dance in a multitude of ways. First and foremost, the school and festival brought leading choreographers together so that modern dance could be seen as a full-fledged movement, not merely individual choreographers working independently. The choreographers began to formalize their teaching and codify their approaches to technique through the necessity of teaching both beginning and advanced students side by side with their competitors. In addition, the choreographers were able to spend the summer away from the hustle, bustle and summer heat of New York City, giving them space mentally and physically to create new work with costumes, music, and sets supplied. Employment or at least living expenses were provided for their company members and accompanists. Childcare, if needed, was made available. These financial arrangements were imperative, as the Bennington School of the Dance coincided with the Great Depression.

For the professional-track students, they could come to Bennington and study a variety of techniques in one place in a pastoral environment and make connections with fellow students as well as faculty members and company members. The physical education teachers, who made up the largest portion of the student population until 1940 and came from all 48 states (Alaska and Hawaii were not states at that time), were able to learn a vibrant new subject to take back to their students and add to the physical education curricula at their schools and colleges. This spread the ideas of modern dance across the country. These teachers also began bringing modern dance choreographers to their schools to teach workshops and perform — thus enhancing what was known as the "gymnasium circuit," allowing for longer, sustained touring for modern dance companies.

And lastly, other summer dance schools and festivals began to model themselves on the Bennington School of the Dance, including what is now called the American Dance Festival and was in many ways a continuation of the Bennington project. The Bennington School of the Dance ended in 1942 primarily because Bennington College, in order to lower amounts of fuel used to heat the college, began closing longer during the winter months and then ran the spring semester far into the summer months leaving little time for a summer program. This was a grave necessity during the World War II years because of fuel conservation and rationing. A few years after the war, in 1948, Hill initiated the New York University–Connecticut College School of the Dance and the American Dance Festival located on the Connecticut College campus. Many of the Bennington faculty were employed there, and the curriculum was similar. This festival still runs today at Duke University.

The impact of the Bennington School of the Dance was immense, and yet it was a school like any school (in some basic ways) with perpetual problems to overcome and faculty and students with differing needs to be accommodated. Each person arrived with their own expectations and left with their individual collected knowledge. There were triumphs and setbacks on a personal and school-wide level. It is in these fine points that I believe the school comes to life. Although I have also documented the "facts" of the school, these vibrant stories are the heart of this book.

1

Bennington:
An Historic Milepost

"It was the historical time and the socio-dynamics of that time that made modern dance possible."[1]—*Alwin Nikolais*

Martha Hill's Recollection

Hill presented the following paper at the American Dance Symposium held in Wichita, Kansas, August 1968. It is an in depth summary of the Bennington School of the Dance that begins with the historical context of dance in the United States, followed by descriptions of the school's founding, continuation, closing, follow-up activities, and legacy.

HILL'S BIOGRAPHY

Martha Hill (1900–1995) was born in East Palestine, Ohio in what she liked to refer to as the Bible belt. She attended the Battle Creek Normal School of Physical Education where she began her teaching career following graduation. In the subsequent years, she taught at Kansas State Teachers College, University of Oregon, and the Lincoln School of Teachers College of Columbia University. Hill studied and performed with Martha Graham while earning a bachelor's degree from Teachers College of Columbia University. In 1930, she began teaching at New York University soon becoming the Director of Dance in the Physical Education Department of the School of Education, and earning a master's degree from NYU in 1941. In addition to her teaching duties at NYU, Hill became a professor at Bennington College in 1932, and the director of the Bennington School of the Dance summer program in 1934. In 1948, she was the founding director of the NYU–Connecticut College School of the Dance, and she became the first

Mary Josephine Shelly (left) and Martha Hill at the Bennington School of the Dance, 1937 (photograph by Edith Vail, a student at the school; courtesy Suzanne Brewer, Vail's niece).

director of the Dance Division at Juilliard in 1951. For her enormous contributions to dance and dance education, she was awarded six honorary doctorates and various other awards.

HILL'S ACCOUNT[2]

"There is a tide in the affairs of men" to be taken at the flood.[3] And such tides occur periodically in the arts. It is difficult now to say whether it was through wisdom, insight, clairvoyance, determination or sheer happenstance that the Bennington School of the Dance and the Bennington Dance Festival were initiated in 1934. Perhaps something of each was in the first planning.

In retrospect, there could not have been a more felicitous falling out of circumstance—the time, the place, the people, for the creation of a new center for the already burgeoning American dance. In *America Dancing*, published in 1936, John Martin wrote "The Bennington School of the Dance, an autonomous department of Bennington College, though still young, is already the most important dance institution in the country."[4] Bennington College had opened in the fall of 1932, in the teeth of a Depression, with the banks closing in the spring of 1933. Its courageous and distinguished young president, Robert Devore Leigh, its enterprising young faculty, and its first class of 85 adventurous students were in the business of way breaking. Part of the so called "progressive education" wave, the College was unique in its liberal views which included

1. high intellectual standards, freed from the dry and stuffy concomitants that had been the pattern for women's colleges;

2. a community organization far ahead of its time; and

3. a full acceptance of the arts, including the performing arts in their active form, as respectable and valued avenues of education.

In that first year, 1932–1933, the College held a symposium on "Modernism in the Arts" in which dance was represented along with the other arts, both in concerts and in discussions. As a comparatively young dance director, it was my responsibility to shape a dance major, one of the first, if not the first, in the country to be free of hampering ties—dance being recognized as an independent art with its own nature, function and disciplines. (At that time, dance in education was commonly allocated to physical education or was occasionally subservient to theatre arts or music.)

9

Dr. Leigh was not only interested, he was enthusiastic in his support and belief in the dance. In fact, in those early years, he participated in my faculty dance group whose membership also included such other distinguished members as the poet Genevieve Taggard, the educator and later to be college president Lewis Webster Jones, the artist Edwin Avery Park, the physicist Paul Garrett, and others. Those were experimental years for everyone at Bennington—learning by doing and by opening one's mind. The College community in a few years saw dance concerts by Martha Graham and her company, Doris Humphrey and Charles Weidman and their company, Hanya Holm and her company, Harald Kreutzberg, Agna Enters, and others, as well as visiting student groups such as that of New York University.

During the 20s and 30s, a flood tide was building in the dance. After an ebb tide of the ballet in America, there were the beginnings of a new wave. There had been limited new theatrical directions shown by Maude Allan, Loie Fuller and Gertrude Hoffman. Emanations from the teachings of François Delsarte and Emile Jaques-Dalcroze were filtering into the ballet and the new dance. Ruth St. Denis and Ted Shawn, pioneer founders of a new American way of dance with their Denishawn Dancers were wielding their many-faceted influence. And over all hung that symbol of freedom — heroic and romantic — Isadora Duncan. Out of this, in the 20s came those divine rebels: Martha Graham in 1923 and Doris Humphrey and Charles Weidman in 1928.[5] Co-existing in Germany, there was to be found part of the same tide of discovery and anti-authoritarian experimentation in the work of Mary Wigman, Rudolf von Laban and Kurt Jooss. Wigman came to the USA on her first solo tour in 1931 and her first group tour in 1933. Young dancers today are sometimes under the misapprehension that the American modern dance was an offshoot of the German dance. Any similarities that might have been evident in the early work of the German and American dancers may be traced to the common influences of the post–World War I period.

In 1930–1931, the Wigman School opened in America with Hanya Holm as its director. The unique contribution of Hanya's method besides its thorough movement training, was its development of space awareness so basic to the German dance and so little brought to a conscious level in the American dance. (We Americans have specialized in a dance of action rather than in a dance of reaction — the dancer as active agent has been

10

our mystique. As a young pioneer country pushing out our frontiers, this is understandable.) Since these early days, Hanya has not only established a flourishing center for American dance in Colorado Springs through the initial imaginative sponsorship of the then-president of Colorado College, Thurston Jynkins Davies [Hill's husband], but has added luster to the American musical show in her fine choreography.

Helen Tamiris should also be mentioned as a theatre influence and pioneer in the modern dance. She made her concert debut in 1927 after a period of theatre dance. After the season of Dance Repertory Theatre in 1930 and 1931, she again returned to a theatre career, first with the active Group Theater, then producing dance works for the Federal Theatre of the Works Progress Administration, and then scoring her great successes with musical shows on Broadway.

In 1932, the New Dance Group and School were established. Those were the days of "Dance as a weapon in the class struggle" and of "Dances of Protest." This was the period of development for Ballet Theatre [launched in 1939] now American Ballet Theatre with its great repertoire. [In 1930], Léonide Massine produced *Rite of Spring* with the Philadelphia Orchestra, with Martha Graham in the leading role and Leopold Stokowski conducting.

There was activity on the West Coast, too. In 1928, Lester Horton was beginning to develop his dance theater. Out of his company have come such outstanding dancers and leaders as Bella Lewitzky, Alvin Ailey, Janet Collins, Carmen de Lavallade, James Mitchell, Joyce Trisler, and James Truitte.

To complete this very brief sketch of a period, certain important centers for dance activity should be noted, all of them in New York City. Antedating the Denishawn School, from 1915 onward, Irene and Alice Lewisohn of the Neighborhood Playhouse, were concerned with dance productions first at their Grand Street Playhouse (now the Henry Street Playhouse), and later uptown at the Manhattan Opera House and the then Mecca Temple which is now New York City Center. From 1925 onward, Joseph Mann of the Student Dance Recital Series presented dance concerts at the Washington Irving High School, moving later to the Central High School of Needle Trades. From 1930, John Martin's course at the New School for Social Research entertained and educated large audiences for the new American dance. William Kolodney, distinguished director of the

92nd Street Y. M. & Y. W. H. A. has always been a true friend of the dance providing a hospitable home for dance education and production from 1935 onward. In addition, there was a Brooklyn Museum series.

In education, the first Modern Dance Symposium (much like the Regional Ballet Festivals of today) was organized for the east at Barnard College in the spring of 1932. Unfortunately this movement did not become a national one. The country was not yet ready for it. (The National Dance Section of the American Association for Health, Physical Education and Recreation which was to prove so strong a champion of the new dance was just then getting under way.)

In addition to all this activity, there was a tremendous schedule of dance concerts at theatres on and off Broadway every Sunday and there was touring in America. (The period of government subsidy for export of America's art was to come later.) And most importantly, there was Bennington's summer neighbor, Jacob's Pillow Dance Festival, the entire project of Festival and School having started in 1930 when Ted Shawn bought land in Lee, Massachusetts.

So, back to the Vermont hills and our Bennington story. I said there could have been no more felicitous time, place, or people for the creation of a new center for the burgeoning American dance. I have given a brief picture of the times and the people. The place? In the green hills of Vermont, the College facing Mount Anthony — a proper summer resort. The facilities: a small theatre; an Armory converted by the theatrical genius of Arch Lauterer into a perfect dance theatre (a stage within a stage, his fins or louvres making it possible to fill or empty the stage in an instant as if by magic, Lauterer magic); many studios, some of them made from the large living rooms of the college houses; but above all, the free and positive atmosphere of Bennington, the style of the place, established with the founding of the College.

President Leigh, Mary Josephine Shelly and I were the planners. Martha Biehle and Natalie Disston and Esther Rosenblatt and others were our helpers. And the faculty was like a Who's Who of the American dance: Martha Graham; Hanya Holm; Doris Humphrey; Charles Weidman; Louis Horst; Arch Lauterer; John and Louise Martin; Pauline Lawrence; Norman and Ruth Lloyd; Bessie Schönberg; the fellows of 1937 who produced original new works for the Festival: Esther Junger, José Limón, and Anna Sokolow; and the fellows of 1938: Eleanor King, Louise Kloepper, and Marian Van Tuyl. There were the resident composers: Wallingford Riegger, Gregory Tucker, Hunter Johnson, Robert McBride, Lionel Nowak, Norman Lloyd, Alex North, and others. Resident poets and playwrights included: Ben Belitt, John Malcolm Brinnin, Howard Moss, Robert Penn Warren, Francis Fergusson and others. Resident photographers included: Barbara Morgan, Thomas Bouchard and others. The new young critic Walter Terry and the established John Martin provided dance criticism.

In 1949, in *The Borzoi Book of Modern Dance*, Margaret Lloyd wrote:

> In some ways, the Bennington years were the most important years in the whole history of the American modern dance. Bennington made possible the first full-length, large-scale productions by supplying the plant and equipment. It provided the artist with a place to live, to dance, to work, and material in large groups to work with. The impress of the festival performances had a lasting effect, not only on those who saw them, but on those who took part in them. In addition to the stir of experiment, the salvos of excitement, the miracles of attainment, shared by audiences and performers, the workshop participants had the inspiration of artistic leadership, the experience of being one of a composite selfhood, bigger than personal selfhood, that was diversified by the size, personality and facility of each dancer.[6]

The Bennington years fall into three periods. First, 1934–1938 with a full curriculum of study in dance and related fields such as music and theatre production and with a festival incorporating a "workshop" idea, the artist-choreographers composing for large groups — augmented concert companies. The second period was a single year, 1939, when the whole school moved to Mills College in California in answer to pleas and invitations from the West Coast to share the riches of Bennington with another section of the country. In the third and final period, up to World War II, 1940–1942, back to Vermont, the Bennington School of the Dance became the Bennington School of the Arts and the Festival was expanded to include music and drama. Otto Luening was the director of music and Francis Fergusson was the director of drama. An expanded offering of classes, seminars and workshops was initiated, and there were many exciting opportunities for collaborations between the performing arts. For example: the production of *The King and the Duke* was a dramatic adaptation by Francis Fergusson, who also directed it, from Mark Twain's *Huckleberry Finn*, with an original score for small orchestra by Gregory Tucker, choreography by myself, sets designed by Holly Bottomley; and the staging of an opera, Mozart's *The Impressario* with multiple collaborations under Otto Luening's direction.

1942 was the final year of the Bennington School of the Arts that closed due to war restrictions on travel and materials and due to the participation of faculty, students, and the College in the war effort. After the close of the School, Bennington College continued its championing of the dance within the restrictions of the war years.

Martha Graham and members of her company and Louis Horst were in residence at the College during late spring of the school year 1943, producing *Deaths and Entrances* (Choreographed by Graham; Music by Hunter Johnson; Set design by Arch Lauterer; Costume design by Edythe Gilfond) in the College Theatre on July 18. Again in 1944, Bennington College provided a place for rehearsal, with reciprocal enrichment of the College program, when Martha Graham and her company and Louis Horst took up residence in the late spring.

Although Doris Humphrey retired from performing in 1945, she continued to teach and choreograph. In July of 1946, Bennington presented the premieres of two new Humphrey works prepared at the College: *The Story of Mankind* (Choreography by Humphrey; Music by Lionel Nowak; Set design by Michael Czaja; Costumes by Pauline Lawrence) and *Lament for Ignacio Sanchez Mejias* (Choreography by Humphrey; Music by Norman Lloyd; Set design by Michael Czaja; Costumes by Pauline Lawrence).

The change in the Bennington College calendar and the impossibility of securing the Bennington Armory as a theatre along with the limitations which were inevitable in the years immediately following World War II made the resumption of the Bennington School of the Arts inadvisable if not impossible. In a few years, however, a new locale was sought. Through that search, Connecticut College at New London was discovered with its new Palmer Auditorium. It had a young president with imagination and courage—Rosemary Park, and a director of summer session — John Moore, who was devoted to the arts. And a director of the dance during the college year, Ruth Bloomer, who had been a student participant in the Bennington years. So, the New York University–Connecticut College School of the Dance came into being in 1948 with Connecticut College carrying on alone after the first few years. [The performance portion of the summer program was called the American Dance Festival, and that name was eventually taken for both the school and performance festival that moved to Duke University in 1978.]

What is our heritage from those Bennington years? First of all, it fed

14

the roots of a movement and not the leaves. Second, it brought into being a body of important dance works, many of them masterpieces and many of them charting new directions for the art. Third, it developed a new generation of dancers and choreographers and of collaborative artists, and it revolutionized the teaching of dance in America. Fourth, it established a broad concept of dance as an art and gave its commitment to freedom for the art and the artist to develop (to "do his own thing" as the current phrase goes), and for the student to live for a while in the stimulating atmosphere of artists "at work" in the production of their art. But over all and above all, Bennington exemplifies the persistence of a dream that became a reality through the collaborative effort of a group of people working together with mutual trust and respect and with continual fresh energy for the future.

2

1933: Planning the School

"I know at the very beginning, I was very fearful because Bennington had been so good to the dance in furthering it in the college, that I was afraid that Bennington would lose its shirt on the summer school."[1]—Martha Hill

Administrative Director Mary Josephine Shelly's recollections for the years 1933–1939 were written in the early 1970s for possible publication in a book about the Bennington School of the Dance that Shelly and Hill were working on in collaboration with Bennington College. In her account that follows and that was to have been a part of the book, Shelly mentions that Hill secured for the school the "greats" of modern dance at that time in the United States—Martha Graham, Hanya Holm, Doris Humphrey, and Charles Weidman. This was imperative in working toward the school breaking even because these choreographers were known quantities. Shelly makes no mention of the choreographer Helen Tamiris who was not included in the Bennington project.

Tamiris had established herself as a significant voice in modern dance by 1934 along with Graham, Holm, Humphrey, and Weidman the four choreographers who would provide the backbone for the school. However, Hill expressly commented about Tamiris: "I think she didn't have as definite, or developed, body of technique."[2] Graham, Holm, Humphrey, and Weidman had begun to codify their technique by the early years of Bennington so that it was taking on form and structure, but Tamiris' concept of technique was perhaps looser. She used less formal structure, choosing to focus more on inner actions and working with the personal movement styles of her students as opposed to molding them in her own vision. Tamiris was also moving back and forth from concert work to commercial work. Hill said, "She didn't just have one aim for her dancing: she was spreading out more, into more fields."[3] (That Charles Weidman was working on Broadway during some of the time period of the Bennington School of the Dance is ignored in terms of its relevance

to Tamiris or that Hanya Holm would work extensively on Broadway post–
Bennington.) In addition, some felt that Tamiris' modern dance concert work
had a more popular leaning to it than the other "modern" choreographers. Hill
herself said that she attended all of Tamiris' concerts and enjoyed them, and
yet the accessibility may have made her look more to other choreographers for
the Bennington School of the Dance. The four choreographers who were chosen
became known as the "Big Four" of modern dance, rightly or wrongly, largely
because the Bennington School of the Dance helped secure their reputations as
such.

Mary Josephine Shelly's Recollection

SHELLY'S BIOGRAPHY

Mary Josephine Shelly (1902–1976) attended the Battle Creek Normal
School of Physical Education where she met Martha Hill. She continued
her education at the University of Oregon earning an A.B., and at Teachers

Mary Josephine Shelly (left) and Hanya Holm at the Bennington School of the
Dance at Mills College, 1939 (photographer unknown, courtesy Special Collections, F.W. Olin Library, Mills College).

College of Columbia University earning an M.A. She taught at Battle Creek Normal School from 1923 to 1924 and was a faculty member at the University of Oregon, the University of Chicago, Teachers College of Columbia University, and New College of Columbia University. Administrative Director of the Bennington School of the Dance/Arts from 1934 to 1941, she joined the regular staff at Bennington College in 1938 as educational assistant to President Leigh and faculty in drama and the arts. She would return to the college in 1946 as director of admissions and then in 1953 as director of personnel. Her years working at Bennington College were interspersed with time in the military. During World War II she was a lieutenant commander in the Women's Naval Reserve, and was also in the WAVES, and then in 1951, she became the second director of women in the Air Force. In 1954, she began working for the Girl Scouts as a public relations director, retiring in 1966. Shelly often went by the nickname "Mary Jo."

SHELLY'S ACCOUNT[4]

What happened at Bennington more than four decades ago has come to seem inevitable. Actually, the launching of the Bennington School of the Dance in 1934 resembled more of an act of faith than a predestined success. At that date, no one even imagined the Festival which later emerged to make dance history of the first order.

Merely to recap the Bennington years so long after they ended would be pointless except for their relevance to the present. The current lively renascence in the performing arts and, specifically the role of an authentically American style of dance in that renascence justify taking a fresh look. Furthermore, while there are many who recall vividly their participation in the School and the Festival, it generated few who know the whole story. I am one of those few, and the view taken here is as much from behind the scenes as in front of them.

Setting the Scene

An art as ancient as dance, like its sister arts, survives by rebirths. Almost unnoticed, certainly unannounced, one came in the 1920s and 1930s. Innovation suddenly began intruding upon a comfortably quiescent classical style, overthrowing tradition from contest to costume, breaking all the established rules, provoking consternation along with excitement.

Full documentation of this period belongs in some other story. Only those aspects that lead to the Bennington years need be briefly recalled.

For all their eventual impact, at first the innovators of modern dance were a scattered if stubbornly persistent minority. Their existence could easily be ignored if one preferred to do so. Avoidance merely required staying at home on intermittent evenings, usually Sundays, and almost exclusively in New York. A comparative few, including dissenters, chose not to do so. Arguments ensued. Intermissions were noisy with them. The verbal brickbats that flew testified to the vitality of the innovation but hardly guaranteed a spectacular future. The opportunities for public appearance were too few and far between, too hard to come by.

By early 1930, another way had to be found to make clear this was no passing phenomenon. A unification of all the components of the new form — artists, students, audience — in one place, for a sufficient time to dramatize its power and its permanence became imperative. Demands, especially in the arts, are seldom met just because they should be. Conventional sources of support — patrons, foundations and the like — existed in plenty. But not for dance, even at that time for ballet, much less for a disturbing upstart. The answer would have to be an unconventional one, which indeed it was.

Origin

The answer might have been found elsewhere than at Bennington College except for two reasons — the character of the college in general, and, in particular, two people who were there.

Innovation had prompted the College's founding, shaped its whole plan and drawn to it people eagerly responsive to such an atmosphere. Among the College's convictions about a true liberal education was that active practice of the arts directed by practicing artists, belonged indispensably to it. The inclusion of dance in this category, not as a beneficial exercise, not as a footnote to art appreciation, but as a serious discipline for body, intellect and spirit came about almost by chance. It was the kind of benign chance that ran through so much thereafter — the meeting of two unselfconscious pioneers. They were Robert Devore Leigh, first President of the College, and Martha Hill, destined to create the dance project that evolved within the College and formed the base for the Bennington School of the Dance and Festival.

Dr. Leigh, appointed four years before the College opened, was commissioned during that interval to rove the halls of academia from coast to coast, scrutinizing the young and the designs their elders had for educating them. He saw much to adopt and at least as much to reject. Among his rejections were didactic teaching and passive learning, hence his evaluation of the arts as exemplars of his view that education should have experiential components. He discovered, as a commonplace of all the colleges he visited, a required program of physical education. Since he planned no such standardized elements in the Bennington curriculum, such a requirement was unnecessary. Dance would be offered but never as other than a free choice by the participants.

At what point and precisely why Dr. Leigh saw dance as belonging in the status of an art, is not clear. Suffice that the results prove the fact. It may have been during a visit to Barnard College during the first of a series of dance symposia held in New York. In any event, at the Barnard symposium he came upon Martha Hill whose dance students from New York University were a participating group. It appears that he found a kindred spirit. Certain it is that Dr. Leigh asked Martha to come up to Vermont to explore the idea of instituting the first independent study of dance as a major field by any American college.

Martha and Dr. Leigh traveled together to the unfinished campus on a windy March day of 1932. Martha demurred. Already busy with a full-time dance program within the Physical Education Department of the School of Education at New York University, Bennington seemed far away, even uninviting. The steel skeleton of the Commons building looked, she said, like a setting for *Mourning Becomes Electra*. Something alien must have risen in the New England wind that day to confront a native-born Middle Westerner. She did not take into account Robert Leigh's persistence. Having found a colleague suited to the purposes he had for the College, he was not to be denied. So Martha came, commuting weekly between the diverse institutions and the two unlike worlds of young students of Bennington College and New York University, bringing to both those first principles that make dancing good.

In the fall of 1933, the College, triumphantly one year old, had been noted by newspapers for its atmosphere of creativity. The summer just past, however, had for all its loveliness — perhaps because of it, seemed to Robert Leigh an open invitation to another venture in tune with the College's spirit. He had already secured from the College Trustees permission to seek an appropriate summer enterprise. Martha Hill, aware of the urgent need to foster the art in which she was immersed, was a jump ahead of him. She had not only a plot, but also a plan. Several other arts — music, drama, writing, had found congenial summer homes in New England. Why not dance and why not at Bennington? So on that Saturday, the two movers and shakers met again in consultation. Just what passed between them at Cricket Hill, the farmhouse of the venerable estate given to the College as its home, remains unrecorded. Suffice to say that the Bennington School of the Dance headed toward reality. Thus the origin.

Before the Beginning

Some alchemy of clairvoyance, wisdom, and sheer determination were at work that day. Dr. Leigh possessed an ever-present little black notebook for such occasions. One could wish it still survived among the archives. Fortunately, the gist of what he wrote is known — Martha's and his specifications for the first center for the modern dance in America, its prospective opening session only months away. Awesomely simple specifications — secure only the then acknowledged greats, not one, but all of them; and figure out how to pay the bills. The first task was Martha's; the second, Dr. Leigh's.

Dr. Leigh's calculations covered the practical matters of approximately four percent return to the College on its investment for the use of the campus; an announcement issued at the College's expense as one in its series of bulletins; and (here both originators must have held their breath) a minimum of forty-three students paying $190 a piece, a visionary maximum of sixty. This would do it. Everyone would be housed, fed, given places to work, and the faculty and staff reimbursed for about what it would cost them to go: get there and back.

Then came Martha's sally forth to capture the greats of the new movement of modern dance. She did it. Wary of the whole notion of so unlikely a rustic hegira, they nevertheless agreed—Martha Graham, Hanya Holm, Louis Horst, Doris Humphrey, John Martin, and Charles Weidman. These were to constitute the so-called visiting staff, none of them for the full season, but each for stipulated intervals. The permanent staff was at this juncture a non-existent entity except for Martha Hill.

Besides the precaution of asking none of the notables to spend more than a short part of the planned six weeks in remote Vermont, students could also enroll for either of two half-semesters or for the whole time. Daring as the originators were, they saw no reason to crowd their luck.

One further embellishment of the plan was the prompt incorporation of the visiting staff into an impressively named Advisory board with Dr. Leigh as chairman; Professor John Coss of Columbia University, a College trustee; Dorothy Lawton, Director of the Music Library and its Dance Collection of the New York Public Library; and Professor Jay B. Nash of New York University. This delicately balanced combination was designed to act in cooperation with Bennington College and the gatherings of the Board. It was not a meaningless invention. In time, and in turn, each member of it did speak vociferously on more than one subject. Also in time, its membership grew substantially.

Dr. Leigh and Martha Hill having committed the College to support a rapidly approaching summer enterprise of substantial size, there had to be found an expanded permanent staff, or else the work to be done between now and July 1934 would evaporate and the enterprise with it. There were as the most obvious items in a list that grew longer as the day grew shorter: (1) An announcement must be written that would magnetize those forty-three, if not sixty, students; (2) Figuring a modest percentage of the take from its circulation, a sizable mailing list had to be drawn up; and (3) The resources of a college campus must be studied for adaptation to an activity heretofore never accommodating anything faintly resembling what did invade that peaceful New England hill-top in the summer of 1934.

As though to certify the rightness of the idea, a solution was at hand. The College then maintained a New York office, concerned with the logical business of raising endowment funds, for the College blithely opened in the [Great] Depression without one. Its presiding genius was Martha Biehle, a scholarly Wellesley graduate, and the idea and practice of modern dance could not have been further from her. Upon her unsuspecting head, descended a large share of the illogical business of helping to get this fanciful show on the road. She served for five subsequent years.

Also lurking nearby elsewhere employed in New York was a confirmed Bennington College enthusiast and ardent modern dance watcher, who lacking any artistic credentials, did qualify as an administrator. By reason of my addiction to the College and the art, I joined the tribe. Thus in that first winter the permanent staff became the two Martha's and myself as, respectively, Director, Executive Secretary, and Administrative Director. Needless to say, job descriptions remained unwritten. We just did whatever came next, and as quickly as we could.

The work, as it had to be for many more years, got done. Five thousand bulletins, eight pages thin, labeled Volume II, Number Three in the College series and entitled "The Bennington School of the Dance at Bennington College, Summer 1934" went out far and wide in February of that year. The bulletin contained a short thesis of its purpose, a listing of "permanent" and "visiting" staff, a program of study to be offered, a substantial amount of practical information about how to arrive and live there, the cost, and a new mysterious sentence. To wit, "work will be done out of doors on the dance green, and in the orchards and garden, whenever possible." Doubtless, this was a lure to fresh air fiends because any lure to secure the magic number would have been considered legitimate at this expectant moment. At any rate, dancing on the green there later was, but not the kind implied by the "work" and no one was ever glimpsed com-

Dancers on the lawn at the Bennington School of the Dance, 1934 (photographer unknown, courtesy Bennington College).

posing an opus among the trees of the small orchard or in the still smaller garden. The permanent staff waited. When the forty-third registration came, they relaxed. When the sixtieth came, they celebrated. With the arrival of the hundred and third, they closed enrollment. There were no more beds.

Available beds, like other available and unavailable accommodations, had already been surveyed. Six of the twelve student houses were allotted to the School, every bedroom to be cleared of the students' personal possessions, living rooms stripped to provide studios. Only later was it learned that dancers resting from their labors leave their silhouettes on bare walls, and they can't be sure about what they are doing without long portable mirrors of which the College originally possessed only one. Where some of the furniture went to be stored, where canvas to protect the walls, and more mirrors came from, no one but an unsung hero, one Murray McGuire, Assistant to the Superintendent of Buildings and Grounds, knows. He and others like him belonged, without proper portfolio, to the permanent staff through all the summers.

A few small living rooms to practice would never be enough. The main dining room of the newly built Commons and old structures bearing the place names of another day, had to be used. The Carriage Barn, the Brooder, the Chicken Coop, became instead Studio this or that. Every nook and cranny was searched for space. The only theatre, top floor of the Commons, an afterthought when the building was put up, betrayed its original function as an attic. But the Commons stage with its small proscenium would serve to incite dancers to use space in unexpected ways. The productive use of the wrong shaped stage, in fact, symbolizes what really took place. Like all the other transposed spaces, the stage contained, over the years, dancing equal in excellence to that housed in the most elegant of accommodations. Improvisation devised the workspaces. Inspiration was to fill them.

And so, at last, planning ended, and reality set in.

3

Summer of 1934:
The Beginning

"All of the publicity for Bennington sounded—when they sent out fliers—as though this would be a lovely vacation."[1]*—Ruth Lovell Murray*

Dates: July 7–August 18, 1934
Location: Bennington College, Bennington, Vermont

Physical education teachers would make up the largest percentage of the population of the school until 1940. One reason is that modern dance was just beginning, and there were only a small number of professional or professionally inclined dance students in the 1930s. A second reason is that the school was running during the Great Depression, and many people were struggling financially. Eva Desca Garnet, a dancer who was a student at the Bennington School of the Dance in 1936, vividly recalls having "to save up a lot of money to go there."[2] The physical education teachers were employed at schools and universities, so had some financial stability and the means to pay tuition for summer programs. They also looked for professional development opportunities, although they often had little understanding of what this professional dance climate would actually be like.

As Murray suggests above, the physical education teachers had been guided by the promotional brochure to envision the summer as an idyllic vacation in which they might learn some modern dance. The intense schedule when they arrived caused more than one to exclaim that they had to go down the stairs by sliding on their "rears" for the first week because their legs were so sore. For the summer of 1934, Hill and Shelly had the foresight to set up the schedule of teachers of modern dance technique so that Hill taught for a week first and then a week at the end, with the professional choreographers in the middle. In this manner, students, many of whom had not studied modern dance before,

25

had an introduction to overall techniques of modern dance to start the session off and a wrap-up of sorts to end. Claudia Moore (Read) suggests that the opening week classes taught by Hill probably reduced injuries significantly because Hill eased students' bodies into learning a new way of moving.[3]

Mary Josephine Shelly's Recollection[4]

The daily northbound passenger train of the Rutland Division of the New York Central was due in North Bennington in the afternoon. It doesn't run anymore, but it did on July 7, 1934. The Up-Flyer, as all good Benningtonians called it, got to North Bennington by tailing behind the Empire State into Albany, being hauled out backwards across the Hudson River, and after a discreet pause, puffing leisurely by itself up the Vermont Valley.

On July 7, 1934, the transportation facilities of the College were assembled under the cupola of the North Bennington station to await the first contingent of the first student body of the Bennington School of the Dance. The students came from half the states in the Union. They did not all come by train. Two even came on a motorcycle. Most, however, came on the Flyer, pouring out onto the platform as excited as the reception committee, but not as scared. It took longer to load the buses than it did to make the short run to campus. Dancers carry a great deal of luggage although they end up in no more than skin-tight work clothes.

As far as could be foreseen, all was in order — a nameplate on every door, advance baggage in place, registration forms ready, vacated faculty apartments prepared for visiting staff. The preparations turned out to be just too neat. To name only a few of the upsets, there were first the students — the youngest fifteen, the oldest forty-nine, some of whom did not care for their roommates. Shuffling of the people and baggage followed. There was the student who, after one night, could not sleep for the sounds of the quarter hours on the Commons clock. Oddly enough, she returned for several summers, being housed farther and farther away from this annoyance but never finding complete peace. There were those who missed the Up-Flyer and had to be fetched from Albany, an event that occurred annually. Then, when the visiting staff came for their stint, there were Charles Weidman's cat and Martha Graham's dogs. The permanent staff, conscious of using borrowed quarters for the summer faculty and guests, worried. But not for long. There was no time for contemplating what would happen after the session ended and regular inhabitants returned, only for what must be done in the next few minutes.

One preliminary to getting down to business in hand had been worded in the first bulletin under the vastly simplified heading "Costume." The bulletin said, "The work costume is a washable leotard, procurable for a small sum at the College store."[5] The purchase was a small matter, but finding the correct fit for a hundred and three human figures definitely was not. Once more good fortune prevailed in the person of Ethel Haviland from Wright and Ditson in Boston who had been contracted to produce the aforesaid washable leotard. Ethel knew from long experience what lay ahead. She had brought not only every conceivable size, but also a consummate patience that lasted through the years of repeating the ordeal of outfitting the School.

Everything fell into place when work actually began. Not everything stayed that way. Fortunately, those responsible for seeing to things never supposed they would. The detailed report of that first session, required each year thereafter by the College trustees from Martha Hill as Director and myself as Administrative Director, differs in notable degree from the picture sketched in the eight pages of the original announcement.

The first section of the report, "The Plan," cites the obligations to be met. In short, the goals of the School were:

1. To offer a program of dance study cross-sectioning the significant contemporary trends;
2. To ensure a diversified student group;
3. To promote audience education
4. To use the College plant for a suitable project in adult education;
5. So far as possible, to operate autonomously of the College, and finally,
6. To be self-supporting and non-profitmaking.

A cross-section the program surely was. Students moved quickly from study of one technique to another, a week of each, with continuity provided by the full session study of fundamentals of movement, composition, music for dance, teaching methods and materials, and a laboratory course in staging and lighting. For this work, to the permanent staff were added Gregory Tucker of the College music faculty, Bessie Schönberg, then study-

Martha Graham with one of her dogs at the Bennington School of the Dance, circa 1934 (photographer unknown, courtesy Bennington College).

ing and assisting Martha Hill at the College, and Jane Ogborn of the College drama faculty. The report also notes the significant departure of extending the time allotted to three courses because their importance became so obvious: Music Related to Movement, Louis Horst; and Dance History and Criticism, John Martin; and the beginning course in dance composition under Bessie Schönberg. Between the lines, the report was really saying that the energy let loose that first modestly planned session had burst its bounds.

On the score of a diversified student body, the cold statistics hardly reflect the diversification. As noted, their age spanned three generations, the report solemnly stating the average age as 27.48 years. The highest percentage were teachers of dance mostly from colleges and universities, with the next largest group being college students. But the true diversification was one of personalities and aptitudes. Doubtless among the hundred and three, no two went back where they came from with an identical sense of accomplishment but, for certain, none went back unaffected by so intense and kaleidoscopic an experience.

The plan promised to promote audience education. The Festival was yet to come. The report included only the understatement that the four artists who came as visiting teachers each presented to the School and the public, a recital. The top floor of the Commons was never after the same place. These recitals were virtuoso performances. If anything was needed to electrify the student audience, these so-called recitals did it. The first season, the public was for the most part from the nearby area but they were bearers of the word as subsequent events proved.

If the plan called for the plant to be used, little doubt remained about that by August when the last student departed. Autonomous administration, however, turned out to be impractical. All manner of College officials and faculty became involved from Myra Jones, the Comptroller and Gladys Leslie, the Librarian, to the President himself. Finally, the School met the requirement to be self-supporting but failed to be non-profit making. The oversubscribed student enrollment, the fact that all but a handful came for the full six weeks, and the capacity audience for the recitals left a balance over expenses of $682.06. The figure speaks for itself.

It might be interjected here that between 1934 and 1940, although roughly only half a million dollars came into and went out of the exchequer, costs were always met, and surpluses if any were minuscule. Today, half a million dollars hardly merits against the cost incurred by all and the grants made to some of the performing arts. To the American form of dance struggling for recognition so long ago, no one even contemplated giving half a cent. Donors were never sought, nor was anything ever spent to secure the voluminous publicity eventually received. Only the people who were there and the Colleges — Bennington for all but one year, Mills for the 1939 session — gave everything they had to give. The gift more than sufficed.

A sudden quiet fell on the Bennington campus on August 19, 1934. Everyone had gone. The first session was over. But so clearly was it only the beginning of something wholly unanticipated that the quiet was scarcely the order of the day for the small corps of planners. Weary but elated, they sat down to contemplate what to do next. Two things for certain — recognize the wide range of ability among students by remodeling the program of study and respond to the irresistible push for more opportunity to create and perform on the part of the artists. When re-planning was completed, the prospectus for the second session bore only one resemblance to the innocent picture drawn so many months before. But neither in 1935 nor thereafter did the essential purposes change. Changes in the plan came because the two originators had unwittingly opened a floodgate and a waiting tide had swept in.

Sybil Shearer (1912–2005)

The following letters by Sybil Shearer were written at the Bennington School of the Dance, summer 1934. The first volume of Shearer's autobiography Without Wings the Way is Steep, *from which the following letters are reprinted, was published in 2008.*[6]

SHEARER'S BIOGRAPHY

Born in Toronto, Ontario, Canada, Sybil Shearer was a leading pioneer of modern dance. After graduating from Skidmore College, she attended the Bennington School of the Dance as a regular student in 1934, as a Humphrey-Weidman Company member in 1935, and as an assistant teacher to Doris Humphrey in 1936. In New York, she worked with the Humphrey-Weidman Company and Agnes de Mille. She made her solo debut at Carnegie Hall in 1941, after which Shearer moved to Chicago. She continued developing her movement style, following her unique creative voice, and working extensively with the photographer, Helen Balfour Morrison.

SHEARER'S LETTERS

Letter 1: 1934 undated, from Bennington, Vermont

To Myself:

Last night out in the storm I was inside of a painting. Everything was colored; the yellow trees, the purple sky on one side. The purple trees and

Sybil Shearer at the Bennington School of the Dance, circa 1934 (photographer unknown, used with permission from the Morrison-Shearer Foundation).

the yellow sky on the other melted always from grays to blues and then to rose and back to yellow so easily and gradually that it made the enormous flashes of purple and red lightning stand out in contrast to the quietness of the constant changes. Then, today, Martha Graham arrived. She came just as the warm haze of the afternoon was smoldering everyone, and like the burning lightning, she made a scene alive with interest. Some who knew her rushed to greet her, and Louis Horst sprang into action as well as his bulk would allow and hurried down the path to see the genius, (which everyone agrees to be a fact) to give her a kiss, and take her hand.

Practice at five o'clock was disturbed several times when Miss Schönberg ran to the balcony to see what was going on below. Laughing with her soft accent she explained to us it was only Martha Graham who could make her so excited.

Bessie Schönberg at the Bennington School of the Dance, circa 1934 (photographer unknown, courtesy Bennington College).

Miss Schönberg is delightful. She has a long nose, slightly tilted upward, a narrow girlish smile, a pale freckled face and long brown crinkly hair which she does in two braided knots at the back or in one band wound about her head. She is rather large and well-shaped and quite freckled. Her gradual departure from an interesting reserve is making her a far more interesting person to me, and I dearly hope to become friends with her before too long.

I have discovered today that it is not the same thing to be a solo dancer and a creative dancer any more than it is the same to be a concert pianist and a composer. They both acquire the same fame perhaps but how much more desirable to be creative! Everyone has told me that I have something the other dancers around me have not, and I imagined it could only be creative talent. I find I was mistaken about my confusion of these two talents, but I have yet to discover my further possibilities and not lose hope. Hope and work only will do it.

Letter 2: July 19, 1934

[*Written to Miss Champlin who was a professor at Skidmore College.*]

Dear Miss Champlin,

You wanted my first impressions of Bennington, but they are so far away now, almost a week and a half, that I feel very settled. The first week of dancing, however, was marvelous and I went at everything with such gusto. I thought I was the most happy person on earth for the first little while, but Martha Graham's technique has somewhat dimmed my enthusiasm. It is almost like trying to learn ballet in one week. It seems quite futile and a little boring to do the same thing every day.

Miss Graham treats us as though we are morons. She talks baby talk to us, and I hate to be told that I look like an "anxious female" when I stick my chin out because another part of my anatomy hurts, and when I am not in the least sentimental about self-expression. She takes for granted that we have all spent every precious moment before meeting her in the soft, flowing movements of calling to the skies or the balloon of our self-expression. I am trying to be just to her because of your advice, but it is hard to see everyone sticking our chins out in admiration of Miss Graham's genius, and remain unaware of my own reactions.

I met Fannie Aronson the first day, and I like her very much, but I do not know her well enough yet to talk to her or draw her story out. In fact I have a feeling that I do not have the power to draw anyone out despite the fact that I am intensely interested in them. I was talking to Fannie this evening in her room, and then went for a walk in the long dark grass behind the college. She feels that Bennington is anything but loose, and that Perry-Mansfield was much more sociable and creative in its atmosphere. Certainly it is very difficult for me to become acquainted with the older people who are interesting because they are satisfied with their own group. Those who welcome you with a sickening smile are the most forlorn and devitalized gym teachers who are here not only to learn the latest methods in the dance, but also to watch others rather than create themselves.

Miss Schönberg is a particularly delightful person, but one with whom it is most difficult to become acquainted because of her reserve; though with the older people she has a most hilarious good time. I have made no attempt to know her, but this next week Miss Graham will be gone and I hope most of the great desire to play up to her among the elite and the administration will be gone as well. Miss S. seems to think she is particularly wonderful. Doris Humphrey will not create such adoration, I know, because Louis Horst and his devotion to Martha are an enormous influence on the community.

I know that as far as technique and advancement are concerned, I have done as well as anyone (because of my adaptable body) but I have become rather involved mentally as to whether I have any creative ability. And we are all terribly worried about Mr. Horst's class Movement & Music. If I could only come to know the worthwhile people! I feel so insignificant! The only way to get over that is to make my work noticeable, for I am afraid my personality is lacking in the demanded exuberance. Marion Shang [Streng] of Barnard and Marian Knighton of Sarah Lawrence are the two most popular people on campus and they are both at least 30 or 35.[7]

Letter 3: July 21, 1934 from Bennington, Vermont

Dear Miss Champlin,

Your letter arrived yesterday, and I was glad to hear from you. No, I have not yet read *Nijinsky* [*Diary of Vaslau Nijinsky*], though someone gave me the money to buy it for graduation.

Last night I saw an entirely different Martha Graham and, you will be glad to know, a more pleasing one. She gave her recital and I can assure you — she is a genius. I have absolutely never seen anything so moving. She did her great and famous solo *Dithyrambic*. The one which moved me the most, however was the first of her *Frenetic Rhythms, Wonder*. She is such an entirely different person in action than she is on the classroom floor. Her designs were perfect and her movements superb. I cannot imagine anyone dancing with more life and vitality! She is just what I have been imagining as perfect for the past several years, and anyone who wishes to be as splendid as she is will have to approach dancing from another side, for I am sure that she has gone the limit in her style.

I still have no desire to study with her, for I am afraid of her dogmatism, though I would like to be proficient in her technique. It is all-embracing, and she used the same basis as ballet.

Her costumes were marvelous in color and in shape. She makes her own, and 15 minutes before the curtain opened she was sewing the last stitches into her newest creation. The lighting in *Lamentation* was very interesting. There were three medium spots, one from each side, and one from directly above. They cut three streams of light across the black velvet curtains, focusing themselves on the dancer wrapped in a light purple jersey, which was a long rectangular piece of tubing that encircled her entire body including her head. Her movements were all within this cloth, and she was seated upon a box.

But I fear that you will never arrive at the end of this letter as it is, I feel it is time to stop.

Fannie wants to be remembered to you.
With very much love,
Sybil L. S.

Letter 4: July 30, 1934 from Bennington, Vermont

[*Barbara Brown was an actress friend.*]

Dear Barbara,

Before I left your home your aunt Edith told me that you were in a summer stock company. I was so thrilled that I wanted to congratulate you immediately, but my rushed plans prevented it until now. Please write and tell me what plays you are putting on and all about the company, etc. I am anxious to hear.

35

I shall surely be in New York this fall, perhaps around the first of October. So I shall see you. It is a dreadful job trying to decide where to live and what to do exactly. I have pretty well decided to be a dancer, however, and am thinking of applying for a scholarship at the Neighborhood Playhouse where Martha Graham and Louis Horst teach. If you know anything about it, I would love to have you tell me.

Doris Humphrey is here at Bennington this week and is a very good teacher. I would like to get into her understudy group and eventually into the group, as they seem to have the faculty of making a little money whereas Martha Graham's group is as poor as possible.

Have you ever seen Graham dance? I did for the first time this summer and I find she is marvelous, really a genius. I ushered at her recital. It was unbearably hot and all her costumes are woolen, but despite discomfort on both sides, the audience was captivated by the dancer.

Quite a crowd came over from Putney, a summer theatre near here, and we had seats in the middle reserved for them. One very eccentric little man tried to leave his little round beret on one of the front seats to save it for himself. When I told him he must sit in his own seat, he looked like a disconsolate boy with his lower lip sticking out. He came to me at every intermission and begged to sit in the front row (all seats were taken). I told him he could sit on the floor, because he just had to see (he lisped) Miss Graham's comedy interpretations. Later I saw him usurp someone else's seat, but I decided to let him alone because he was sitting so straight and looking so intent.

It is just grand to be here for six weeks doing nothing but dance and listening to music.

Most sincerely,
Sybil L. Shearer

Letter 5: July 31, 1934 from Bennington, Vermont

Dear Miss Champlin,

Here it is the fourth week already and Hanya will be here on Sunday. You must come while she is here!

Everything has been going well for me. I am taking a tonic steadily to keep up the strenuous work. But the time has flown so that I feel as though I have accomplished nothing. I believe that I have received the most benefit from Louis Horst's class. It is a constant creating of dances, which is agony in itself but great joy at the same time.

I had a long talk with Louis yesterday. I began by asking him about the Neighborhood Playhouse. We agreed that it was far better to be successful artistically than successful financially (so I guess I shall have to be contented with poverty all my life).

Louis is a very nice person, for he said if I did not like New York, I could go back home and teach. I said vehemently, "Never!" and he smiled. Now we always smile when we see each other. I am going to do a rigadoon tomorrow and I am just praying that he will see something good in it.

With much love & remember me to your mother.
Sybil L. S.

Letter 6: August 7, 1934 from Bennington, Vermont

Dear Miss Champlin,

Your splendid letter arrived yesterday morning, and I have been in very high spirits ever since. In fact I cut all my morning classes and went out into my favorite field to create a dance called "Enthusiasm." Flock by flock, the cows, horses, and sheep came from their different pastures and looked over the fence at me. The cows were the most impressed, because they find it so hard to move quickly (the dance was a failure for Louis was in a bad temper and said it was animation not enthusiasm, so I am trying a different approach for tomorrow).

You asked if I was convinced of the virtues of the modern dance. I can frankly say — not until yesterday. In fact I wrote and mailed a letter to the School of American Ballet over the weekend.

As to going to Skidmore, I can think of nothing more inspiring than being near you. But as long as dancing remains in the hands of physical eds I have no chance. If, however, it should become part of the dramatic major, there would be room for expansion and real work. Of course, my aim has always been for dancing rather than teaching, but I am beginning to realize more and more that one needs nourishment in order to dance, and that just dancing does not earn nourishment. I have a positive horror, however, of getting into a rut the way Miss Hill has. She cannot do any technique but her own, and that can be summed up in side pulls and suspensions. I would want to keep working and creating continually and your suggestion sounds splendid. I am really very thrilled to think that you want me.

As to Humphrey, I have almost forgotten her. She is so put in the shade by Hanya, and to think that last week I wrote to my friends that I had hopes of entering her understudy group! I don't yet know whether I am jumping at conclusions or whether the existing sensation of having found something new will extend into my real aim.

My best love to you,
Sybil L. S.

P.S. I also found out about sentimentality, which has bothered me enormously. It is a kind of self-expression without form. It is all right in itself and in the private life of an individual, but not all right in public because it is formless and artless. This is what Louis and all the modern dancers have been trying to tell us when they used the word *distortion* as a means to art.

SLS

Facts and Figures, 1934

Total Enrollment of Students: 103 (does not include company members)

Select Students

Fannie Aronson, Ruth Bloomer, Berta Ochsner Campbell, Delia Hussey, Virginia Keene, Marian Knighton (Bryan), Naomi Lubell, Claudia Moore (Read), Ruth Murray, Barbara Page, Helen Priest (Rogers), Sybil Shearer, Marion Streng, Marian Van Tuyl, Mildred Wile

Faculty and Curriculum

Martha Hill, Director

Mary Josephine Shelly, Administrative Director

Modern Dance
Taught by Martha Graham July 16–20
Assistant — Dorothy Bird (Villard)
Accompanist — Dini de Remer

Taught by Charles Weidman July 23–27
Assistant — Gene Martell
Accompanists — Pauline Lawrence and Jerome Moross

Taught by Doris Humphrey July 30–August 3
Assistant — Cleo Atheneos
Accompanist — Jerome Moross

Taught by Hanya Holm August 6–10
Assistant — Nancy McKnight (Hauser)
Accompanist — Harvey Pollins

Fundamental Techniques
Taught by Martha Hill
Assistant — Bessie Schönberg
Accompanists—Ruth Lloyd and Norman Lloyd

Dance Composition
Taught by Martha Hill
Assistant—Bessie Schönberg
Accompanists — Ruth Lloyd and Norman Lloyd

Music Related to Movement
Taught by Louis Horst
Assistant — May O'Donnell
Accompanist — Dini de Remer

Teaching Methods and Materials
Taught by Martha Hill

Music for Dancers
Taught by Gregory Tucker

Production
Taught by Jane Ogborn

Dance History and Criticism
Taught by John Martin

Practice
Supervised practice taught by Bessie Schönberg

Select Concerts, Demonstrations and Events

July 11
Barn Quadrangle

Lecture-Discussion on the Modern Dance by John
 Martin

July 15
Lounge

Discussion of Current Events

Thomas Brockway of the Social Studies Division of
 Bennington College

July 18
Barn Quadrangle

Lecture-discussion on the Modern Dance

Martha Graham

July 20
College Theatre

Martha Graham as a Soloist, Accompanied by Louis
 Horst

Dance Prelude
Choreographed by Martha Graham
Music by Nikolai Lopatnikoff

Lamentation
Choreographed by Martha Graham
Music by Zoltan Kodaly

Dithyrambic
Choreographed by Martha Graham
Music by Aaron Copland

Satyric Festival Song
Choreographed by Martha Graham
Music by Imre Weisshaus

Ekstasis—Two Lyric Fragments
Choreography by Martha Graham
Music by Lehman Engel

Primitive Canticles—Ave and Salve
Choreography by Martha Graham
Music by Heitor Villa-Lobos

Sarabande—from Suite *Transitions*
Choreography by Martha Graham
Music by Lehman Engel

*Frenetic Rhythms—Wonder, Renunciation, and
 Action*
Choreography by Martha Graham

Music by Wallingford Riegger
Voice — Norman Lloyd

Harlequinade — Pessimist and Optimist
Choreography by Martha Graham
Music by Ernst Toch

July 22
Lounge

Discussion of Current Events
Thomas Brockway and Dimitry Varley

July 24
Lounge

Lecture-discussion on "The Bennington College
    Plan"
President Robert D. Leigh

July 27
College Theatre

Doris Humphrey and Charles Weidman, accompanied
    on the piano by Vivian Fine and Pauline Lawrence

Three Mazurkas
Choreographed by Doris Humphrey
Performed by Doris Humphrey and Charles Weidman
Music by Alexandre Tansman

Counterpoint No. 2
Choreographed and performed by Doris Humphrey
Music by Harvey Pollins

Memorial — To the Trivial
Choreographed and performed by Charles Weidman
Music by Jerome Moross

Rudepoema
Choreographed by Doris Humphrey
Performed by Doris Humphrey and Charles Weidman
Music by Heitor Villa-Lobos

*Two Ecstatic Themes — Circular Descent and Pointed
    Ascent*
Choreographed and performed by Doris Humphrey
Music by Nikolai Medtner and Gian Francesco
    Malipiero

Kinetic Pantomime
Choreographed and Performed by Charles Weidman
Music by Colin McPhee

Alcina Suite
Choreographed and performed by Doris Humphrey
    and Charles Weidman
Music by George Frideric Handel

July 28 Lounge	Analysis and Demonstration of Musical Forms Norman Lloyd

July 30
Lounge
	Lecture-discussion on "Physics Applied to Human
	    Movement"
	Paul Garrett of the Science Division of Bennington
	    College

August 1 Lounge	Lecture-discussion on the Modern Dance Doris Humphrey
August 2 Sculpture Studio	Sculpture Show Simon Moselsio of the Art Division of Bennington College

August 3
College Theatre
	Gregory Tucker, Piano Recital
	Concerto in D Minor by Antonio Vivaldi, *Thirty-Two*
	    Variations in C Minor by Ludwig van Beethoven,
	    Etudes Symphoniques by William Schuman, *Two*
	    Dances from L'Amour Sorcie by Manuel De Falla,
	    Sonatina by Carlos Chavez, *Fourth Sonata* by Leo
	    Ornstein

August 4 Science Lecture	Showing of Moving Pictures Ruth Bloomer and E. Crosby Doughty
August 5	Show of Paintings by Jane Welling
August 5	Movies taken of the school by Kenneth Bloomer and E. Crosby Doughty
August 5 College Theatre	Piano Recital — J.S. Bach, Organ Fugues for Four Hands Ruth and Norman Lloyd
August 6 Science Lecture Room	Illustrated Lecture on "The Background of Contemporary American Painting" Jane Welling of Wayne University, Detroit, Michigan

August 8 Barn Quadrangle	Lecture-discussion on the Modern Dance Hanya Holm
August 10 College Theatre	Hanya Holm and Students of the Bennington School of the Dance

Demonstration of Techniques from the Modern
German Dance
By Hanya Holm and Selected Group of Students
Assisted by Nancy McKnight (Hauser)
Harvey Pollins, Pianist

Compositions under the Direction of Martha Hill
Assisted by Bessie Schönberg
Pianists: Ruth and Norman Lloyd
Choreography by students: Ellen Adair, Ruth
Alexander, Ruth Bloomer, Christine Dobbins,
Charlotte MacEwan, Ruth Murray, Berta
Ochsner

Compositions based on Pre-Classic Forms under the
Direction of Louis Horst
Assisted by May O'Donhell and Dini de Remer
Choreography by students: Betty Fleming, Marie
Heghinian, Berta Ochsner, Marian Van Tuyl

August 11 Studio 1	Demonstration Dance Lesson Margaret H'Doubler, University of Wisconsin, Guest Teacher
August 11 College Theatre	Maude Adams with Company in *Twelfth Night*
August 12 Lounge	Discussion of Current Events Dimitry Varley
August 12 Lounge	Lecture on "Modernism in Poetry" Genevieve Taggard of the Literature Division of Bennington College
August 13 Science Lecture	Showing of Moving Pictures from the Dance Department of the University of Wisconsin; courtesy of Margaret H'Doubler

August 14 Commons Practice	Community Sing Ruth and Norman Lloyd, Accompanists
August 15 Lounge	Round Table Discussion on "The Future Plan of the School" President Leigh and members of the School
August 16 Commons Theatre	Recital — Discussion of Music from Pre-Classic to Modern Louis Horst Solo Dance, May O'Donnell Review demonstration of Completed Work from Mr. Horst's class in Music Related to Movement
August 17 Lounge	Symposium on the Modern Dance John Martin, leader

4

Summer of 1935:
The Workshop Began

"What the artist needed most was a place to develop his work for the future season."[1]*— Martha Hill*

Dates: July 5–August 17, 1935
Location: Bennington College, Bennington, Vermont

After the first summer, Hill and Shelly developed their idea to provide more support for the choreographers in terms of production. They devised what they called "the five year plan" in which each of the artists-choreographers would present choreographic premieres, produced by the Bennington School of the Dance, in one of the following three summers — Humphrey and Weidman would share a year. In the summer of 1938, all four artists would have new works produced. They began alphabetically according to last name with Martha Graham being highlighted in the summer of 1935. The choreographer designated for each particular year taught a "workshop" for which students were especially chosen for their aptitude and interest in professional careers in dance, thus creating two levels of instruction: the General Program and the Workshop Program. Several students in the workshop programs would eventually join the dance companies of one of the choreographers represented.

Bennington College faculty member Arch Lauterer, by many accounts, was a genius of stage design. In the summer of 1935, he literally transformed the Vermont State Armory. It already had a very small stage, but he expanded that by using most of the main floor as performance space, and seating most of the audience in the balcony. On stage, he used "fins" instead of traditional curtained legs. This revisioned Armory was first used for Martha Graham's performances in 1935 and became an integral component of the festivals of subsequent years.

Mary Jo Shelly's Recollection[2]

Everything expanded. No one any more waited for a sixtieth enrollment. A hundred were scheduled and a hundred and twenty-eight were
admitted before enrollment had to be closed. And, sign of the future, two
men came as students. The cost went up ten dollars. The relationship of
the School to the College became more formalized as an autonomous unit
with a special Board of College Trustees overseeing matters in general and
making honest women of the Director and Administrative Director by
legally appointing them on recommendation of the President. The School
now had its separate Advisory Board with the College President still as
chairman. These actions reflected no friction. Doubtless some of the
Trustees were as surprised as everyone else at what had transpired. But
Trustees of the College like this one took surprises in stride. And everyone
concerned felt more comfortable, especially since the Directors had recommended and received approval for not just one, but four more sessions.

These formalities remained invisible to the participants in the 1935
session. Evident to them were the two distinct, interrelated divisions within
the curriculum:

- The General Program — an enlarged and refined version of the 1934
  plan
- The Workshop Program — first in a projected series of four — fore-
  runner to the Festival.

Together these answered the two pressing needs faced after the preceding
summer. The evolution to two programs was a solution found almost spontaneously, requiring less a hard search than the application of common
sense to the self-evident. They appeared to be more right than appeared
at first glance. The broader scope of the General Program gave room for
everyone in it to work at the proper pace. The Workshop Program
promptly belied its modest title by exploding into such dancing that the
small College Theatre clearly could not contain it. Somewhere a theatre
of adequate dimensions had to be found. The plan called for the Workshop
to be directed in turn by each of the four artists, beginning with Martha
Graham in this 1935 session. The workshop group, the 1935 announcement
stated, "will be composed of ten resident members of Miss Graham's Concert Dance Group and a limited number of students of advanced ability

46

in modern dance, not otherwise members of the School during the current session, who will be admitted for the period of six weeks as members of the concert group."[3] (In the end, there would be twelve members of Graham's Concert Dance Group.) Anyone who judged themselves qualified could apply. Miss Graham and the Director would decide. Of the seventy applicants, twenty-four met the test.

To underscore the significance of the Workshop Program is by no means to minimize the worth of the General Program. Each gave fresh impetus to the other. More importantly for the long run, together they began building a base for modern dance, far beyond the confines of the school, one stretching across America and beyond.

From the outset, there had been the possibility that some students might want academic credit transferable to their own institutions. A proper record form existed. Over the years, a bare handful of these ever came out of the files. Such paraphernalia as traditional credit hours, examinations, prescribed courses of study, would have been irrelevant. Sheer enthusiasm was enough. Both during the whole first session and in the General Program thereafter, students freely chose the kind and amount of work they would do. Any restrictions, like success or failures, were the students' own doing. The cry from students for genuine participation in shaping their own education was never heard at this school.

In the announcement for the 1935 session, a short section appeared entitled "Additional Program," the first paragraph being called Concerts. It stated, "The Concert Series of the 1935 session arranged primarily for the members of the School without admission fee, will be open to a limited number of the public. The series will include: a concert by Tina Flade; a lecture by John Martin; a joint concert by Doris Humphrey and Charles Weidman; and a third concert by Martha Graham and the workshop group."[4] (Tina Flade replaced Hanya Holm who was on leave for this season.) This was a marked change from the so-called recitals of 1934. No words ever written fell farther short of describing what happened.

If the inadequacy of the Commons Theatre had been demonstrated earlier, this time the evidence from the first three weeks was overwhelming. The "limited number of the public" turned out to be a mass assault. Students wanting to enroll had been for two seasons turned away for lack of housing. Now an audience wanting to be in on the excitement had to be cut off for lack of another inch into which to squeeze seating. And why

47

not? The consciousness of a parallel move toward a new form in Germany led by Mary Wigman had not been lost on the American public. They recognized the name Hanya Holm from the first session. They wanted to see another representative of the same school, Tina Flade. As for hearing what John Martin (dance critic of the prestigious *New York Times* and at that writing the only fully authorized dance critic extant) had to say about "The Ancient Art of the Dance," one couldn't afford to miss that.

Then there were Doris Humphrey and Charles Weidman and their professional company brought to Bennington for the occasion. That evening's program included among the six numbers, a trilogy to be completed later. No wonder that with the clamorous demand to be in the audience for such a series, that weeks before the fourth event was scheduled, everyone involved with staging the series was less delighted at the pace of things than anxious about how to cope with it. Driven by necessity and blessed with great good fortune, there came a historic moment, not merely in the story of the Bennington years, but in the whole story of modern dance. The great good fortune was the presence of a person not even listed among the dance faculty. He belonged to the College Drama Division. His name was Arch Lauterer.

Arch not only knew the Commons Theatre intimately, he had also looked hard at modern dance which he considered to be the most promising form of theatre he had come upon in his career as a stage designer and director. At some undated time, he had known also what would surely happen at the School. The miracle came in

Arch Lauterer at the Bennington School of the Dance, 1938 (© Barbara Morgan, Barbara Morgan Archive).

48

his discovery of what to do about it. There existed in the town of Bennington, four miles away, the Vermont State Armory, an unadorned rectangular brick building with a large open floor, a three-sided shallow balcony, and a stage one-tenth the size of the Commons stage.

Arch saw it differently. The tiny stage interested him only as an incidental space within the theatre he had already sketched in his mind while prowling around this unlikely structure. He then transferred the sketch to paper. Here, he proposed, was where Martha Graham and the Workshop Group and all the workshop groups thereafter would perform. The balcony would serve and so would temporary seating at floor level. There would be no curtain, only fins angled along each side of the open space for instantaneous entrances and exits. The lighting would come from equipment hung overhead from the bare metal beams, unconcealed but unobtrusive because all focus would be upon the dancing.

The most succinct account of the whole incredible sequence of events is to be found in a section of the program for the two performances that took place on August 14 and 15, 1935. It read:

> *Panorama*, the first Workshop production, with Martha Graham as choreographer and solo dancer, is the result of six weeks of work with the thirty-six dancers of the Workshop group composed of twelve members of Martha Graham's Dance Group and twenty-four students of the Bennington School of the Dance. The choreography for *Panorama* was begun by Martha Graham on July 15. The technical work by Jane Ogborn, the composing of the music by Norman Lloyd, and the construction of the mobiles by Alexander Calder were begun the following week. The designing and execution of the setting and lighting by Arch Lauterer have been carried out in the final half of the session. The music has been directed by Louis Horst. Students under the direction of Jane Ogborn have assisted in the technical work.[5]

Panorama, the climax of the program, was not the only work for which technical provisions so passingly mentioned had to be made. It was preceded by *Celebration*, danced by the Concert Group; as well as *Sarabande* from the suite *Transitions*, and *Frontier* from the suite *Prospectus*, both of which were solos danced by Martha Graham. All had of course been performed earlier, but probably never since danced under quite the same circumstances nor to a more intent audience.

In addition to thinking about the stage and the seating-cost, there was also transporting every needed item (down to the last thumbtack) from the campus to the Armory, establishing dressing rooms, and creating a box office. The music obviously had to be played on something other than the Armory's one rickety upright. And before any of the preparations could so much as begin, there was the Vermont contingent of the National Guard to be reckoned with. It was, after all, their Armory. Furthermore, while it had often accommodated appropriate civic events, no one had ever proposed to turn it into a theatre for, of all things, dancing. Also, August was the season for the annual summer encampment of the National Guard, and the Armory was the place where preparations were made for it.

Negotiations with the commanding officers of these latter-day Green Mountain Boys fell to me. Nothing even faintly suggested the disruption that would ensue. Negotiations in Vermont take time. They are conducted at proper length, full of suspenseful pauses indicated by the unpronounceable New England "eyah," signifying not necessarily a "yes" or a "no," only with luck, a "maybe." Payment was not in question. A federal facility could not be rented. It could only be occupied. And occupied it was. The Guard would be off to camp. No one else had a use for the place in the interim. Might as well let the new college (the commanding officer disbelieved in the very existence of the School) use it. So into my nervous waiting hands came the precious keys. We were in.

There was little time. The Guard would take off only days before the opening night. A magical part of Arch's gift was the ability to figure time within the half hour as he invariably figured expense within a fraction of the last ten-penny nail. His figuring included driving himself to the limit and inciting every co-worker to do the same. The setting and lighting — a large understatement of the labors ahead — could be left to him and Jane Ogborn and those students who helped as an unpremeditated part of the study of dance production. Arch never seemed to worry. Only the angle of an errant lock of black hair ever betrayed the pitch at which things were having to move. Other matters belonged to the list of worries of its Director and her helpers. Somehow, star dressing rooms were rigged backstage; the basement arranged for the company who would arrive at stage level via an outdoor staircase; a box office provided by a providentially located half door to a small room off of the miniature lobby. Even the fact that dancers do not eat ordinary food just prior to performance, must be seen to. There were other chores now forgotten.

There is something about southwestern Vermont weather in August that is anti-dance. It expresses itself in violent thunderstorms accompanied

Backstage at the Vermont State Armory, 1938 (© Barbara Morgan, Barbara Morgan Archive).

by on and off deluges of rain. In all the summers of dancing in the Armory, this evil genius never failed to make an appearance. Lights flickered. The overloaded area designated as a parking lot turned to muck. No one ever seemed to mind. For this first event only one performance had been scheduled until advance demand necessitated announcing a second one. Although the audience for the two evenings numbered over a thousand, demand still exceeded capacity, even though the weather was its characteristic self.

Martha Biehle, in the box office collecting the one dollar admission which remained the same throughout the Festival, had her hands full. So I, flanked by a loyal band of strong-arm helpers, literally drove the excess audience back out into the rain.

A custom peculiar to the Bennington years first appeared that August of 1935. A new form of applause developed — the beating of heels on the floor, later to prove something of a hazard. Among other unlooked for developments, the critics had come from the *New York Times*, the *Herald*

51

Tribune, the *Boston Daily Eagle*, the *Christian Science Monitor*, and other New England papers, as well as from magazines like *Theatre Arts Monthly* and *Newsweek*. Throughout the session, visitors had kept turning up — musicians, writers, people from the theatre, educators, and just plain interested spectators. This tide of students and audience, swelled by the season. The real aficionados began early to plan vacations to coincide with performances. The tide swelled but accommodations for them were less than elastic, especially the capacity of the Armory, maximum five hundred seats and little standing room, which must always allow room first for the students from the School and only after that for the public.

And so, after the close of the second season, as after the first, the planners had to do some re-planning.

Ruth Lloyd's Recollection

Ruth Lloyd wrote up her recollections of Bennington in December of 1977. McPherson minimally edited her writings and included a short paragraph Lloyd wrote in her diary on May 11, 1981. The edits and inclusions were approved by her son, David Lloyd who spent some of his earliest years at Bennington.

Lloyd's Biography

Ruth Rohrbacher Lloyd (1910–2002), born in Buffalo, New York, was the wife of composer Norman Lloyd with whom she coauthored several books and played professional four-hand piano. She graduated from New York University in 1933 after which she taught at the Lakemont School in New York. She accompanied classes and performances at the Bennington School of the Dance from 1934 to 1941, and later at Connecticut College School of the Dance. Lloyd joined the faculty at Sarah Lawrence in the 1940s and continued teaching there for over twenty years after which she taught at the State University of New York–Purchase.

Lloyd's Account[6]

The path to Bennington, for me, started when I was an undergraduate at NYU, majoring in music education. The [Great] Depression had hit,

Ruth and Norman Lloyd outside the Commons at the Bennington School of the Dance, 1938 (© Barbara Morgan, Barbara Morgan Archive).

and I needed some money to augment the little bit my parents could send me as an allowance. I was sent, by sheer luck, to the Physical Education Department, where an accompanist was needed for some dance classes. The teacher was Martha Hill. Fortunately I had always been a good sight-reader and had always done a lot of improvising on my own. I was excited about playing for Martha — she knew music and was interested in doing things with music and dance. I don't remember exactly what those things were — my experience was meager — but Martha owned a large pile of music. Fine music that I didn't know. I had the feeling that there would be possibilities here for a musician to have a good time with music, dance in music, and dance education.

Later, when I was teaching in the wilds of Central New York State (Starkey Seminary near Elmira, NY), and Norman, who had also been at NYU, was trying to survive and get going in his professional life in New York City, I urged him to get in touch with Martha Hill. They met, and the result was a collaboration in music and dance that lasted for many years.

Because Norman was so unusually good at his work at NYU, Martha invited him in 1934 to come in as an accompanist to a new kind of summer school in dance at Bennington College. First he had to have an audition with Louis Horst — which he passed. Next, he was asked to recommend another accompanist, and since I had originally recommended him, I think he felt it was time to return a favor, and so he recommended me. We had also gotten married the year before (April of 1933), but had been living apart because of our jobs. So we were able to start our life together at Bennington. We were to be paid $50 and our living. Our rooms were a suite in Swan House consisting of 2 bedrooms and a connecting bath — our first home. We were thrilled to be there. It was so beautiful. We were the babies of the group, and I think we were "appreciated" by all and sundry. It never occurred to us to question this; we gave unstintingly of what we thought was wanted of us. The conversations at faculty meals were so marvelous — I didn't say anything for almost the entire 6 weeks. We ate as if there would be no tomorrow, and as far as we knew there might not be one.

The first summer at Bennington, we served as accompanists for the technique and composition classes of Martha Hill and Bessie Schönberg. It was an exciting time of discovering modern dance and meeting the great dancers — Martha Graham, Hanya Holm, Doris Humphrey, and Charles Weidman, each of whom spent a week of teaching and doing performances

54

Norman Lloyd at the piano; Martha Hill behind him at NYU, circa 1936 (photographer unknown, courtesy New York University Archives Collection).

in the tiny College Theatre. John Martin, of the *New York Times*, was there for the first and sixth weeks. I think we strongly hoped we would be accepted by these remarkable people. And we definitely wanted to have a part in this highly charged art movement.

The students that first summer were in most cases teachers from physical education departments throughout the country, and they were intensely interested in giving dance a place in their curricula. Bennington, that first summer, was designed to be a "sampler" — a time for the dance teachers to get acquainted with dance as it was happening in New York City. Credit Martha Hill and Mary Jo Shelly for that idea. They knew what it was like to be teaching dance in Michigan, Oregon, and Kansas.

It didn't take long for us to be integrated into the Bennington community — or should I say the community of dancers. But I still remember the trepidation I felt as I put hands to the keyboard for the first class of the session — my first real modern dance class in every way. (My earlier work with Martha Hill had been, strangely enough, in tap classes.) This was semi-old stuff to Norman who had played for Martha Hill's modern classes at NYU.

It is hard to remember now what that first summer at Bennington was like. Most of the population was very much involved with their own work in dance — but there was a great deal of socializing. We found that our playing of four-hand jazz on the patio after dinner was enjoyed by many, including ourselves. It was a recreational activity for us, certainly not a chore. (We continued this in most of the summers that followed. In the charming series of Bennington After Dinner drawings by Betty Joiner, we always appear at the piano at the back of the scene.)

The next summer was more memorable — it was the time of Norman's writing of *Panorama* for Martha Graham. We went to Bennington and had a reunion with all of our dancer friends. Some of them we had seen, but many we had not. But there was a peculiar thing about Bennington. Even after not seeing someone for a whole year, friendships were picked up where they had left off— a phenomenon that still exists among those of us who were at Bennington "in the old days."

That summer of 1935 was wild. I continued to play for Martha and Bessie's classes and added the rehearsal classes for Louis Horst's Pre-Classis and Modern Forms classes. Norman taught his first classes in what we later called Rhythmic Training, as Gregory Tucker went on leave of absence. (Greg was a talented member of the Bennington College Music Faculty who later moved to MIT He came from the Eastern Pennsylvania coalfields, as did Norman. And by coincidence, they had known each other as very small boys. Now their paths crossed again.) Greg had taught exciting classes in Dalcroze Eurhythmics. But Norman and I felt that dancers needed to know more about the possibilities that lay in the area of tempo extremes, rhythmic counterpoint, phrasing, etc., as well as understanding the tremendous varieties of rhythmic organization. In 1935, we used a lot from our own Dalcroze background and just tentatively began to introduce our ideas, based on what we had seen lacking in dancers' musical background. (Music is such a great discipline for dancers. All the greatest and even near-great choreographers have known this. It is a pity that so many dancers today ignore music, but, then, it's their loss.)

So much for Rhythmic Training, Norman was "invited" by Martha Graham to compose the score for a new work [*Panorama*] — the first full-fledged workshop production to be given at the end of the summer. Since an "invitation" from Martha was stronger than a request from the Queen, and as "unrefuseable," Norman agreed. (There was no exchange of money in this commission. Like most of the music written for dance at Bennington, it was done as part of the six week job at the Bennington School of the Dance.)

Finding time to write a 40 minute score, while teaching a new course for the first time, was difficult. But even more difficult, was finding a piano to use. The Bennington music faculty were highly suspicious of dance musicians and were not going to allow their precious pianos and studios to be used by any of them. So Norman wandered from dormitory to dormitory, looking for a living room piano on which to try out his ideas.

Martha was in the throes of composing the dance, which would then be shown to Norman. He then would write a piece of music, and it would be tried with the dancers, as though having a dress fitting. Somehow or other, the score was finished. Norman stayed up all night putting the score in shape for Louis Horst and the five musicians who made up the usual Graham orchestra.

Arch Lauterer had re-designed the Bennington Armory so that it was a marvelous full stage. There was room for an audience of only about 150, as I remember. Alexander Calder had designed two mobiles for the dance. The first was a set of primary colored discs, suspended from pulleys. Each disc was attached to a wrist of one of the five dancers. The effect was stunning, with the dipping and rising space patterns counterpointing the slow-moving, earthbound movement of the dancers. But Calder's second mobile never worked. He had designed a huge wooden machine, jointed so that it could leap across the whole stage like a jagged bolt of lightening. Something went wrong either in the design or the execution of the design. The joints of the machine responded arthritically at best. So this mobile never made it to the Bennington Armory.

Panorama was a local, two night triumph at Bennington. It had no other performances, in part, because it was made expressly for the floor of the Bennington Armory and utilized a Workshop group of twenty-four dancers plus Graham's company of twelve. (Among the workshop group were such dancers as Nadia Chilkovsky, Jane Dudley, Helen Priest (Rogers), Muriel Stuart, Theodora Wiesner, and Marian Van Tuyl.) Also the press reception did not help. John Martin was cool. The left wing press was hostile — referring to the "Yankee Doodle" quality of the music. (This was a year before Americana became fashionable. Timing in an art is important in many ways!)

In subsequent summers at Bennington, we were involved not only with the School, I playing for classes and Norman teaching, but also with the end of summer festival. Other musicians came with the artist-teachers, including Dini de Remer who accompanied Graham's classes by playing only low, bass tone clusters to give the beat. Norman wrote *Quest* for Charles Weidman; *Dance of Work and Play* for Hanya Holm; and several short interludes for José Limón as well as a work for Louise Kloepper — both two of the young choreographer fellows. He also poured out a multitude of short pieces for student compositions, none of which lasted in the form of dance pieces but occasionally turned up in some of his scores for documentary films. (This was the period when Gebrauchsmusik was part of many composers' ideology — that is music written to be used, maybe only once, and then tossed away. There was music of this kind written during the Bennington summers.)

Every class at Bennington had an accompanying musician. Some of the artists-teachers added hand drums to heighten the intensity and help push the students across the floor. Except for the music used in Louis Horst's classes, most of the accompaniments were improvised. Even in the dance composition classes, while short pieces of music were sometimes used as a basis for movement sketches, often the movement phrases were composed by the dancers with suitable improvised music added as a background by the accompanist.

This was not the kind of music that conservatories prepared one to do, so, to add to the small available pool of dance musicians, Louis and Norman set up a special training course for aspirant dance accompanists. Louis's solution was to select the best dance done as the solution to a dance composition assignment. These dances would have been done to music, selected by the dance student from various choices given to her by Louis. The selected dance would then be shown to the composers in the dance musician class—*without* music. Discussion would follow — and the composers sent off to write their own scores to the dance. (A typical assignment for the composers would be a Bourrée from Louis' Pre-classic Dance form class and a Blues from the class in Modern Dance Forms.)

The composers usually had to write their scores overnight. At the next meeting of the musicians' class, the dances would be tried with every piece of music written for it. It was a little like trying on many costumes to see which one really fit and made the wearer comfortable. The effect of different scores on the same movement phrase was most instructive.

One of the ordeals for the student composer was playing his work in front of Louis, who had strong feelings about how dance music should be played: the music could be soft but solid; there was no place in dance music for romantic rubatos; but dance musicians had to breath with the dancers and thereby make subtle cadences and phrasing; and the music had to MOVE. Louis always played for his classes. He said that he got something from the feel of the keyboard that made the dances more tangible to him. And what a magnificent pianist he was! I shall never forget the sound of Copland's *Piano Variations* rolling across the campus as he and Martha Graham rehearsed Martha's *Dithyrambic*.

Norman worked with the student composers as an intermediary and interpreter for Louis whose emphasis was so thoroughly on the dance. The young musicians were often overwhelmed and confused by Louis' high-level aesthetics, and they needed someone to reconcile what they had been hearing with what they thought they knew. Norman and I taught improvisation to the musicians — and those few dancers who wanted to come to grips with the materials of music — and Norman gave a special course in compositional techniques to those who were weak in music composition or those who wanted to go beyond what they had learned in music school classes. (Norman had composed music most of his life and had studied with Vincent Jones at NYU and, later, with Aaron Copland; Copland used to argue with Alex North, who shared a lesson period, against writing so much dance music. "You should be writing concert music," he said. But this was before he wrote *Billy the Kid* or *Rodeo*.)

Louis was truly a wonderful artist and musician. We both learned a tremendous amount about contemporary music from him — he had an insatiable curiosity about new music. Later, when Norman became a member of the music faculty at Sarah Lawrence College, one of his new colleagues, who prided himself on *his* knowledge of contemporary music, expressed astonishment at Norman's breadth of musical background.

The classes for dance musicians paid off. From them came quite a few musicians who dedicated much of their musical lives and professional skills to the field of dance: B. J. Walberg, Esther Williamson Ballou, Freda Miller, Hazel Johnson, Evelyn Lohoefer, and Carl Miller, plus many others.

The adventurous spirit of the modern dance pioneers led them to seek out young composers — and even those not so young — to write scores for their dances. The monetary rewards were small — but the opportunity to have one's music performed and heard in public was very enticing. Such opportunities in the concert field were hard to come by. That was why Bennington was able to have ballet-length modern dance scores by such composers as Wallingford Riegger, Alex North, Hunter Johnson, Harrison Kerr and Greg Tucker. We were involved in most of these as a piano team or, if there was a small instrumental ensemble, Norman conducted, and I played.

The workload for us, and probably for everyone, was staggering. But through it all, we never felt put-upon. No one told us we shouldn't work so hard — and anyhow, it was wonderful to be doing it with all those extraordinary people. What we saw, heard, did, and felt during those earthshaking summers became the matrix of our adult philosophy as well as providing many components of our professional equipment.

Because of Bennington, we both spent considerable time with dance during and after the Bennington years. We played for all kinds of dance classes: modern, folk, tap, stage show, cabaret — you name it, and we did it. We played for the Humphrey-Weidman Company for a few years, until their tours got to be too long. We had to decide whether to go on the road and give up teaching or stay close to home base. We chose the latter.

Martha Hill gave us a chance to play for classes and to develop dance courses for the dance students at NYU. Marian Knighton Bryan, whom we had met during the first Bennington summer, hired us to play for the dance classes at Sarah Lawrence and do some teaching. Bessie Schönberg soon joined the Sarah Lawrence faculty, and we spent many fruitful years together. There, I was in the lovely position of being able to be a tyrant about dance students and their need to use "live" music.

We also played for Hanya Holm on what must have been one of the first television programs of dance, in 1938. And one or the other of us helped Louis whenever Graham used two pianos instead of her small chamber ensemble. For a while, we felt like regular occupants of the Guild — now the American National Theatre and Academy, playing a concert for a different dancer or dance company every Sunday.

Norman went his own way, joining the music faculty at Sarah Lawrence, then moving to Juilliard, to Oberlin, and to the Rockefeller Foundation. He never lost touch with dance though. He taught dancers about music at Juilliard, and wrote scores for Doris [Humphrey], José [Limón], and Martha Hill. While at Rockefeller, he remembered Bennington and how wonderful it was for choreographers to have their companies together for six weeks, so he started a series of residencies for dance companies.

Perhaps that was a key to the importance of Bennington. We heretofore unemployed or underemployed musicians and dancers had six weeks with all necessities and creature comforts provided. Six weeks every summer to be allowed to work to the limit of one's strength! Play for classes all day, squeeze a rehearsal in here or there, rehearse the whole evening without the interruption of classes — it was a different world. There had to be live musicians because — it is hard to believe that there was such a time — there were no tape recorders. (There also were no photocopiers which is why there exists in most cases only one copy of a composer's score from those Bennington days.)

I still think that modern dance is short-changing itself by tolerating taped and other canned music. The aliveness is more important than the dancer seems to be able to realize. There is the excitement, the danger, if you will, of human unpredictability. However, the living and breathing musician doesn't have much place with today's modern dancers. So, after a year's teaching and playing at the new State University of New York campus at Purchase — working with Bill [William] Bales, who I first met at Bennington, and getting to know a whole new group of fine students, I decided to join my husband in a new kind of life called "retirement." We decided that it was time for us to get down on paper some of the things we had learned about teaching. One book is out — *Creative Keyboard Musicianship* — based in large part on classes we taught at NYU and Bennington. Another book is on the way, and another in the planning stage.

Bennington is the past, and it is an emotional experience to look back. But I prefer to look ahead. And one of the things I look forward to is the day when "live" musicians for the modern dance are no longer referred to in quotes.

Facts and Figures, 1935

Total Enrollment of Students: 132 (does not include company members)

Select Students

General Program: Ruth Alexander, Fannie Aronson, Natalie Disston, Betty Joiner, Helen Knight, Welland Lathrop, Hermine Sauthoff, Gladys Taggart, Florence Warwick[7]

Workshop Program: with Martha Graham: Miriam Blecher, Prudence Bredt, Nadia Chilkovsky, Evelyn Davis, Jane Dudley, Nancy Funston, Alice A. Gates, Mildred Glassberg, Mary Anne Goldwater, Marie Heghinian, Merle Hirsch, Gussie Kirshner, Edith Langbert, Naomi Lubell, Mary Moore, Helen Priest (Rogers), Pearl Satlien, Kathleen Slagle, Muriel Stuart, Maxine Trevor, Marian Van Tuyl, Florence Verdon, Theodora Wiesner, Collin Wilsey

Faculty and Curriculum

Martha Hill, Director

Mary Josephine Shelly, Administrative Director

General Program

Modern Dance
Taught by Martha Graham July 8–August 17
Assistant — Bonnie Bird, Dorothy Bird (Villard), Gertrude Shurr
Accompanist — Dini de Remer

Taught by Tina Flade July 8–20
Assistant — Nancy McKnight (Hauser)
Accompanist — Ruth Hunt

Taught by Doris Humphrey July 22–August 3
Assistant — Letitia Ide
Accompanist — Pauline Lawrence

Charles Weidman August 5–17
Assistant — José Limón
Accompanist — Jerome Moross

Techniques of Dance Movement
Taught by Martha Hill and Bessie Schönberg
Accompanists — Ruth Lloyd and Norman Lloyd

Composition in Dance Form: Pre-Classic Forms
Taught by Louis Horst
Assistants — May O'Donnell and Anna Sokolow
Accompanists — Ruth Lloyd and Alex North

Composition in Dance Form: Modern Forms
Taught by Louis Horst
Assistant — Anna Sokolow
Accompanist — Alex North

Dance Composition
Taught by Martha Hill
Assistant — Bessie Schönberg
Accompanists — Ruth Lloyd, Norman Lloyd, Alex North

Elements of Music
Taught by Norman Lloyd

Basis of Dramatic Movement
Taught by Louise Martin

Stagecraft for Dancers
Taught by Jane Ogborn

Dance History and Criticism
Taught by John Martin

The Dance in Education
Led by Martha Hill and Bessie Schönberg

Special Studies in Dance[8]
Taught by Martha Hill and Mary Josephine Shelly

Practice
Supervised rehearsal

Workshop Program

Technique
Taught by Martha Graham, July 8–August 17

Assistant — Bonnie Bird, Dorothy Bird (Villard), Gertrude Shurr
Accompanist — Dini de Remer

Choreography
Rehearsals and Production with Martha Graham

Supplemental Study in Courses from the General Program

Select Concerts, Demonstrations, and Events

July 13
College Theatre

Tina Flade, solo concert, accompanied by Ruth Hunt

Dance in the Early Morning
Choreography by Tina Flade
Music by Henry Cowell

Paeans
Choreography by Tina Flade
Music by Dane Rudhyar

Obsession of the Spiral
Choreography by Tina Flade
Music by Ruth Crawford

Sinister Resonance
Choreography by Tina Flade
Music by Henry Cowell

Two Sarabandes
Choreography by Tina Flade
Music by Arcangelo Corelli

Elegy
Choreography by Tina Flade
Music by Alejandro Garcia Caturla

*Fire Cycle — Fire Preservation, Fire Torture, Fire
    Purification*
Choreography Tina Flade
Music by Henry Cowell

July 27
College Theatre

John Martin, Dance Critic and Author — Lecture on
    "The Ancient Art of the Modern Dance"

July 28	"An Evening of Revolutionary Dance"
College Theatre	Presented by the New Dance League

Greeting
Choreographed and danced by Anna Sokolow
Music by Vissarion Shebalin

Three Negro Poems
Choreographed and danced Miriam Blecher
Poems by Frank Horne and Langston Hughes

Themes from a Slavic People
Choreographed and danced by Sophie Maslow
Music by Bela Bartok

Affectations: Ennui and Sentimentale
Choreographed and danced by Merle Hirsch
Music by Alexander Scriabin and Maurice Ravel

Dilemmas: Aesthete and Liberal
Choreographed and danced by Jane Dudley
Music by Arthur Honegger and Sergei Prokofiev

Fatherland: Persecution and Defiance
Choreographed and danced by Lily Mehlman
Music by Arthur Honegger

Agitation
Choreographed and danced by Marie Marchowsky
Music by Gyorgy Kosa

Woman from *The Disinherited*
Choreographed and danced by Miriam Blecher
Music by Parnas

Impressions of a Dance Hall
Choreographed and danced by Anna Sokolow
Music by Louis Gruenberg

Forward
Choreographed and danced by Sophie Maslow
Music by Alex North

Time is Money
Choreographed and danced by Jane Dudley
Music by Sol Funaroff

American Sketches, One of the West, Two of the South, One of the East
Choreographed and danced by Lil Liandre
Music by Louis Gruenberg

August 3
College Theatre

Doris Humphrey and Charles Weidman with their Concert
Dance Group, accompanied by pianists Vivian Fine and Pauline Lawrence

New Dance
Choreographed by Doris Humphrey and Charles Weidman
Music by Wallingford Riegger
Performed by Doris Humphrey, Charles Weidman, and Group

Traditions
Choreographed by Charles Weidman
Music by Lehman Engel
Performed by José Limón, William Matons, Charles Weidman

Life of the Bee
Choreographed by Doris Humphrey
Performed by Doris Humphrey, Letitia Ide, and Group

Studies in Conflict
Choreographed by Charles Weidman
Music by Dane Rudhyar
Performed by José Limón, Charles Weidman, and Group

Memorial—To the Trivial, To the Connubial, To the Colossal
Choreographed by Charles Weidman
Music by Jerome Moross
Performed by Charles Weidman and Group

Alcina Suite
Choreographed and Performed by Doris Humphrey and Charles Weidman
Music by George Frideric Handel

Humphrey-Weidman Concert Group: Helen Bach, Morris Bakst, George Bockman, Jerry Brooks, Noel Charise, Beatrice Getson, Letitia Ide, Ada Korvin, José Limón, Katherine Litz, Joan Levy, Katherine Manning, William Matons, Edith Orcutt, Beatrice Seckler, Sybil Shearer, Mildred Tanzer

August 10
College Theatre

A Recital of Modern Music

Julian DeGray, pianist

Performed works by J.S. Bach, Arnold Schoenberg, Igor Stravinsky, Ernesto Halffter, Francesco Malipiero, Sergei Prokofiev, Maurice Ravel, and Alexander Scriabin

August 15
The Armory

Martha Graham and her Dance Group, and the Workshop Group

Louis Horst, Musical Director

Setting and Lighting designed and executed by Arch Lauterer

Celebration
Choreographed by Martha Graham
Music by Louis Horst
Performed by the Dance Group

Sarabande from the suite *Transitions*
Choreographed and Performed by Martha Graham
Music by Lehman Engel

Frontier from the suite *Perspectives*
Choreographed and Performed by Martha Graham
Music by Louis Horst

Panorama—*Theme of Dedication, Imperial Theme, Popular Theme*
Choreographed by Martha Graham
Music by Norman Lloyd
Performed by Martha Graham and the Workshop Group

Martha Graham's Concert Group: Anita Alverez, Bonnie Bird, Dorothy Bird (Villard), Ethel Butler,

Lil Liandre, Marie Marchowsky, Sophie Maslow, Lilly Mehlman, May O'Donnell, Florence Schneider, Gertrude Shurr, and Anna Sokolow

Workshop Group: Miriam Blecher, Prudence Bredt, Nadia Chilkovsky, Evelyn Davis, Jane Dudley, Nancy Funston, Alice Gates, Mildred Glassberg, Mary Anne Goldwater, Marie Heghinian, Merle Hirsch, Gussie Kirshner, Edith Langbert, Naomi Lubell, Mary Moore, Helen Priest (Rogers), Pearl Satlien, Kathleen Slagle, Muriel Stuart, Maxine Trevor, Marian Van Tuyl, Florence Verdon, Theodora Wiesner, and Collin Wilsey

Accompanied by Hugo Bergamasco — flute, H. Tafarella — clarinet, J. Youshkoff — bass clarinet, V. Peretti — trumpet, H. Denecke, Jr. — drums

August 16	Final Demonstration of student work (no program located)
August 16	Forum — Panel Discussion under the chairmanship of Edward C. Lindeman

5

Summer of 1936:
The First Festival

"You probably are very aware — that in those days it was a serious thing; ballet dancers didn't talk to modern dancers."[1]— Eugene Loring

Dates: July 3–August 15, 1936
Location: Bennington College, Bennington, Vermont

1936 was the first year of the full-fledged festival performances, with four of the nine performances held at the Vermont State Armory for the first time. Doris Humphrey and Charles Weidman were the featured choreographers each working with their own workshop group of student dancers. In addition to the festival performances, Lincoln Kirstein's Ballet Caravan performed for the first time at the Bennington School of the Dance. Eugene Loring who was a choreographer and dancer with Ballet Caravan, noted, "the fact that they let a small ballet company perform there I thought was an absolute miracle."[2] Considering the separation that existed between ballet and modern dance during this time-period, Ballet Caravan performing at Bennington was unlikely and somewhat extraordinary, but in a way anticipated the future when ballet and modern dance would become increasingly connected. Ballet Caravan member Erick Hawkins met Martha Graham which would have far-reaching results in a multitude of ways. Another new development was the offering of formalized programs in "Music Composition for the Dance" and "Choreography."

Mary Jo Shelly's Recollection[3]

To designate the summer of 1936 as marking the advent of the Festival is to an extent incorrect. True, the term appeared for the first time to iden-

69

tify the series of occasions open to the public. Actually, festivity had pervaded the School since it began, and the series of events open to the public bore an earlier date. In the third season, however, the term did appear for the first time out loud in print. Again, the 1936 chapter of the story is best told by reference to the report to the College trustees, annually presented by the Directors after it was all over. It begins by reiterating the five purposes, never from the beginning lost sight of: a unified program of study in all aspects of the modern dance; a widely diversified student body; audience education; suitable use of the College facilities during the summer recess; at moderate cost to the students, a self-supporting and non-profit-making enterprise serving these ends. It stands as an astonishingly mild manifesto for a veritable revolution.

The report also reiterates that the School's organization for the third session remained the same. It did to the extent that the General Program actually the expanded 1934 program, and the Workshop Program, initiated the year before, would go on. The latter, however, was doubled to provide one workshop for women students directed by Doris Humphrey, and a separate one for men directed by Charles Weidman. And two new programs, one in Choreography and the other in Music Composition for the Dance were less new developments, than formal recognition of what already existed. The Festival Series of Concerts, also already extant, got its new name and, remembering the clamor of the audience, was increased from five events to nine.

Expansion, likewise, affected the faculty size. By 1936, the teaching group had grown by approximately one third, including now, of necessity, a resident photographer Thomas Bouchard to supply the demands of the media and technical assistants to help stage the Festival Series. Including this session, fifty-two persons had been faculty and staff members, the majority for more than one session.

By this third year, the total student count for all three summers exceeded four hundred. It was possible to analyze who they were. In this session, enrollment reached a hundred and sixty-six (students and company members), over a hundred percent increase from the maximum hoped for two years before. And every year, applicants had to be refused admission. In 1935 and this year, seventeen percent were returning for a second time, and seven students were veterans of all three sessions. The sound character of the General Program showed in fact that three out of four students

Charles Weidman and Doris Humphrey at the Bennington School of the Dance, 1938 (© Barbara Morgan, Barbara Morgan Archive).

chose all or some part of it. The age range this year spanned three generations but although the average age had gone down about three years since 1934, the majority still were college or university teachers spread out across the country. In 1936, the overall charge, not covering the uniform work costume, went up another ten dollars to $210. Everyone, regardless of program of study chosen, paid that same fee. The only forms of scholarship were provision to pay the fee in installments if needed, or a few partial rebates in exchange for services on some job.

No one cared about differences in economic status any more than they did about other kinds of distinctions among the student body. Every kind of differences did exist. The School aimed at exactly this realism. Attitudes colored by regional and professional interests, a range of ability from beginner to established artist, a wide age span, divergent and often controversial social and political points of view — these strong contrasts within the School community gave it its unique quality. A common concern — modern dance, unified the group, brought it together physically and held it together psychologically.

Men continued to be overwhelmingly outnumbered — five students in the Workshop Program and the six members of Charles Weidman's Concert Group. They at least found themselves in company with men on the faculty. This situation, like the whole composition of the School, mirrored the state of affairs in modern dance as a whole in this period.

The new Program in Choreography was directed by Martha Hill and Louis Horst, who were joined by John Martin to form a Committee for auditions. They discouraged six of the ten students who applied for the new program, and transferred them to the General Program. The four who survived met a challenging assignment. No attempt was made in accepting them this year or thereafter to lower the standards to admit more students. If this, the first opportunity of its kind to be offered in a school of modern dance, were to serve its purpose, that standard must be defensibly high. In addition to supplementary courses in the General Program, each of the four completed and presented in demonstration, with elementary costuming and staging of their own devising, two full-length compositions — either a solo and a group number or a combination of the two in which they also danced. In addition, three of them rehearsed and presented for criticism, dances previously composed. The work was judged not only on choreographic accomplishment including the conception chosen and the method of treatment, but also on their own competence as directors of a group, their success in handling rehearsals, and the contribution they had made to the dance experience of the students from the General Program who had volunteered to act as their groups.

The other new addition, the program in Music Composition for the Dance, had ten applicants, six of whom transferred to the General Program, either because of realization that the standard set was too high or that they preferred a more diversified plan of work. Two other students participated in part of the program and wrote music for student dance compositions. The program was divided between the technique of keyboard improvisation and class accompaniment for dance, and a variety of problems in music composition for dances composed by students both in the General Program and the Program in Choreography.

The amount of work done and brought to finished form under Louis Horst, director of the program, and Norman Lloyd, who together conducted the work, was illustrated in the final student demonstration. Of the twenty-five dances presented, the majority having several sections, seventeen used music written by students. The music showed not only command of a variety of styles and forms, but a competent grasp of the principles governing the relationship between music and modern dance.

The two new programs proved their point. The scope of study within the School gained a new dimension, one that reflected growing aspects of the modern dance as a whole and which foreshadowed further developments within the School itself.

As in the two previous sessions, beyond the classes held, there had been a series of evening meetings designed to supplement regular work. For these, members of the faculty of the School and of the College were drawn upon, and visiting speakers were invited. In 1934 and 1935, these had been of great interest to students. Now in 1936, although numerous such events were held, student interest in them diminished. Work was growing more intense and crowding over into otherwise free time. The student body was becoming a more experienced group, concerned more deeply with independent creative activity and less in need of other stimulation than that coming from direct involvement in the primary studies in which they were engaged. Also, significantly, the inauguration of the Festival Series of Programs in the Modern Dance, climaxed by the Workshop Concerts in the Armory, were preceded by eight other eventful evenings in the College Theatre. Using the term for the first time, John Martin gave a classic survey of the scene in a lecture called "The American Dance," the gist of his landmark book, *America Dancing*, published in the same year. Earlier during the School session, the School had been host to the two debut concerts of the Ballet Caravan, directed by Lincoln Kirstein, and to a concert by students of the School who were members of The New Dance League with Anna Sokolow as guest artist. These evenings were followed by two solo concerts by Martha Graham and two concerts by Hanya Holm and her concert group. Then, on the final evenings of the session, came the four concerts in the Armory by Doris Humphrey and Charles Weidman with their concert groups and the students from their workshops.

The name Festival had truly been earned. The total audience for the Series including the members of the School, exceeded three thousand. What it would have been if there had been room for all who wanted to be there remains uncounted as it had been before and would be again in seasons to some.

Again on August 12 and 14, 1936, the opening salvo of a passing thunderstorm. Again, the village clock struck nine. Again, the house lights went down and the spotlights on. Then, the first two sections of Doris Humphrey's great trilogy *Theatre Piece, Part I* and *New Dance, Part II*, composed previously and danced during the 1935–1936 New York Season but now redesigned and restaged. The significance of Weidman's *Quest*, the title of the new work by Charles Weidman, which followed, is best found in the program note:

> The artist, in his endeavor to find or create conditions under which he may achieve full and free expression, encounters many obstacles, in many lands. Today he struggles alone with nothing but his inner strength to aid him. Perhaps tomorrow he will unite his forces with those of his fellows and reach his goal.[4]

Despite its serious intent, *Quest* displayed some of those moments that have marked Charles Weidman as one of the greatest and most gentle satirists of all that is silly and pretentious. The message of the program note had special meaning for those present. One hope of the Bennington School had been to alleviate the aloneness of the dancer's struggle. *Quest* repeated on August 13 and 15, was made even more interesting by the first full recognition of the gift possessed by the leading member of Charles' concert group, José Limón.

On these same dates, came the final part of Doris' trilogy, *With My Red Fires*. Now that whole brilliant drama was complete. It is doubtful if anyone who was in the Armory that evening has forgotten the event. A privileged few remained afterward to watch Thomas Bouchard photograph

Doris Humphrey at the Bennington School of the Dance, 1934 (photograph by Lionel Green, courtesy Bennington College).

the production. By the early hours of the morning, the exhausted company was allowed go home. Only Doris remained, standing like a vengeful arrow at the top of the central structure of Arch's stage. Finally, even Bouchard gave up and sank down on the bottom step of a ladder. Came the quiet question, "Are you through, Tom?" He was, and Doris descended the stage and disappeared. The printed picture still exists. So does the one of the watchers of a great choreographer, a great work, and a great woman. The 1936 session was over.

May O'Donnell's Recollection

Dawn Lille interviewed May O'Donnell on September 9, 1999, on Elizabeth McPherson's behalf as O'Donnell preferred to be interviewed by someone she knew. McPherson was, at the time, working on her dissertation. She transcribed and edited the material to develop the following narrative.

O'DONNELL'S BIO

May O'Donnell (1906–2004) was at the Bennington School of the Dance from 1934 to 1936 as an assistant to Louis Horst and as a member of the Martha Graham Dance Company. She was at Bennington again in 1938 to assist Martha Graham and to perform in the premiere of *American Document*. Born in Sacramento, California, she studied and performed with Estelle Reed in San Francisco, and after moving to New York City studied with Martha Graham. She was a soloist with Graham's company from 1932 to 1938, rejoining as a guest artist from 1944 to 1952. In 1939 she presented the first program of her own work, and founded the San Francisco Dance Theatre. From 1950 on, she would focus much of her energy on her own choreography, creating more than 50 dances over the course of her career. She established the May O'Donnell Concert Dance Company in 1974, and the company toured nationally and internationally through the 1980s. O'Donnell created her own modern dance technique which is still taught today, and she counts among her students such dance luminaries as Gerald Arpino, Robert Joffrey, and Ben Vereen. She was married to the composer Ray Green.

May O'Donnell (left), Sophie Maslow, and others in Martha Graham's *American Document* at the Bennington School of the Dance (© Barbara Morgan, Barbara Morgan Archive).

O'DONNELL'S ACCOUNT[5]

The Bennington School of the Dance brought together people like Martha Graham, Doris Humphrey, Hanya Holm, and Charles Weidman (some of the people that were very involved in dance at the time) with the idea of giving modern dance the chance to project itself. And of course the idea was marvelous because here dance was beginning, but the gym teachers all across the country, they didn't have dance, they didn't know dance. So, suddenly if there was a place where they could come and get some kind of basic training, it would be wonderful for them. But at the same time, Martha Hill and Mary Jo Shelly didn't want the educational aspect entirely. They wanted to present concerts in modern dance with people like Martha Graham, and Doris Humphrey, and Hanya Holm, and so on.

Martha Hill and Mary Jo's big job was to see that it was going to work, that everybody would have their own space. Bennington College was very wonderful that they would let them use the campus in the summer because they had all these dorms. We were set up in single dorms so that different people and different companies could be in their own space. It was a big adventure. I don't remember just the first day I was there, but you could see it was going to work. Martha Hill and Mary Jo had to spend an awful lot of time keeping everybody happy. And they had worked out I'm sure with the teachers that were coming, like Martha Graham and Doris Humphrey, that they would teach at a professional level besides the educational work that was taught.

To explain the educational dance, I believe they had simple exercises in those classes. I was so involved with Martha Graham's group that I didn't pay too much attention to what was going on elsewhere, but it was almost like two programs going on at once. I remember one year, they had the critic John Martin do a series of lectures on dance, and that was in the big auditorium open to everybody. So there was time when there would be a little mixture. Also, sometimes in the dorms, some of the people were mixed because there were maybe not enough of the serious dancers to fill one dorm. But usually they tried to keep us together.

Louis Horst was teaching what he called his Pre-Classic Dance Forms, and I was his assistant. The class was a hard problem for some of the students. First we'd have them do some of the basic historical dance and its original steps (as much as Louis knew) and rhythm. Then, they'd take that same rhythm and make up their own dance to it. Well, those gym teachers like Marion Streng and the whole bunch they were good-natured characters, but it was hard. I'm sure at the end of the day they'd go back and have a good drink of whiskey to keep their spirits up.[6] They'd jump on me, of course, to help them, and I would do the best I could.

78

The gym teachers loved to watch our rehearsals with the Graham Company. I got to know some of them and kept in touch through letters. Some of them got the idea of having the dance companies out to their colleges, or they would invite somebody to come and teach. They said, "Look, we'd love to have our students and the people see some of this modern dance. If we can get the college to give us just a little money, then you could set up a little tour and then that way people would know about modern dance, and they might take our classes and be easier for us to teach." It worked out in a very nice way. I must say, Martha Hill and Mary Jo were very open to the possibilities because this was the beginning of it. People didn't know much about Martha Graham or Doris Humphrey. Graham and Humphrey had done concerts, but not much outside of the limitations of where they lived. They hadn't gone on big tours. It was out of the Bennington School of the Dance that the tours started.

I was maybe on two concert tours with Martha Graham going around the country. She knew that people were going to be puzzled and all of that. I remember the first concert we did was, I think, in Greeley, Colorado. People didn't know you were supposed to watch the stage. My god was that torture! I think at the end of a write-up in the paper the author said, "Boy, we'll put them on the football team!"

In 1939, the year the Bennington School of the Dance was at Mills College out in California, that's when I met José Limón. At that time, I had gone to San Francisco, had left Graham. Martha Hill and Mary Jo asked me to do a concert there during the summer, and that's when José came to me and he said, "May, I'd like to come and work with you."

Mary Jo and Martha Hill were wonderful directors because they were gym teachers themselves. Martha Hill seemed to me very placid. I never saw her with a temper. Mary Jo, she was kind of more, well, strident than Martha Hill and more excitable. I always thought of her as an Irishman. Very friendly, but you didn't feel anything artistic at all. I think Martha Hill was much more in the artistic vein. Martha Hill had danced with Martha Graham, but for a short time and early on. I think she was smart enough to know what to put most of her energy into. Martha Hill kind of just quietly and in a very practical way knew what needed to be done in her life, which was, of course, always connected with education. She just loved, evidently, teaching, and I think she practically taught to the end of her life.

But anyway, the two of them managed, and it was quite a hard thing to manage that first year and *every* year after that actually. And there was never time to really get *too* acquainted with much of anybody. You were just happy that the things that were set up would work. Martha Hill and Mary Jo had this big sea of folks, the gym teachers, and when something goes wrong you have to see the administrator. So, I think Martha Hill and Mary Jo worked very hard, but I never saw them lose their tempers. They managed to somehow or another just be very calm, and if there was a storm, they just waited for it to finish. They were very nice. You never felt that they were putting any pressure on you or anything. They saw to it that the arrangements were right so that Martha Graham could take her group to a place and rehearse; where there could be a place for Doris Humphrey to rehearse; and at the same time take care of all of us that had to be working all the time because we were working toward a concert at the end of this deal; to keep Louis Horst happy; and this bunch of people in education happy. And we all had to be fed. They worked it out so that everybody could get something out of the program. It was quite a big adventure.

Without Martha Hill and Mary Jo, it might have taken much longer to open the doors of the country for people to see and study modern dance. The Bennington School of the Dance students came from all over the country. From their studies, they saw they had a chance to do something in dance. You didn't have to be a ballet dancer. Even if it was simple, some of them were smart enough to know, "Okay, that's simple, but maybe I can build on it." And, they would begin to experience things themselves, and began to put on concerts. Modern dance is a way to express oneself. That seemed to mean a lot to people because what you did in movement was something that came out of you, that you felt. And so, all in all I would give both Martha Hill and Mary Jo a crown, but especially I'd put jewels in Martha's.

Martha Hill encouraged that whole sweep of modern dance coming into its own, and becoming accepted. She probably early on discovered that she maybe couldn't or for some reason wasn't a performer, but she then encouraged other people to be performers and to know more about it. At the Bennington School of the Dance, she didn't just stick to Martha Graham or this one or the other. If somebody did something interesting and good, she was open. I would give her a very high reward in heaven.

Facts and Figures, 1936

Total Enrollment of Students: 148 (does not include company members)

Select Students

General Program: Elizabeth Bloomer (Betty Ford), Natalie Disston, Margaret Erlanger, Margaret M. Isaacs, Truda Kaschmann, Helen B. Knight, Barbara Mettler, Phyllis P. Van Fleet, Florence Warwick, and Geneva Watson

Workshop Program: Patricia Amster, Otto Asherman, Nanette Atchinson, Edgar Barclift, Anita Brady, Lynn Buchanan, Lillian M. Burgess, Betty Carper, Maxine A. Cushing, Eva Desca (Garnet), Lois Ellfeldt, William N. Garrett, Harriette Ann Gray, Helene E. Hetzel, Frances Kinsky, Frederic W. Lane, Jr., Beatrice Lovejoy, Anne E. MacNaughton, Ethel Mann, Alice Marting, Frances McDonald, Eloise Moore, Jane Perry, Kaya Russell, Selma Silverman, Mary Tracht, Bernice Van Gelder, Theresa Willman, Mildred Zook

Program in Choreography: Fannie Aronson, Ruth H. Bloomer, Margery Schneider, Marian Van Tuyl

Program in Music for Dance: Elizabeth Gottesleben, Beatrice Hellebrandt

Faculty and Curriculum

Martha Hill, Director

Mary Josephine Shelly, Administrative Director

Thomas Bouchard, Photographer

General Program

Modern Dance
Taught by Martha Graham (July 20–August 1)
Assistant — Dorothy Bird (Villard)
Accompanist — Dini de Remer

Taught by Hanya Holm (August 3–15)
Assistant — Nancy McKnight (Hauser)
Accompanist — Harvey Pollins

81

Taught by Doris Humphrey (July 6–August 1)
Assistants — Joan Levy, Katherine Manning, Sybil Shearer
Accompanist — Pauline Lawrence

Taught by Charles Weidman (July 6–August 1)
Assistants — José Limón and William Matons

Techniques of Dance Movement
Taught by Martha Hill and Bessie Schönberg
Assistant — Marjorie Church
Accompanists — Ruth Lloyd, Jean Williams, Esther Williamson

Composition in Dance Forms (Pre-Classic) and Modern)
Taught by Louis Horst
Assistant — May O'Donnell
Accompanists — Dini de Remer, assisted by Jean Williams and Esther
    Williamson

Composition in Dance Forms (Modern)
Taught by Louis Horst
Assistant — May O'Donnell
Accompanists — Ruth Lloyd, assisted by Jean Williams and Esther
    Williamson

Dance Composition: Introductory Section
Taught by Bessie Schönberg
Accompanists — Ruth Lloyd, Jean Williams, Esther Williamson

Dance Composition: Intermediate and Advanced Sections
Taught by Martha Hill
Assistant — Bessie Schönberg
Accompanists — Ruth Lloyd, Jean Williams, Esther Williamson

Basis of Dramatic Movement
Taught by Louise Martin

Elements of Music
Taught by Norman Lloyd

Percussion Accompaniment for the Dance
Taught by Nancy McKnight (Hauser)

Stagecraft for Dancers
Taught by Sally Brownell

Dance History and Criticism
Taught by John Martin

Seminar in Dance Criticism
Taught by John Martin

Workshop Program

Women's Workshop—Director, Doris Humphrey
Technique
Taught by Doris Humphrey
Assistants — Joan Levy, Katherine Manning, Sybil Shearer
Accompanist — Pauline Lawrence

Choreography
Rehearsals and Production with Doris Humphrey
Accompanists — Pauline Lawrence, Ruth Lloyd, Norman Lloyd
Assistant — Nancy McKnight (Hauser) — percussion
Composer — Wallingford Riegger

Dance History and Criticism
Taught by John Martin
Workshop students joined students in the General Program for this course.

Men's Workshop—Director, Charles Weidman
Technique
Taught by Charles Weidman
Assistants — José Limón and William Matons

Choreography
Rehearsals and Production with Charles Weidman
Accompanists — Clair Leonard and Norman Lloyd
Composer — Norman Lloyd

Dance History and Criticism
Taught by John Martin
Workshop students joined students in the General Program for this course.

Supplemental Study in the workshop or other programs of the school

Program in Choreography

Co-Directors, Martha Hill and Louis Horst
Modern Dance

Composition in Dance Form—Modern Forms
Dance Composition—Advanced Section
As well as recommended courses from the General Program

Program in Music Composition for the Dance

Director, Louis Horst
Music Accompaniment
Taught by Norman Lloyd

Music Composition
Taught by Louis Horst

As well as select courses from the General Program

Select Concerts, Demonstrations, and Events

July 4	Display of Fireworks
July 5	Community Sing Ruth and Norman Lloyd, Accompanists
July 10 College Theatre	Lecture-demonstration, Doris Humphrey and Charles Weidman and their Concert Groups

July 11
College Theatre
	Piano recital of J.S. Bach, George Frideric Handel,
	    Domenico Scarlatti given by Julian DeGray,
	    member of Music Division, Bennington
	    College

July 14 College Theatre	Illustrated lecture on growth of plant forms Robert Woodworth, member of the Science Division, Bennington College
July 16 Lounge	Lecture-discussion, "The Bennington College Plan" Mary Garrett, Director of Admissions, Bennington College
July 17 College Theatre	Concert, Ballet Caravan, accompanied by pianist David Stimer
	Encounter Choreographed by Lew Christensen Music by Wolfgang Amadeus Mozart

Harlequin for President
Choreography by Eugene Loring
Music by Domenico Scarlatti

*Divertissements—Mazurka, Morning Greeting,
Pas de Deux, Gitana, Can-Can, Pas Classique,
    Rhapsody*
No choreographer listed
Music by Francisco de la Torre, Mikhail Glinka,
    Benjamin Godard, Georg Liebling, Franz
    Liszt, Franz Schubert, Johann Strauss
Danced by Ruby Asquith, Ruthanna Boris,
    Gisella Caccialanza, Harold Christensen,
    Lew Christensen, Rabana Hasburgh, Erick
    Hawkins, Albia Kavan, Charles Laskey,
    Eugene Loring, Annabelle Lyon, Hannah
    Moore

July 18
College Theatre

Lecture-demonstration, Lincoln Kirstein and
    members of Ballet Caravan

July 18
College Theatre

Concert, Ballet Caravan

Promenade
Choreographed by William Dollar
Music by Maurice Ravel

Pocahontas
Choreographed by Lew Christensen
Music by Elliott Carter

*Divertissements—Rhapsody, Can-Can, Morning
    Greeting, Valse, Gitana, Pas Classique, March*
No choreographer listed
Music by
    Francisco de la Torre, Benjamin Godard,
    Georg Liebling, Franz Liszt, Francis Poulenc,
    Sergei Prokofiev, Franz Schubert, Johann
    Strauss

Danced by Ruby Asquith, Ruthanna Boris, Gisella Caccialanza, Harold Christensen, Lew Christensen, Rabana Hasburgh, Erick Hawkins, Albia Kavan, Charles Laskey, Eugene Loring, Annabelle Lyon, Hannah Moore

July 20
Lounge
Informal Discussion for students teaching dance in secondary schools, led by Martha Hill

July 22
Barn Lecture Room
Lecture-demonstration on Laban Dance Script, Irma Dombois-Bartinieff and Irma Otto-Bets

July 23
Barn Lecture Room
Lecture-demonstration on Laban Dance Script, Irma Dombois-Bartinieff and Irma Otto-Bets

July 25
College Theatre
Lecture, "The American Dance," John Martin, 1st Program of the Festival Series

July 26
College Theatre
Concert, Members of the New Dance Group with Anna Sokolow as guest artist(no program found)

July 28
College Theatre
Lecture-demonstration, Martha Graham and three members of her concert group

July 30
Lounge
Lecture-discussion, Thomas Bouchard, photographer

July 31 and August 1
College Theatre
Concert, Martha Graham, 2nd and 3rd Programs of the Festival Series

Praeludium
Choreographed and performed by Martha Graham
Music by Paul Nordoff

Lamentation
Choreographed and performed by Martha Graham
Music by Zoltan Kodaly

Frontier
Choreographed and performed by Martha Graham
Music by Louis Horst

Satyric Festival Song
Choreographed and performed by Martha Graham
Music by Imre Weisshaus

86

Imperial Gesture
Choreographed and performed by Martha Graham
Music by Lehman Engel

Sarabande
Choreographed and performed by Martha Graham
Music by Lehman Engel

Building Motif
Choreographed and performed by Martha Graham
Music by Louis Horst

Ekstasis
Choreographed and performed by Martha Graham
Music by Lehman Engel

Act of Piety from the suite *American Provincials*
Choreographed and performed by Martha Graham
Music by Louis Horst

Harlequinade — Pessimist and Optimist
Choreographed and performed by Martha Graham
Music by Ernst Toch

Accompanied by Hugo Bergamasco —flute,
    H. Tafarella — clarinet, V. Peretti — trumpet,
    J. Youshkoff— bass clarinet, S. Gershek — drums,
    R. Lloyd — voice

August 2 Barn Quadrangle	Lecture, "Abstractism in Literature and Other Arts" Irving Fineman, member of the Literature Division of Bennington College
August 4 Lounge	Display of dance costumes from Aldrich and Aldrich under direction of Elaine Scanlan
August 5 Barn Lecture Room	Lecture, "Backgrounds of American Painting" Jane Welling
August 6 College Theatre	Piano recital of J. S. Bach, Francis Poulenc, Wallingford Riegger given by Ruth Lloyd and Norman Lloyd
August 7 and 8 College Theatre	Concert, Hanya Holm and her Concert Group 4th and 5th Programs of the Festival Series

Salutation
Choreographed by Hanya Holm
Music by Henry Cowell
Performed by the group

In a Quiet Space
Choreographed and performed by Hanya Holm
Music by Franziska Boas

Drive
Choreographed and performed by Hanya Holm
Music by Harvey Pollins

*Dance in Two Parts — A Cry Rises in the Land and
    New Destinies*
Choreographed by Hanya Holm
Music by Wallingford Riegger
Performed by Holm and the Group

Dance Stanzas
Choreographed by Hanya Holm
Music by R. Jurist
Performed by Dora Brown, Hanya Holm, Melvene
    Ipcar

Sarabande
Choreographed and performed by Hanya Holm
Music by Harvey Pollins

City Nocturne
Choreographed by Hanya Holm
Music by Wallingford Riegger
Performed by the group

Four Chromatic Eccentricities
Choreographed and performed by Hanya Holm
Music by Wallingford Riegger

Primitive Rhythm
Choreography by Hanya Holm
Music by Jacques Barzun
Performed by Holm and the Group

Members of the Group: Louise Kloepper, Dora
    Brown, Margaret Dudley, Carolyn Durand,
    Melvene Ipcar, Nancy McKnight (Hauser),
    Elizabeth Waters

Accompanists: Harvey Pollins and Thomas
    McNally — piano, Elizabeth Gottesleben —
    percussion

August 8	Showing of sculpture
	Moselsio's Studio, Simon Moselsio, member of the Art Division, Bennington College
August 9 College Theatre	Piano recital given by Jean Williams and Esther Williamson
August 10 Lounge	Lecture-demonstration on the modern dance, Hanya Holm
August 12, 14 The Armory	Concert, Doris Humphrey and Charles Weidman with their Concert Groups, 6th and 8th Programs of the Festival Series

Theatre Piece
Choreographed by Doris Humphrey and
    Charles Weidman (one section, "In the
    Theatre")
Music by Wallingford Riegger

    Prologue (Assignment of Roles)
    performed by Doris Humphrey and Group

    Behind Walls
    performed by Doris Humphrey and Group

    In the Open (Hunting Dance)
    performed by Edith Orcutt, Charles Weidman
      and Group

    Interlude
    performed by Doris Humphrey

    In the Stadium
    performed by George Bockman, José Limón,
      Katherine Manning, and Group

In the Theatre (choreographed by Weidman)
performed by Katherine Litz, Katherine
  Manning, Charles Weidman

The Race
performed by Doris Humphrey and Group

Epilogue (The Return)
performed by Doris Humphrey and Group

New Dance
Choreographed by Doris Humphrey and Charles
  Weidman (one section, "Third Theme")
Music by Wallingford Riegger

Prelude
performed by Doris Humphrey and Charles
  Weidman

First Theme
performed by Doris Humphrey and Group

Second Theme
performed by Doris Humphrey and Group

Third Theme (choreographed by Charles
  Weidman)
performed by Charles Weidman and Group

Processional
performed by Doris Humphrey, Charles
  Weidman, and Groups

Celebration
performed by Doris Humphrey, Charles
  Weidman, and Groups

Variations and Conclusion
performed by Groups with selected soloists

Members of Doris Humphrey's Concert Group:
Louise Allen, Letitia Ide, Ada Korvin, Miriam
Krakovsky, Joan Levy, Katherine Litz, Katherine
Manning, Edith Orcutt, Beatrice Seckler, Sybil
Shearer, Lily Verne

Members of Charles Weidman's Concert Group:
William Bales, George Bockman, Kenneth
Bostock, José Limón, William Matons

Workshop Groups (see p. 81)

Workshop Groups (see p. 81)

August 13, 15   Concert, Doris Humphrey and Charles Weidman
The Armory   with their Concert Groups and students of the
                 School Workshops, 7th and 9th Programs of the
                 Festival Series

With My Red Fires
Choreographed by Doris Humphrey
Music by Wallingford Riegger

> *Part I— Ritual*
> *Hymn*
> performed by Katherine Litz, Charles
>   Weidman, Concert Groups, and Workshop
>   Group
>
> *Search and Betrothal*
> performed by Katherine Litz, Charles
>   Weidman, Concert Groups, and Workshop
>   Group
>
> *Departure*
> performed by Katherine Litz, Charles
>   Weidman, Concert Groups, and Workshop
>   Group
>
> *Part II— Drama*
> *Summons*
> performed by Lillian Burgess and Maxine
>   Cushing
>
> *Coercion and Escape*
> performed by Doris Humphrey and Katherine
>   Litz
>
> *Alarm*
> performed by Doris Humphrey and Workshop
>   Group

91

Pursuit
performed by William Bales, José Limón,
  William Matons, and Workshop Group

Judgment
performed by Katherine Litz, Charles
  Weidman, Concert Groups and Workshop
  Group

The Characters in *Part II:*
  Choric Figures: Lillian Burgess and Maxine
    Cushing
  Young Woman: Katherine Litz
  Young Man: Charles Weidman
  Matriarch: Doris Humphrey

Quest
Choreographed by Weidman

Music by Clair Leonard and Norman Lloyd
  (Transition)

Prelude
performed by Group

Emergence
performed by Doris Humphrey, Charles
  Weidman, and Group

Allegory
performed by Doris Humphrey and Charles
  Weidman

Trivia (Patronage)
performed by Harriet Ann Gray, Katherine
  Manning, Edith Orcutt, Beatrice Seckler,
  Sybil Shearer, Charles Weidman

Transition
Performed by William Bales, José Limón,
  William Matons, and Group

Kulturreinigung
Performed by Charles Weidman and Group

Trivia (Anthropometry)
Performed by William Bales, William Canton,
   Philip Gordon, José Limón, William Matons,
   Charles Weidman

Allegory
performed by Doris Humphrey and Charles
   Weidman

Pro Patria
Performed by José Limón, William Matons,
   Charles Weidman, and Group

Allegory
performed by Doris Humphrey and Charles
   Weidman

Convergence
performed by José Limón, William Matons,
   Charles Weidman

Affirmation
performed by Doris Humphrey, Charles
   Weidman, and Group

Members of Doris Humphrey's Concert Group:
Louise Allen, Letitia Ide, Ada Korvin, Miriam
Krakovsky, Joan Levy, Katherine Litz, Katherine
Manning, Edith Orcutt, Beatrice Seckler, Sybil
Shearer, Lily Verne,

Members of Charles Weidman's Concert Group:
William Bales, William Canton, Philip Gordon,
Paul Leon, José Limón, William Matons

Workshop Groups (see p. 81)

August 15 Final demonstration of Student compositions in
dance and music

Dance Composition demonstration under the
direction of Martha Hill and Bessie Schönberg
Works by students: Caryl Cuddeback, Truda
Kaschmann, Helen Knight, Fara Lynn

Pre-Classic Forms under the direction of Louis Horst
Works by students: Karen Burt, Marjorie Church,
Ruth Diamond, Barbara Mettler, Phyllis Van
Fleet, Florence Warwick
Modern Forms under the direction of Louis Horst
Works by students: Ruth Bloomer, Alice Gates,
Isabelle Katz, Tosia Mundstock, Margery
Schneider, Marian Van Tuyl

Program in Music Composition for the Dance
Choreography by students: Fannie Aronson, Ruth
Bloomer, Margery Schneider, Marian Van Tuyl

Danced to music compositions by students:
Elizabeth Gottesleben, Beatrice Hellebrandt,
Jean Williams, Esther Williamson

6

Summer of 1937:
The Final Workshop Program,
the Fellowships

"Look, in those days nobody had a chance to do anything. You had to work like a fiend to just do something, and to have the opportunity to work some place for six weeks and be chosen to represent [modern dance] it's a great honor."[1]—*Anna Sokolow, fellow of 1937*

Dates: July 2–August 14, 1937
Location: Bennington College, Bennington, Vermont

The premiere of Hanya Holm's Trend *and the first Fellows program, in which Esther Junger, José Limón, and Anna Sokolow were selected to choreograph and present their own works, were the big events of the summer of 1937. The Fellows were clearly well chosen as each were successful choreographers, particularly Limón and Sokolow who would make major contributions to modern dance.*

Mary Jo Shelly's Recollection[2]

By the fourth session, there was no need to revise, only to add one important element to the whole plan. The pattern of study continued with the four established programs — General Workshop, Choreography, Music for the Dance, and the last of the planned Workshops. Enrollment rose to one hundred and fifty-nine, including four men, and still conveying approximately the same age range and geographical spread from coast to coast. It was again oversubscribed. The simple statistics show an unabated tide.

95

But the planners, gratified by the present usefulness of the School and the Festival of the Modern Dance, had an eye on the future. Hence, the introduction of the new element, the fellowships. These were to aid directly in the training of future leaders. For testimony to the fulfillment of that purpose one need only name the first young dancers selected from among the fifteen nominated by the Directors and the Advisory Board of the School: Esther Junger, José Limón, and Anna Sokolow.

Holding a fellowship meant two things: the modest essentials for doing independent work and having it publicly presented as part of the Festival; and the obligation to produce a new group work worthy of the opportunity. The essentials comprised: living; a small stipend for travel and miscellaneous expenses; studio space; accompanist services; and, for public presentation — staging, costuming, and music. Each fellow chose, through audition, student volunteers from the General Program to form a company of ten or twelve dancers. These dancers carried also a full schedule of classes, all rehearsals taking place outside of class hours with very limited rehearsal time in the Armory. Many of them appeared there on the evening of the fellows' concert for the first time in a professional production.

The list of composers of the music contains names equally significant — Henry Clark, Norman Lloyd, Morris Mamorsky, Jerome Moross, Alex North, and Harvey Pollins. And in addition, for the concerts, the list included Ruth Lloyd, Robert McBride, and Esther Williamson. A young designer, Betty Joiner, planned all of the costumes for the new works; and Gerard Gentile of the College faculty, the settings and lighting. Norman Lloyd was musical director.

The Festival still had the form of a series of events scheduled throughout the session, but for the first time all were held in the Armory. It began July 2 and 3 with Doris Humphrey and Charles Weidman and their companies. After the opening number *To the Dance*, *Theatre Piece* and *New Dance* followed. On July 24, the Ballet Caravan returned for a second time under the auspices of the School. Martha Graham gave solo concerts on July 30 and 31 including two new numbers: *Opening Dance* and *Immediate Tragedy*.

The finale began on August 12 with the concert by the fellows. Esther Junger presented two solos and a suite, danced by Miss Junger, José Limón, and the group, all three works choreographed at Bennington. Part II of the evening was José Limón's three part suite, *Danza de la Muerte*, with opening and closing sections danced by the group, and a solo interlude

José Limón at the Bennington School of the Dance, 1937 (photograph by Edith Vail, courtesy Suzanne Brewer).

Anna Sokolow at the Bennington School of the Dance, circa 1937 (photographer unknown, courtesy Suzanne Brewer).

danced by Mr. Limón. The concert was completed with two solos by Anna Sokolow, previously composed and performed, and a four-part suite *Façade-Exposizione Italiana*, choreographed at Bennington and danced by Miss Sokolow and the group.

The fourth summer closed with the Workshop concerts. On August 13 and 14, Hanya Holm, her concert group and the workshop students she had trained, took the Armory stage. The program opened with four numbers from the repertoire, three performed by the concert group, and one by Hanya Holm with the group. The fifth number was unique among all the Workshop concerts. *Prelude* composed at Bennington, was danced by the two young groups — the professional company and the workshop group. Then came *Trend*, the product of the summer's intensive preparation — a many faceted commentary on human trial and triumph. Combining group and solo sections, the solos danced both by Hanya and by

Hanya Holm (left) and Company in *Trend* at the Bennington School of the Dance, 1937 (© Barbara Morgan, Barbara Morgan Archive).

four members of her company, it was in two sharply contrasting sections. The closing part of each section, first "Cataclysm" and finally "Resurgence," indicate the dramatic theme of the whole work.

The workshop plan was completed. Four new titles had been added to the list of major modern dance works: *Panorama, Quest, With My Red Fires,* and *Trend.* Acting on the conclusions to be drawn from this summing up, the plans for the fifth session were made.

Helen Alkire's Recollection

Elizabeth McPherson interviewed Helen Alkire by telephone on July 13, 2008, with the assistance of Lucy Venable. McPherson then transcribed and edited the material. This version was revised/corrected by Helen P. Alkire and Lucy Venable at Alkire's home February 13, 2011.

ALKIRE'S BIOGRAPHY

Helen Alkire (b. 1916) attended the Bennington School of the Dance in 1937 and 1940, and visited briefly in 1938. Professor Emerita of Dance at The Ohio State University (OSU), Alkire came from a musical family, and was interested in dance her entire life. Fortunately, she had excellent teachers of dance, including Stella J. Becker, and, as a student at Ohio State, Geneva Watson and Hermine Sauthoff. She completed a B.S. in Ed., and an M.A. in Dance at Ohio State, and worked toward a doctorate at Columbia University. As a student Alkire participated in all department dance productions at OSU, and was a member of Orchesis (a dance club formed by Margaret H'Doubler at the University of Wisconsin that became active in several universities in the United States). She gravitated strongly to modern dance because it was not confined to a strict technical style. She studied the German Expressionist technique pioneered by Mary Wigman and known as the "Wigman Technique." She worked closely with Hanya Holm at the Bennington School of the Dance, and became familiar with some of the great pioneers of modern dance such as Martha Graham, Doris Humphrey, José Limón, and Anna Sokolow at Bennington and Connecticut College. She founded the Department of Dance at Ohio State University in 1968 and chaired the department until 1983. She was awarded an honorary Doctor of Education degree by OSU in 1990 in recognition of her outstanding achievements and the importance of her contributions to the field of dance in higher education.

ALKIRE'S ACCOUNT[3]

The first time I was at the Bennington School of the Dance was 1937. I was a junior in college at Ohio State University, and Geneva Watson, one of her teachers there, as well as my studio teacher Stella J. Becker, whom I studied with as a child, suggested that I go to Bennington. Geneva Watson had been there in 1936, and was eager to have me go, which I decided to do. Hanya Holm was putting together an auxiliary group to add to her permanent company. You applied to get in, and my teachers wrote letters of recommendation. So I was with Hanya there all summer working on *Trend* which was her first major piece choreographed in this country.

It was quite an experience to work on *Trend*—very interesting to work with Hanya. She was very precise and very demanding. As an example, we used to rehearse in the Armory in the town of Bennington. And there were ramps going up onto the stage and then down into the auditorium. As we left the stage Hanya would sit below with this little baton in her hand and smack the top of your foot as you passed by. You were supposed to place your foot so that your arch was held high. It was very difficult to do. I don't think

Helen Alkire, circa 1930s (photographer unknown, courtesy Helen Alkire).

101

many of us could do it. The rehearsals were endless before we actually presented the dance. We worked all day and half the night. But when we performed *Trend* in the Bennington Armory, the ovation at the end was unbelievable. I think it went on for 5 minutes. I was so impressed.

We were up very late while they filmed it. They would film 3 or 4 minutes and then stop and then go back and overlap. So it took forever. It was in the early days of amateur filming, at least in modern dance. No one seems to know what happened to that film.

Hanya asked if I was going to be in New York and if I would be interested in doing the New York version of *Trend*. But I was in school, and I knew I couldn't leave school to go to New York, so I had to say no although I was even more interested in performing after being in *Trend*.

As an auxiliary member of Hanya's group, I could take Hanya's technique class only. I didn't take any others. It was a no-no to go into a Graham or a Weidman class or into any other class. You had to study with only one person. That was pretty much what happened for everybody in the school at that time. Other people may have risked it. I really don't know. I was too busy working on *Trend*.

Hanya Holm's *Trend* at the Bennington School of the Dance, 1937 (© Barbara Morgan, Barbara Morgan Archive).

102

The other course that I was able to take besides Hanya's technique class was a drumming course, and it was taught by Franziska Boas. We had to beat the drum with one rhythm but do another rhythm as we went across the floor which required complete concentration. I can remember once concentrating so much on what my feet were going to do and what my hand was going to do on the drum while I was gazing toward Franziska that she said, "Don't stare at me. That's not going to help you get it." And I just about keeled over. It was so difficult, you know, like doing a triplet in 4/4 time or something.

I remember Martha Hill and Mary Jo Shelly handing out the practice outfits that were cotton and sort of a cream color. There was a bra top and tight pants, and a skirt that fell about midway down the calf, which you wore when you went to dinner in the dining room.

The following summer of 1938, I went to the University of Wisconsin to work with Berta Ochsner and perform in her work called *Immediate Comment*, which was performed the next year in New York. At the end of that session at the University of Wisconsin, we drove up to Bennington

Students in percussion class at the Bennington School of the Dance, 1937 (photograph by Edith Vail, courtesy Suzanne Brewer).

for the last two weeks of their session. I think it was mostly just to see concerts and attend a lecture of some sort. Records seem to show that I also went to the Bennington School of the Arts as a student in 1940, but my strongest memories are of being there in 1937.

As I recall, people came from all over the United States to go to Bennington. It was the first time you could get together with people who were interested in modern dance or American dance, not that I put the ballet down, because I trained in ballet all during my childhood, but you could talk about the same things, and you could have the same goals. It was a wonderful experience.

I think Bennington was a very important school for the whole country. I think it influenced many people. And I am so grateful that I had the opportunity to go there. And I went to Connecticut College [Connecticut College School of the Dance] about every summer after that. It was at Connecticut that Louis Horst and I got to be great friends. I became his unofficial assistant for a short time. I loved Louis. He was great. I found him to be very helpful in many ways. Of course he was insisting that I stay in New York. He said, "You don't want to go back to Oblivion, Ohio." And I said, "But Louis, things have to happen in Ohio as well."

Going to the Bennington School of the Dance spearheaded the rest of my life. I was always interested in performance. I thought maybe I wanted to be a performer, and that was just emphasized a bit more by being in *Trend*. But when I returned to the university after the summer at Bennington, the physical education department offered me a graduate assistantship that of course I accepted. I was very flattered and honored. I stayed on another year to continue my assistantship and complete my master's degree. I still didn't know what I wanted to do — be a performer or be a teacher, but I got to the place where I loved teaching. I also thought if the Bennington School of the Dance can happen with all that wonderful dance, and all those wonderful artists, why can't it happen at a university? After I got my masters degree, OSU hired me as an instructor. Another teacher and I taught the technique and choreography classes. My aim was to establish a dance major. It was a long-term process because I had to first develop courses, and then I had to get a major in Physical Education because there was no College of the Arts at that point. I went to see Martha Hill once to ask her advice on developing a department of dance, but my best advice came from Merce Cunningham when he told me, "You just begin." In 1968,

OSU established the College of the Arts, and invited Dance to come in as a Department. The idea that had begun in 1937 had finally happened.

When I was at Bennington, I thought why can't I have visiting artists of young people so they can come to OSU and choreograph and have time to do it the way they wish? I had got to know Anna Sokolow that summer of 1937, and we were friends for the rest of her life. She was one of our first visiting artists along with Jack Moore and Viola Farber and others. In that way the Visiting Artists Program came out of the Bennington experience as well. The Bennington effects were far-reaching.

Facts and Figures, 1937

Total Enrollment of Students: 147 (does not include company members)

Select Students

General Program: Elizabeth Bloomer (Betty Ford), Pauline Chellis, Jean Erdman, Rose Koenig, Eleanor Lauer, Gertrude Lippincott, Naomi Lubell, Elizabeth Lyons, Barbara Mettler, Ruth Murray, Alwin Nikolais, Mildred Shaw, Theodora Wiesner

Workshop Students: Mary Standring Adair, Helen Alkire, Mary Alice Andrews, Carol Beals, Caryl E. Cuddeback, Elizabeth Ann Davis, Hermine Dudley, Helen J. Ellis, Marianne Elser, Mary R. Gillette, Margaret Jewell, Helen B. Knight, Hildegarde Lewis, Caroline Locke, Victoria H. Payne, Josephine Reddin, Ruth E. Riley, Harriet Roeder, Jeannette Saurborn, Dorothy M. Smith, Edith Vail, Florence Warwick, Martha Wilcox

Program in Choreography: Fannie Aronson, Ruth H. Bloomer, Margery Schneider, Marian Van Tuyl

Program in Music for the Dance: Beatrice Hellebrandt, Margaret Lidy

Faculty and Curriculum

Director, Martha Hill

Administrative Director, Mary Josephine Shelly

Photographer, Thomas Bouchard

Fellows: Esther Junger, José Limón, Anna Sokolow

General Program

Modern Dance
Martha Graham July 30–August 14
Assistant — Dorothy Bird (Villard)
Accompanist — Dini de Remer

Hanya Holm July 2–31
Assistants — Louise Kloepper, Elizabeth Waters, Lucretia Wilson
Accompanist — Harvey Pollins

Doris Humphrey July 2–17
Assistant — Edith Orcutt
Accompanist — Pauline Lawrence

Charles Weidman July 19–31
Assistant — George Bockman
Accompanist — Yolanda Lorenz

Techniques of Dance Movement
Martha Hill and Bessie Schönberg
Assistant — Hortense Lieberthal (Zera)
Accompanists — Ruth Lloyd and Esther Williamson

Composition in Dance Form — Pre-Classic Dance Forms
Taught by Louis Horst
Assistant — Mildred Wile
Accompanists — Dini de Remer and Ruth Lloyd

Composition in Dance Form–Modern Forms
Taught by Louis Horst
Assistant — Mildred Wile
Accompanists — Morris Mamorsky, assisted by Ruth Lloyd

Dance Composition — Introductory Section
Taught by Bessie Schönberg
Accompanists — Ruth Lloyd, Morris Mamorsky, and Esther Williamson

Dance Composition — Intermediate and Advanced Sections
Taught by Martha Hill
Assistant — Bessie Schönberg to Intermediate Section
Accompanists — Ruth Lloyd, Morris Mamorsky and Esther Williamson

Dramatic Basis of Movement
Taught by Louise Martin

Laboratory in Composition
Supervised by Martha Hill, Louis Horst, John Martin
Accompanists — Margaret Lidy, Ruth Lloyd, Morris Mamorsky and Esther
    Williamson
For the fellows and students enrolled in the Program in Choreography

Elements of Music
Taught by Norman Lloyd

Percussion Accompaniment
Taught by Franziska Boas

Dance History and Criticism
Taught by John Martin

Seminar in Dance Criticism
Taught by John Martin

Workshop Program

Hanya Holm, Director
Technique and Choreography
Taught by Hanya Holm (working on *Trend*)
Assistants — Louise Kloepper, Elizabeth Waters, Lucretia Wilson
Accompanists — Harvey Pollins, piano; Franziska Boas and Carolyn
    Durand, percussion
Musical Director for the performance, Norman Lloyd
Composer of *Trend*, Wallingford Riegger

Percussion Accompaniment
Taught by Franziska Boas

Dance History and Criticism
Taught by John Martin

Program in Choreography

Directors, Martha Hill and Louis Horst
Courses from the General Program
Modern Dance

Techniques of Dance Movement

Composition in Dance Forms — Modern Forms

Percussion Accompaniment

Program in Music for the Dance

Director, Louis Horst

Music Accompaniment
Taught by Norman Lloyd

Music Composition
Taught by Louis Horst

Select Concerts, Demonstrations, and Events

July 2 and 3 The Armory	Doris Humphrey, Charles Weidman and their New York Concert Groups

To the Dance
Choreographed by Doris Humphrey
Music by Clair Leonard
Danced by Doris Humphrey, Charles Weidman, and Group

Theatre Piece
Choreography by Doris Humphrey (Charles Weidman choreographed "In the Theatre" section)
Music by Wallingford Riegger

> *Prologue (Assignment of Roles)*
> Danced by Doris Humphrey and Group
>
> *Behind Walls*
> Danced by Doris Humphrey and Group
>
> *In the Open (Hunting Dance)*
> Danced by Edith Orcutt, Charles Weidman, and Group
>
> *Interlude*
> Danced by Doris Humphrey

In the Stadium
Danced by George Bockman, José Limón,
Katherine Manning and Group

In the Theatre
Danced by Katherine Litz, Katherine Manning,
Charles Weidman

The Race
Danced by Doris Humphrey and Group

Epilogue (The Return)
Danced by Doris Humphrey and the Group

New Dance
Choreography by Doris Humphrey (Charles
Weidman choreographed "Third Theme" section)
Music by Wallingford Riegger

Prelude
Danced by Doris Humphrey and Charles
Weidman

First Theme
Danced by Doris Humphrey and Group

Second Theme
Danced by Doris Humphrey and Group

Third Theme
Danced by Charles Weidman and Group

Processional
Danced by Doris Humphrey, Charles Weidman,
and Group

Celebration
Danced Doris Humphrey, Charles Weidman,
and Group

Variations and Conclusion
Danced by William Bales, George Bockman,
Doris Humphrey, José Limón, Katherine Litz,
Edith Orcutt, Sybil Shearer, Charles
Weidman and Group

Members of the Group: Doris Humphrey, Charles
Weidman, William Bales, George Bockman,
Philip Gordon, Harriette Ann Gray, Joan Levy,
José Limón, Katherine Litz, Katherine Manning,
Edith Orcutt, Miriam Raphael, Sybil Shearer, Lee
Sherman, Ruth Sloan, Lily Verne

Musical Director, Norman Lloyd
Costumes, Pauline Lawrence
Ruth and Norman Lloyd — piano, M. Goldenberg —
percussion, H. Tafarella — clarinet, V. Peretti —
trumpet

July 4	Display of Fireworks
July 9	Informal Music with Ruth Lloyd and Norman Lloyd, Morris Mamorsky, and Harvey Pollins
July 11 College Theatre	Lecture-demonstration in Modern Dance by Hanya Holm and her Concert Group
July 14 Barn Quadrangle	Lecture-discussion in Modern Dance by Doris Humphrey
July 15 Lounge	Display of dance costumes from Aldrich and Aldrich under the direction of Elaine Scanlan
July 16, 17, and 18 Lounge	Lectures on Dance Notation by Paul Love
July 19 Lounge	Playing and Analysis of Music for Dance Techniques Written by Norman Lloyd and Harvey Pollins — lecture given by Pauline Lawrence, Ruth Lloyd, and Harvey Pollins
July 22 Lounge	Lecture-discussion, "The Bennington College Plan" by Robert D. Leigh, President of Bennington College
July 24 College Theatre	Lecture-discussion "The Classic Dance" by Lincoln Kirstein, Director of Ballet Caravan
July 24 College Theatre	Demonstration of Ballet Technique by Members of Ballet Caravan under the direction of Douglas Coudy

July 24 The Armory	Concert: Ballet Caravan under the auspices of the Bennington School of the Dance

Encounter (Classic ballet in one act)
Choreography by Lew Christensen
Music by W. A. Mozart
Danced by Ruby Asquith, Ruthanna Boris, Harold Christensen, Lew Christensen, Douglas Coudy, Jane Doering, Albia Kavan, Lorna London, Marjorie Munson, Helen Stewart

Yankee Clipper (Ballet-voyage in one act)
Choreography by Eugene Loring
Music by Paul Bowles
Danced by Ruby Asquith, Ruthanna Boris, Harold Christensen, Lew Christensen, Fred Danieli, Jane Doering, Marie-Jeanne, Rabanna Hasburgh, Erick Hawkins, Mary Heater, Albia Kavan, Lorna London, Eugene Loring, Marjorie Munson, Helen Stewart, Audrey White

Show Piece (Ballet Workout in one act)
Choreography by Erick Hawkins
Music by Robert McBride
Costumes by Keith Martin
Danced by Ruby Asquith, Ruthanna Boris, Lew Christensen, Douglas Coudy, Fred Danieli, Jane Doering, Rabana Hasburgh, Marie-Jeanne, Albia Kavan, Lorna London, Eugene Loring, and other ensemble members

Douglas Coudy, Company Manager
Lew Christensen, Ballet Master
Elliott Carter, Jr., Musical Director
David Stimer, Pianist

July 25 College Theatre	Informal Dance Concert by Marian Van Tuyl and Group under the auspices of the American Dance Association

Dances choreographed by Van Tuyl and performed by Ruth Ann Heisey, Eleanor Lauer, Marian Van Tuyl, Theodora Wiesner, Mildred Wile

Salutation
Music by Carlos Chavez
Danced by Marian Van Tuyl

No Retreat
Music by Egon Wellesz
Danced by Ruth Ann Heisey, Eleanor Lauer, Marian Van Tuyl, Theodora Wiesner

Americana: Alone, Together, Public Condolences, Public Rejoicings
Music by Jean Williams and Paul Nordoff
Danced by Ruth Ann Heisey, Eleanor Lauer, Marian Van Tuyl, Theodora Wiesner, Mildred Wile

Triumphant Figure
Music by Esther Williamson
Danced by Marian Van Tuyl

Epilogue to Victory
Music by Jean Williams
Danced by Ruth Ann Heisey, Eleanor Lauer, Marian Van Tuyl

Exhibition Piece
Music by Jean Williams
Danced by Ruth Ann Heisey, Eleanor Lauer, Marian Van Tuyl, Theodora Wiesner

In the Clearing
Music by Gregory Tucker
Danced by Ruth Ann Heisey, Eleanor Lauer, Marian Van Tuyl, Mildred Wile

July 27
College Theatre

Lecture-discussion, "The Relationship Between the Arts of the Theatre" by Francis Fergusson, Chairman of the Drama Division of Bennington College

July 28 College Theatre	Lecture-demonstration in Modern Dance by Charles Weidman, assisted by George Bockman and José Limón
July 30 and 31 The Armory	Concert, Martha Graham Dances choreographed and danced by Martha Graham Louis Horst, Musical Director

Opening Dance
Music by Norman Lloyd

Lamentation
Music by Zoltán Kodály

Frontier
Music by Louis Horst

Satyric Festival Song
Music by Imre Weisshaus

Immediate Tragedy
Music by Henry Cowell

Spectre 1914
Music by Wallingford Riegger

Ekstasis
Music by Lehman Engel

Imperial Gesture
Music by Lehman Engel

Act of Piety
Music by Louis Horst

Harlequinade
Music by Ernst Toch

Hugo Bergamasco —flute, H. Tafarella — clarinet,
V. Perreti — trumpet, J. Youshkoff— bass clarinet,
S. Gershek — drums

July 31 Lounge	Lecture "A Project Theatre for Bennington College" by Arch Lauterer, Member of Drama Division of Bennington College and designer of the plan

August 1 Lounge	Closed conference on the National Dance Conference by Frederick Redefer, chairman, and visiting members of conference Attendance by invitation only
August 1 College Theatre	Informal Music Recital by Edward Glass, Ruth Lloyd and Norman Lloyd, Morris Mamorsky, Harvey Pollins, Esther Williamson of the faculty and staff of the Bennington School of the Dance
August 3 Lounge	Discussion, "The Dance in Education," Martha Hill presiding
August 6 Barn Lecture Room	Lecture, "Why Spain Is Important to You" given by Theodore Newcomb, member of the Social Studies Division of Bennington College Under the auspices of the American Dance Association
August 6 Barn Lecture Room	Lecture, illustrated, showing films of speed and time-lapse photography of natural phenomenon, given by Robert Woodworth, member of the Science Division of Bennington College
August 7 Lounge	Playing of music for dance technique, written by Ellen Boyd, played by Ruth Lloyd
August 8 Barn Lecture Room	Showing of Dance Movies taken by Ruth Bloomer, Helen Knight, and Marian Van Tuyl
August 9 Lounge	Community Meeting of all members of the Bennington School of the Dance to discuss future plans of the schools based on suggestions and criticisms of the groups and to sample opinion on a plan for a permanent central school for modern dance
August 11 Lounge	Lecture-discussion on Modern Dance by Martha Graham
August 12 The Armory	Esther Junger, José Limón, Anna Sokolow — fellows of the Bennington School of the Dance, 1937

Dance to the People
Choreographed and performed by Esther Junger
Music by Jerome Moross

Ravage
Choreographed and performed by Esther Junger
Music by Harvey Pollins

Festive Rites-Processional, Betrothal, Recessional
Choreographed by Esther Junger
Music by Morris Mamorsky
Performed by Esther Junger, José Limón, and
  Group

Danza de la Muerte
Choreographed by José Limón
Music by Henry Clark and Norman Lloyd
  Sarabande for the Dead
  performed by the Group

  Interlude
  performed by José Limón
    Hoch!
    Viva!
    Ave!
  Sarabande for the Living
  performed by the Group

Ballad in a Popular Style
Choreographed and performed by Anna Sokolow
Music by Alex North

Speaker
Choreographed and performed by Anna Sokolow
Music by Alex North

Façade-Esposizione Italiano
Choreographed by Anna Sokolow
performed by Anna Sokolow and Group
Music by Alex North
  Belle Arti
  Giovanezza

Prix Femina
Phantasmagoria

Opus for Three and Props
Performed by Esther Junger, José Limón, Anna
   Sokolow
Music by Dmitri Shostakovitch
   With Pole
   Choreographed by José Limón
   With Hats
   Choreographed by Esther Junger

Esther Junger's Group: Jean Aubry, Dorothy
   Barnitz, Sara Jean Cosner, Victoria Kahn, Frances
   Kronstadt, Eileen Logan, Margaret Ramsay, Rima
   Rodion, Germaine Steffes, Eva Trofimov

José Limón's Group: Pauline Chellis, Gertrude
   Green, Molly Hecht, James Lyons, Alwin
   Nikolais, Peter Terry, James Welch, Emily White,
   Mary Elizabeth Whitney, Mildred Wile

Anna Sokolow's Group: Elizabeth Bloomer, Nina
   Caiserman, Jean Erdman, Natalie Harris,
   Hortense Lieberthal (Zora), Naomi Lubell,
   Elizabeth Moore, Pearl Satlien, Margaret Strater,
   Elizabeth van Barneveld

Musical Director, Norman Lloyd
Accompanists — Norman Lloyd, Ruth Lloyd, Morris
   Mamorsky, Robert McBride, Alex North, Harvey
   Pollins, Esther Williamson

August 13 and 14   Hanya Holm and her New York Concert Group
The Armory   with Students of the School Workshop presenting
                              a New Major Composition

All choreography by Hanya Holm
Salutation
Music by Henry Cowell
Performed by Concert Group

116

City Nocturne
Music by Wallingford Riegger
Performed by Concert Group

Rhythm II
Music by Lucretia Wilson
Performed by Concert Group

Festive Rhythm
Music by Wallingford Riegger
Performed by Hanya Holm and Concert Group

Prelude
Music by Wallingford Riegger
Performed by Concert Group and Workshop Group

Trend
Music by Wallingford Riegger
Performed by Hanya Holm, Concert Group and
  Workshop Group

Members of Hanya Holm's Group: Keith Coppage,
  Carolyn Durand, Marva Jaffay, Miriam Kagan,
  Louise Kloepper, Henrietta Greenhood (Eve
  Gentry), Ruth Ledoux, Lydia Tarnower, Bernice
  van Gelder, Elizabeth Waters, Lucretia Wilson

Students of the Workshop Group: Mary Standring
  Adair, Helen Alkire, Mary Alice Andrews, Carol
  Beals, Caryl Cuddeback, Elizabeth Ann Davis,
  Hermine Dudley, Helen Ellis, Marianne Elser,
  Mary Gillette, Margaret Jewell, Helen Knight,
  Hildegarde Lewis, Caroline Locke, Victoria Payne,
  Josephine Reddin, Harriet Roeder, Jeannette
  Saurborn, Dorothy Smith, Edith Vail, Florence
  Warwick, and Martha Wilcox

Musical Director, Norman Lloyd

Norman Lloyd and Harvey Pollins — piano, Hugo
  Bergamasco — flute, H. Tafarella — oboe,
  J. Youshkoff — bassoon, V. Peretti — trumpet,

S. Gershek — drums, Franziska Boas, Carolyn
Durand — percussion

August 14
College Theatre

Final Demonstrations of Student Work
Dance Composition under the direction of Martha
Hill and Bessie Schönberg: compositions by:
Karen Burt, Mary Cave, Janet Cumming, Ruth
Ann Heisey, Beatrice Hellebrandt, Josephine
Ketcik, Eleanor Lauer, Naomi Lubell, Eva
Trofimov, Theodora Wiesner

Pre-Classic Forms under the direction of Louis
Horst, assisted by Mildred Wile; compositions
by: Pauline Chellis, Gertrude Green, Josephine
Ketcik, Frances Kronstadt, James Lyons, Alwin
Nikolais, Eva Trofimov, Theodora Wiesner

Modern Forms under the direction of Louis Horst,
assisted by Mildred Wile; compositions by:
Karen Burt, Jean Erdman, Ruth Ann Heisey,
Truda Kaschmann, Eleanor Lauer, Barbara
Mettler, Elizabeth Moore, Elizabeth Whitney

*Program in Choreography and Program in Music
Composition for the Dance* under the direction of
Martha Hill, Louis Horst, and John Martin;
compositions by Ruth H. Bloomer, Marjorie
Schneider, Marian Van Tuyl

Summer of 1938:
Culmination of a Plan, or
"the Year of the Tent"

"I had an early morning class in that tent. I don't know if anybody told you, it [had] great big wide stripes. When I'd have people turning or doing anything of that kind in the studio, the bodies would be going around and the stripes would be going around the other way. Oh it used to make me so dizzy!"[1]—Ethel Butler

Dates: July 2–August 13
Location: Bennington College, Bennington, Vermont

Participants at the school who were there for multiple years frequently speak of 1938 as the climax of the nine year project. However, there were quite a few obstacles, including managing the highly creative and idiosyncratic faculty who were all in residence together in the summer of 1938, and perhaps the even more difficult problem—lack of dance spaces. With each choreographer creating work, finding places for everyone to rehearse was more challenging than ever. Arch Lauterer provided one solution in the form of a big striped tent. Other solutions were bussing dancers to the town of Bennington to rehearse at the Vermont State Armory and at North Bennington High School.

Mary Jo Shelly's Recollection[2]

The story of the fifth session, culmination of a plan barely sketched that day in 1933, is best told by reciting its highlights.

Within the curriculum, two significant changes appear, among other lesser refinements. One was a change of title from Workshop Program to Professional Program, meaning more than a change of words. Those who met the requirements for any one of the four groups within this program had to satisfy the most stringent demands. They were to dance as full apprentice members of a concert group, not as students of a workshop.

The second change, the addition of a Program in "Stage Design for Dance" under Arch Lauterer and Martha Hill marked an evolution in the art of modern dance. Like the earlier "Program in Music for Dance," modern dance could no longer function by borrowing ready-made assistance from other arts. Action, accompanist, setting — all had to be of a piece. Dance as true theatre was thus recognized.

On the score of production, the 1938 session amounted to nothing less than sheer daring. The Festival assumed its full form — six performances concentrated in one week in August, made up of three programs, each given twice. It opened with the performance by the fellows selected this year — Eleanor King, Louise Kloepper, and Marian Van Tuyl, followed by Hanya Holm and group, Doris Humphrey and group, then Charles Weidman and Martha Graham and their groups. While the Armory was the scene of action in the evenings, rounding out the Festival, the College Theatre in the afternoon had its own events — a lecture by Curt Sachs on "Dance and Music," one by John Martin on "Backgrounds of the American Modern Dance," a "Program of Music for the Dance" with Louis Horst and nine other composers, a second lecture by Curt Sachs on "Dance, Anthropology, History," and finally John Martin's second lecture "Isadora Duncan and the Modern Dance." One had to pay a dollar to get into the Armory, if one was lucky enough to do so. These afternoon events were free of charge. During the Festival week, the Commons also housed exhibits of photographs of the dance at Bennington by Barbara Morgan and Thomas Bouchard, exhibits of dance costumes by Wright and Ditson, and books on dance from the Kamin Bookshop. Invasion took over the campus; stampede took over the Armory.

Instead of culmination of a plan, 1938 could well be called the year of the Tent. The capitalization it deserved. Since 1936, agreement about use of the Armory, while always approached with due caution, had been reached. This year, the Vermont National Guard had a new schedule, and a new mood prevailed during the customary negotiations. They were not only prolonged but had the possibility of disaster for the already announced ambitious Festival. Maybe the Armory would not be available at all, or at least in time.

Nothing, not even the Vermont National Guard could defeat Arch Lauterer. Obviously, out of the question, in the event of an actual exclusion from his magnificently devised theatre, was containment of such a cycle on the top floor of the Commons. Another imaginative setting, a tent erected beside the Library on campus, would do it. Off Arch went to find one. A dull brown Army tent? Not for Arch. Somewhere on Long Island, discarded long since as a shelter for some part of a racetrack, he came upon his conception of a proper tent, not only capacious, but gaily red and white striped. He bought it, and had it carted to Vermont. By this time, Martha Biehle, custodian of the bluest of the blue-sky budgets ever devised, was only slightly concerned. More was to come — a platform for dancing since that couldn't be done on bare ground and a cable for electrical connections since dancing called for lights.

Suffice it to report that the tent came and was erected in a prophetic wind. The platform and the cable both materialized. Only the wind continued unconquered. Arch had an answer to that. His two technical assis-

Graham technique class in the Tent at the Bennington School of the Dance, 1938. Erick Hawkins in center (© Barbara Morgan, Barbara Morgan Archive).

tants, Edward Glass, already a veteran at assisting Arch, and Henry Seymour, new to it, but brave, would live in the tent and handle it like a ship at full sail, slacking or tightening ropes as the wind dictated. It never blew down. It just leaked. Clearly even to undauntable Arch, it was no home for a festival.

Negotiations with the powers controlling the Armory simply had to be resumed and were. An odd factor entered the considerations. The School and especially the Festival, had become big business for the small town — a fact not to be ignored even if never admitted. At last, if the impossible interval of three days for installation of the theatre and rehearsals in it would do, the place was again ours. Anything that would make opening the Festival on August 4 possible would do. One full rehearsal in the Armory of each performance would have to be enough. The rest of the problem was Arch's, except for one element. Composing and rehearsing for four professional companies and the fellows group had to happen somewhere while the School also went on. Charles Weidman, judged the sturdiest, drew the Tent. The others made do, as they had before, with the spaces in the campus buildings and one off campus, found by chance in an unused loft of uncertain stability. But it, like the Tent, survived the period of preparation.

Installation of the theatre in the Armory was another matter. Arch, long dissatisfied not only with its audience capacity but the floor level seating for the majority of on-lookers, wanted something better this time. He designed bleachers, rising from the floor to balcony, on which folding chairs could be put. Built in advance and erected, it posed a wholly new question — coverage under the liability policy taken out for audience protection in the Armory. The College policy covered only the campus. A proper insurance company official appeared late in the afternoon preceding the first performance, crawled under the unlikely structure with notebook and pencil and emerged to announce the amount of "mobile weight" it would support. Here was the moment when the hazard of the now traditional signal of approbation — the beating of heels on the floor, came instantly to mind. Since nothing was likely to stop it, it would just have to be counted as part of the mobile weight.

It must have been another of the beneficences that seemed to go along with the Bennington project that it did. For six successive evenings, a capacity audience, accompanied by a classic version of the annual summer thunderstorm, filled every seat and beat their heels with good reason. Programs included works composed and danced before and those newly composed and danced for the first time at Bennington, six of them short pieces by the young artists holding the 1938 fellowships, the other four major works by the four resident artists and their companies. As before, works

Martha Graham (Erick Hawkins behind her) in *American Document* at the Bennington School of the Dance, 1938 (© Barbara Morgan, Barbara Morgan Archive.

123

for a group by the fellows drew on qualified students volunteering from among those studying under the "General Program." Financial resources had limited the number in each of the artists' professional companies to six, augmented in each case by a varying number meeting standards set for apprentices.

Another limitation had been set by greatly increased costs of having four professional companies in residence for the full session, and the staging of a Festival of these dimensions. Although total cost to students had risen over five years from $190 to $225, so also had size of faculty, salaries, and the cost of everything needed to support the School and the Festival. The one dollar admission fee for the Festival performances, despite a capacity audience each season for every performance, never paid Festival expenses. In 1938, this source of income was projected to fall far below expenses. Some sacrifice had to be made. For every other season, a small orchestra had been imported. The cost in addition to the impossibility of having satisfying orchestral accompaniment for such an extensive number and

Charles Weidman and others in Weidman's *Opus 51* at the Bennington School of the Dance, 1938 (© Barbara Morgan, Barbara Morgan Archive).

Doris Humphrey and others in Humphrey's *Passacaglia* at the Bennington School of the Dance, 1938 (© Barbara Morgan, Barbara Morgan Archive).

variety of works, made an orchestra out of the question this year. Two concert grand pianos and percussion for some numbers had to be substituted. Under the overall musical direction of Norman Lloyd, there appeared to be no detriment to the effect of the six evenings on the audience from having more limited musical accompaniment. Even the critics, who came in a phalanx to cover the event, failed to take notice of anything other than the breath-taking dancing that, for the last time, filled Arch Lauterer's theatre.

Together with the new works by the fellows, the final festival held in the Armory added still another series of long-remembered titles to the list of major compositions: Doris Humphrey's *Passacaglia*, Hanya Holm's *Dance Sonata*, Charles Weidman's *Opus 51*, and Martha Graham's *American Document*. Not all of them were elsewhere repeated in identical form, but each was conserved in some form in later works. As during preceding seasons, here had been the first chance even to undertake production on such a scale; here had been the first epic demonstration of a new style in an art as old as mankind; here had been creativity at its freest and dancing at its brilliant best. After such a culmination of the original plan, there had to come a new departure. Figuratively and literally that would take place.

Jeanne Hays Beaman's Recollection

Elizabeth McPherson interviewed Jeanne Hays Beaman by telephone on January 28, 2011. McPherson transcribed and edited the interview that was then checked by Beaman in February of 2011.

BEAMAN'S BIOGRAPHY

Jeanne Hays Beaman was born (1919) in San Francisco and began her dance career as a member of the San Francisco Ballet (1938–1940), having previously danced with Michel Fokine in the Hollywood Bowl in 1929. On the West Coast, she studied with Adolph Bolm, William Christensen, May O'Donnell and José Limón, and in New York, she studied at the School of American Ballet and with Martha Graham. She attended the Bennington School of the Dance in 1938. Beaman holds an undergraduate degree from the University of California at Berkley in Art History and an M.A. in Physical Education from Mills College where she worked under the direction of Marian Van Tuyl. As a choreographer, Beaman created three nationally released original ballets for Pittsburgh's WQED, and she choreographed for the Red-

Jeanne Hays Beaman at the Bennington School of the Dance, 1938 (photographer unknown, courtesy Jeanne Beaman).

lands Bowl in California from 1953 to 1955. A pioneer in dance and technology, she wrote several articles on that subject including "Computer Dance" for *Impulse* (1965). Beaman taught at the University of Pittsburgh from 1961 to 1974, and is now Professor Emerita. She was a founder of the American College Dance Festival Association and the Pittsburgh Dance Council. She was the Dance Coordinator for the Massachusetts Arts and Humanities Foundation (1975–1978), dance evaluator for the New England Foundation for the Arts (1979 to 1982), and a member of the Massachusetts Cultural Council (1986–1992). In 2004, Beaman received the Boston Dance Alliance's Dance Champion Award.

BEAMAN'S ACCOUNT[3]

I was only at the Bennington School of the Dance in 1938. By the following summer, I was busy dancing with San Francisco Ballet. I knew about the Bennington School of the Dance because I had a subscription to *Dance Magazine* and had read about it there. I was also studying with a dance teacher Valerie Quandt who kept me informed about things that were going on. I knew about Martha Graham and Doris Humphrey and so on. Since everybody was there that summer, including Hanya Holm and the assistants May O'Donnell for Martha Graham and Louise Kloepper for Hanya Holm, I wanted to go. I was at that time living in Berkeley, California so it was a trek for me to go to Vermont, but a very exciting one.

Martha Hill and Mary Jo Shelly were running the place along with Bessie Schönberg. They saw that things got done. And they all ate lunch together, so they would discuss what was going on and what they needed to do. They were wonderful caretakers of that place. Martha Hill was a very strong person particularly. I remember many years later, I was at a dance conference, and Martha Hill was there. I said that I was hoping to introduce the American College Dance Festival in Pittsburgh the next year. Martha Hill said, "Don't say you are hoping to do it. Say you are *going* to do it." You can just hear her saying that — don't be doubtful at all. And of course I did do it. But she was that sort of a person, a wonderful person.

At the Bennington School of the Dance, I took the general technique program. Bessie actually interviewed me when I was there. As a ballet trained person, I was totally frightened of choreographing anything, so I wasn't electing to take one of Louis Horst's courses because I was terrified of it. When I told Bessie about my dance background, she said "You must take a course with Louis Horst." So that was how I got enrolled in that. I have a funny story to tell you about the first piece of choreography I did for him. He knew by then that I had been trained as a ballet dancer, and he said, "Well at least they teach them how to dance," implying correctly that I had not been trained how to choreograph. But Louis and I became very well acquainted, and we remained very good friends after that session at Bennington. He was a wonderful teacher. I mean he could be caustic, but it was caustic for usually a good reason.

I particularly enjoyed working with Arch Lauterer who was there doing stage designs. Alwin Nikolais and I were interested in that, so we met through playing around with and talking about the use of stage space. At Bennington, we looked at the whole realm of dance — including the staging, and we had sessions on music too. It was not just "Can you choreograph a piece and show it off?" We experimented with other production aspects and also other periods of dance through the Louis Horst choreography method of Pre-classic Dance Forms which gave you a real history of dance in another time. And John Martin, the dance critic lectured too, so I went to that.

I took technique classes with Doris Humphrey, Martha Graham, Hanya Holm, and Charles Weidman. They taught their own classes, but usually had an assistant, one of their company members demonstrating some things, so that they didn't have to do all of the demonstrating.

The Graham technique appealed to me a great deal. It is, of course, so disciplined. The form of the exercises is quite exact, so I enjoyed that technique very much. But as a teacher, the one who was perhaps the most informative to me was Doris Humphrey because she often did improvisations, moving across the floor based on a rhythm or something she gave you. I did one of these improvisations, and I was using arm gestures which were like marching gestures you might do in a parade, and what she said was, "If you do that Jeanne, then everybody is going to think that is the kind of dance you are doing." Well, I had no idea that certain arm gestures had meaning and identification for people who are looking at it. I thought I was improvising something brand new and different, so that was a very informative idea — that you have to remember that certain gestures have preconceived meanings that the audience will recognize. It was an important lesson to learn about using gestures. I also enjoyed Hanya Holm and Charles Weidman's classes very much.

Although I took classes with everybody who was there, there were many people who stayed with one technique. There were very clearly Graham-ites and Humphrey-Weidman-ites, no doubt about it. Some Graham fans did not associate with the Humphrey fans and vice versa, so there was that kind of clannishness, devotion to one or the other. And if you wanted to hop around between the two, you were different than some of them, but there were a lot of people who were mixing everything up too, like me. Later on when I was teaching at the University of Pittsburgh, I brought both Graham and Humphrey-Weidman there. So those connections were important.

The Bennington School of the Dance had a wonderful atmosphere, but my atmosphere was quite colored by the fact that Anna Halprin (Ann Schuman at that time) was on the same floor in the same dorm as I was, and we kind of bonded as two young people right away. She was my friend and my intimate contact. I actually didn't really bond with anybody else although I knew of course who some of the people were, the older ones, and they were friendly and cordial. Anna and I used to fix ice cream cones for ourselves that they should have charged us double for. We filled the cones solid! I remember another students, Marian Ryder. We kept in touch for a while after being at Bennington, and then we lost contact. And I remember being driven by one of the music students, Freda Miller, to Tanglewood. That was my one big outing from Bennington, and it was a real treat. It was my first trip to Tanglewood which I've since enjoyed a lot now that I am a New Englander.

There was much excitement on campus with the festival performances at Bennington. I remember seeing the premiere of Graham's *American Document* (1938) and also seeing Humphrey's *Passacaglia and Fugue in C Minor* (1938). Marian Van Tuyl was one of the fellows that year, and I was in the dance she choreographed. It was very interesting being in it with her. I did not particularly warm to Marian Van Tuyl's choreography, but I did enjoy dancing with her. Teddy Wiesner and I did a duet together. It must have been kind of a "Mutt and Jeff" thing because I am very short and she is rather tall!

José Limón was there at the end of the six week session after having

Jeanne Hays Beaman, third dancer from the left, Marian Van Tuyl, second dancer from the right in darker dress, and others in Van Tuyl's *Out of One Happening*, 1938 (© Barbara Morgan, Barbara Morgan Archive).

been teaching in Colorado. He was absolutely thrilling as a dancer, and he was so happy to be back kind of in his milieu. That was memorable, his return.

In terms of lasting effects on my career, of course I met Marian Van Tuyl at Bennington and went on and took my graduate degree with Marian at Mills College. That is how it affected me directly, an important phase in my career. And the association with Louis Horst, the introduction to choreography, was very important to me. Actually in many ways, Bennington changed my direction as a teacher and a performer away from being a totally ballet dancer. Although I should say that as a ballet dancer, I was also a character dancer. I had studied Spanish dance with the Canseno family and took classes from every visiting teacher, such as Harald Kreutzberg, who came through Northern California.

I went to American Dance Festival at Connecticut College once later on. It was similar to Bennington, but different too. It wasn't as spontaneous as I felt Bennington was. At Bennington, they were trying all sorts of things. Each choreographer was absolutely doing their own style whatever it was. When I was at American Dance Festival, it was much more organized, and there were more levels (1, 2, 3, 4) like a school. At Bennington, it didn't strike me as being like a school. It was where people with talents and ideas they wanted to express and pass on could work, but nobody had organized them into which way each of them was going. Modern dance was still in its formation, less formalized.

The Bennington School of the Dance trained the next generation of modern dancers and choreographers. Anna Halprin was not the only one — Alwin Nikolais, Merce Cunningham, Marian Van Tuyl and Gertrude Lippincott were there too at that time. So that was an important legacy — they trained many of the people who gave the new face to modern dance and dance education in the second half of the 20th century.

Facts and Figures, 1938

Total Enrollment of Students: 150 (does not include company members)

Select Students

General Program: Jean Aubry, Marjorie Browning, Doris Isabelle Ewing, Alma Hawkins, Jeanne Hays (Beaman), Delia Hussey, Lillian Lack, Eleanor Lauer, Gertrude Lippincott, Charlotte Moton[4], Marion Glover Moulton, Alwin Nikolais, Faith Reyher, Ann Schuman (Anna Halprin), Marion Streng, Betty Lynd Thompson, Theodora Wiesner

Apprentice Program:
With Martha Graham: Muriel Brenner, Jean Erdman, Erick Hawkins, Virginia Johnson, Jane Perry, Helen Priest (Rogers), Kaya Russell, Elaine Scanlan, Margaret Strater, Claire Strauss, Eleanor Struppa

With Hanya Holm: Mary Standring Adair, Katherine Bollard, Mary Frances Cave, Elsie Earle, Saralee Harris, Katharine Imig, Beatrice Lovejoy, Charlotte Orlov, Hildegard Spreen, Claire Weigt, Martha Wilcox

With Doris Humphrey: Barbara Beiswanger, Sara Jean Cosner, Gloria Garcia, Maria Maginnis, Ethel Mann, Claudia Moore (Read), Pegge Oppenheimer, Ruth Parmet, Barbara Spaulding, Patricia Urner, Mildred Zook

With Charles Weidman: Pauline Chellis, Maxine Cushing, Eleanor Frampton, Molly Hecht, Maxine Munt, Dorothy Ross, Anne Stern

Program in Choreography: Lillian Shapero, Florence Warwick

Program in Music for the Dance: Ralph Gilbert, Minnie Goodsitt, Freda D. Miller, Drusa Wilker

Program in Stage Design for the Dance: Ruth H. Bloomer, Lois Lord, Philip Stapp

Faculty and Curriculum

Martha Hill, Director

Mary Josephine Shelly, Administrative Director

Barbara Morgan, Photographer

Curt Sachs, Lecturer

Fellows of 1938: Eleanor King, Louise Kloepper, and Marian Van Tuyl

General Program

Modern Dance
Taught by Martha Graham, July 4–August 3, August 11, 12
Assistants — Ethel Butler and May O'Donnell
Accompanist — Dini de Remer

Taught by Hanya Holm, July 4–August 3, August 11, 12
Assistants — Carolyn Durand and Elizabeth Waters
Accompanist — Harvey Pollins

Taught by Doris Humphrey, July 4–August 3, August 11, 12
Assistants — Katherine Manning, Edith Orcutt, Sybil Shearer
Accompanists — Pauline Lawrence and Morris Mamorsky

Taught by Charles Weidman, July 4–August 3, August 11, 12
Assistants — William Bales, George Bockman, Lee Sherman
Accompanist — Margaret Lidy

Techniques of Dance Movement
Taught by Martha Hill and Bessie Schönberg
Assistants — Hortense Lieberthal (Zera)
Accompanists — Ruth Lloyd and Esther Williamson

Composition in Dance Forms, Pre-Classic Forms
Taught by Louis Horst and Mildred Wile
Accompanists — Ruth Lloyd, Dini de Remer, and Esther Williamson

Composition in Dance Forms, Modern Forms
Taught by Louis Horst
Assistant — Mildred Wile
Accompanist — Ruth Lloyd

Dance Composition (Introductory Section)
Taught by Bessie Schönberg
Assistant — Hortense Lieberthal (Zera)
Accompanist — Ruth Lloyd

Dance Composition (Intermediate Section)
Taught by Martha Hill
Assistant — Bessie Schönberg
Accompanists — Ruth Lloyd and students from the Program in Music for the Dance

Laboratory in Composition
Co-directed by Martha Hill and Louis Horst
Accompanists — Margaret Lidy, Drusa Wilker, Esther Williamson
For the fellows and students enrolled in the Program in Choreography

Elements of Music
Taught by Norman Lloyd

Percussion Accompaniment
Taught by Franziska Boas

Experimental Production
Co-Directed by Martha Hill and Arch Lauterer
Assistants — Edward Glass and Henry Seymour

Professional Program

"for intensive technical study under one artist and apprenticeship in the artist's concert group"[5]
Taught by Martha Graham, working on *American Document*
Assistants — Ethel Butler and May O'Donnell
Composer — Ray Green
Accompanist — Ralph Gilbert

Taught by Hanya Holm, working on *Dance Sonata*
Assistant — Carolyn Durand and Elizabeth Waters
Composers — Norman Lloyd and Harrison Kerr
Accompanist — Harvey Pollins

Taught by Doris Humphrey, working on *Passacaglia*
Assistant — Katherine Manning, Edith Orcutt, Sybil Shearer
Accompanist — Morris Mamorsky

Taught by Charles Weidman, working on *Opus 51*
Assistants — William Bales, George Bockman, Lee Sherman
Composer — Vivian Fine
Accompanists — Yolanda Lorenz and Morris Mamorsky

Program in Choreography

Co-Directors, Martha Hill and Louis Horst
Program for students was arranged individually from the General Program

Program in Music for the Dance

Director, Louis Horst

Music Accompaniment
Taught by Norman Lloyd

Music Composition
Taught by Louis Horst

Program in Stage Design for the Dance

Directed by Arch Lauterer
Assisted by Edward Glass and Henry Seymour

Select Concerts, Demonstrations, and Events

July 4	Fireworks
July 8 Lounge	Lecture "Dance in England" by Margaret Einert of the London *Dancing Times*
July 15 Barn Quadrangle	Lecture "Music and The Dance" by Dr. George Beiswanger, Professor of Philosophy, Monticello College

July 17 College Theatre	Concert of Music written for dance: Vivian Fine, RayGreen, Ralph Gilbert, Norman Lloyd, Ruth Lloyd, Morris Mamorsky, Harvey Pollins, Esther Williamson
July 19 Student Lounge	Lecture "New Horizons of the Theatre" by Mr. Francis Bosworth, Program Advisor for the Federal Theatre Project
July 16–23	Exhibit of Federal Theatre Project — photographs and drawings
July 22 College Theatre	Yale Puppeteers "It's a Small World"
July 26 Student Lounge	Lecture "Surrealism in Art" by Mr. Douglas Rigby
July 31 Lounge	Concert — New Music Quarterly Recordings under direction of Mr. Otto Luening
July 31 Student Lounge	Lecture "Space and Time in Music" by Mr. Paul Boepple, Director of the Dalcroze School of Music, New York City, and Conductor of the Dessoff Choirs
August 4 and 8 The Armory	Festival Series Concerts Fellows of the Bennington School of the Dance, 1938: Eleanor King, Louise Kloepper, Marian Van Tuyl

Ode to Freedom
Choreography by Eleanor King
Music by Andrew Law, arranged by John Colman and Norman Lloyd
Danced by: Jean Aubry, Jane Forte, Wanda Graham, Margot Harper, Gertrude Lippincott, Alice M. Mulcahy, Marian Ryder, Ann Schuman (Anna Halprin), Mildred Rea Shaw, Mary Starks

Romantic Theme
Choreographed and Danced by Louise Kloepper
Music by Harvey Pollins

135

Statement of Dissent
Choreographed and danced by Louise Kloepper
Music by Gregory Tucker

Earth Saga: The Coming, The Claiming, Aftermath, The Remaking
Music by Esther Williamson
Choreography by Louise Kloepper
Danced by Shirley Bennett, Marjorie Browning, Mary Gillette, Winifred Gregory, Elizabeth Hayes, Louise Kloepper, Hortense Lieberthal (Zera), May Mendelsohn, Joyce Palmer, Klara Sepmeier

Directions: Flight, Indecision, Redirection
Choreographed and Danced by Marian Van Tuyl
Music by Nikolai Lopatnikoff

Out of One Happening
Choreography by Marian Van Tuyl
Danced by Marian Van Tuyl, Jeanne Hays (Beaman), Lillian Lack, Eleanor Lauer, Marion Moulton, Marjorie Muehl, Polly Ann Schwartz, Marie Prahl, Theodora Wiesner, Olga Wolf
Music by Gregory Tucker

In the Clearing
Choreography by Marian Van Tuyl
Music by Gregory Tucker
Danced by Eleanor Lauer, Marjorie Muehl, Marian Van Tuyl, Theodora Wiesner

American Folk Suite: Bonja Song, Hoe-Down, Hornpipe
Choreography by Eleanor King
Music: *Bonja Song* arranged by Esther Williamson; *Hoe-Down* by Reginald Forsythe; *Hornpipe*— traditional

Danced by William Bales, George Bockman, Wanda Graham, Eleanor King, Ann Schuman (Anna Halprin), Mary Starks, Marian Van Tuyl

136

August 5	First Lecture of the Festival Series
College Theatre	"Dance and Music" by Dr. Curt Sachs
August 5 and 9	Festival Series Concert:
The Armory	*Passacaglia*

Passacaglia
Choreography by Doris Humphrey
Music by J.S. Bach
Danced by Doris Humphrey, Charles Weidman and
  the Concert and Apprentice Groups
Musicians: Vivian Fine and Morris Mamorsky — piano

Dance of Work and Play
Choreography by Hanya Holm
Music by Norman Lloyd
Danced by Hanya Holm and members of her Concert
  Group
Musicians: Franziska Boas — percussion, Norman
  Lloyd and Ruth Lloyd — piano

Dance Sonata
Choreography by Hanya Holm
Music by Harrison Kerr
Danced by Hanya Holm and Members of her Concert
  and Apprentice Group
Musicians: Franziska Boas — percussion, Yolanda
  Lorenz and Harvey Pollins — piano

Variations and Conclusions from *New Dance*
Choreography by Doris Humphrey
Music by Wallingford Riegger
Danced by William Bales, George Bockman, Doris
  Humphrey, José Limón, Katherine Litz, Beatrice
  Seckler, Sybil Shearer, Charles Weidman and
  Concert Group
Musicians: Franziska Boas — percussion, Pauline
  Lawrence and Morris Mamorsky — piano

Hanya Holm's Concert Group: Keith Coppage,
  Carolyn Durand, Henrietta Greenhood (Eve
  Gentry), Miriam Kagan, Caroline Locke, Harriet
  Roeder, Marva Spelman, Elizabeth Waters

Apprentice Group: Mary Adair, Katherine Bollard, Mary Frances Cave, Elsie Earle, Saralee Harris, Katherine Imig, Beatrice Lovejoy, Charlotte Orlov, Hildegard Spreen, Claire Weigt, Martha Wilcox

Doris Humphrey's Concert Group: Billy Archibald, William Bales, Mirthe Bellanca, George Bockman, Harriette Ann Gray, Frances Kinsky, Katherine Litz, Katharine Manning, Edith Orcutt, Beatrice Seckler, Sybil Shearer, Lee Sherman

Apprentice Group: Barbara Beiswanger, Sara Jean Cosner, Gloria Garcia, Maria Maginnis, Ethel Mann, Claudia Moore (Read), Pegge Oppenheimer, Ruth Parmet, Barbara Spaulding, Patricia Urner, Mildred Zook

August 6 College Theatre	Second Lecture of Festival Series "Background of the American Dance" by Mr. John Martin
August 6 and 10 The Armory	Festival Series Concerts: *Opus 51* Choreography by Charles Weidman Music by Vivian Fine Danced by Charles Weidman and Members of his Concert Group: Billy Archibald, William Bales, Mirthe Bellance, George Bockman, Harriette Anne Gray, Katherine Litz, Beatrice Seckler, Lee Sherman And Apprentice Group: Pauline Chellis, Maxine Cushing, Eleanor Frampton, Molly Hecht, Maxine Munt, Dorothy Ross, Anne Stern

American Document
Choreography by Martha Graham
Music by Ray Green
Musical Direction by Louis Horst
Costumes by Edythe Gilfond
Danced by Martha Graham and Members of her Concert Group: Anita Alverez, Thelma Babitz, Ethel Butler, Jane Dudley, Nina Fonaroff, Natalie

138

Harris, Marie Marchowsky, Sophie Maslow, Marjorie G. Mazia, May O'Donnell, Gertrude Shurr

And Apprentice Group: Muriel V. Brenner, Jean Marion Erdman, Erick Hawkins, Virginia Hall Johnson, Jane Lee Perry, Helen Priest (Rogers), Kaya Russell, Elaine Scanlan, Margaret Strater, Claire Strauss, Eleanor Struppa

August 7 College Theatre	Concert of Music Written for the Dance Louis Horst, Chairman Compositions by Vivian Fine, Ray Green, Harrison Kerr, Norman Lloyd, Harvey Pollins, Wallingford Riegger, Gregory Tucker, Esther Williamson
August 9 College Theatre	Third Lecture of Concert Series Dr. Curt Sachs, "Dance, Anthropology, History"
August 10 College Theatre	Fourth Lecture of Concert Series "Isadora Duncan and the Modern Dance" by Mr. John Martin
August 11 College Theatre	Demonstration lesson by Doris Humphrey with members of her concert group and apprentice group Demonstration lesson by Charles Weidman with members of his concert group and apprentice group
August 12 College Theatre	Demonstration lesson by Martha Graham with members of her concert group and apprentice group Demonstration lesson by Hanya Holm with members of her concert group and apprentice group
August 13 College Theatre	Demonstration of student work in the General Program: *Percussion Studies* under the direction of Franziska Boas; compositions by Franziska Boas and Margaret Dudley *Elementary and Intermediate Composition* and *Music for the Dance* under the direction of Martha Hill, Norman Lloyd, and Bessie Schönberg; dance compositions by Dudley Ashton, Jean Aubry, Patricia

139

Balz, Lois Barnes, Inez Baum, Shirlee Brimberg,
Virginia Dean, Frances Dougherty, Jane Eastham,
Dianne Ewell, Doris Ewing, Jane Forte, Ruth
Franck, Wanda Graham, Winifred Gregory, Clara
Harnden, Florence Hartley, Harriet Hathaway,
Jeanne Hays (Beaman), Delia Hussey, Katherine
Hutzler, Barbara Johnston, Marie Louise
Kretchmann, Lillian Lack, Eleanor Lauer, Modena
Lewis, Elizabeth Lyons, Lucille Marks, Mary
McKee, Marion Moulton, Alice Mulcahy, Litia
Namora, Marian Ryder, Ann Schuman (Anna
Halprin), Mildred Shaw, Gertrude Silver, Rose
Strasser, Elizabeth Whitney, Beatrice Wiseman,
Robert Wolff

Pre-classic Dance Forms under the direction of
Louis Horst, assisted by Mildred Wile; dance
compositions by: Shirlee Brimberg, Jeanne Hays
(Beaman), Janet Nash, Alwin Nikolais, Margaret
Patrick, Julia Sanford, Klara Sepmeier, Mary Shaw
(Schlivek)

Modern Forms and Music for the Dance under the
direction of Louis Horst, assisted by Mildred Wile;
dance compositions by Truda Kaschmann, Eleanor
Lauer, Gertrude Lippincott, Alwin Nikolais, Mary
Starks, Elizabeth Whitney, Theodora Wiesner

Experimental Production and *Music for the Dance* under
the direction of Martha Hill, Arch Lauterer,
Norman Lloyd; dance compositions by: Charles
Hinds, Delia Hussey, Gertrude Lippincott, Alwin
Nikolais, Eva Pletsch, Lillian Shapero, Mary Starks,
Philip Stapp, Theodora Wiesner

*Choreography, Music for the Dance, and Stage Design
for the Dance* under the direction of Martha
Hill, Louis Horst, and Arch Lauterer; dance
compositions by Florence Warwick and Lillian
Shapero

8

Summer of 1939:
From East to West

*"The musicians, among whom were Louis Horst, Norman Lloyd,
and Lionel Nowak, conducted classes outdoors under the eucalyptus
trees."[1]—José Limón*

Dates: July 1–August 11, 1939
Location: Mills College, Oakland, California

*The Bennington School of the Dance moved to Mills College in California
for the summer of 1939. All key faculty traveled out to teach, but because their
dance companies did not accompany them due to financial constraints, there
were no festival performances planned. With few to no rehearsals for the senior
faculty, the schedule was more open, and they had leisure time, which was
quite different from the summers at Bennington College. There were, however,
some significant events including a percussion concert directed by John Cage;
a dance concert of work by Ethel Butler, Louise Kloepper, José Limón, and
Katherine Manning; and the filming of the movie short* Young American
Dances, *directed by Ralph Jester.*

*Norman Lloyd indicates that there was a long-term plan discussed, that
every five years, the Bennington School of the Dance would be held at a location
other than Bennington College. They hoped to move to a location in the Mid-
west in 1943, but with the onset of World War II, and the closing of the Bennington School of the Dance, that was not to be.[2]*

Mary Jo Shelly's Recollection[3]

By the time of the 1938 Festival, the departure of 1939 was already
more than a prospect. The Festival program contained the simple announce-

ment that, "By invitation of the trustees of Mills College, the 1939 session of the Bennington School of the Dance will be held at Mills College, Oakland, California. In accepting this invitation to hold a session in the West, the School will share in the significant development of the modern dance in another section of America."

The invitation came out of the natural affinity between the two Colleges — each was noted for services to the arts and for leadership in fostering dance in its own region. The moving spirit behind the idea was Rosalind Cassidy, a member of the Mills faculty, director of the Mills summer session, and a dance enthusiast. [In the margin of Shelly's manuscript are Martha Hill's notes that Marian Van Tuyl also assisted in facilitating the move to Mills for the summer of 1939.]

Although the invitation had been formally blessed by the Trustees of both Colleges, some plain and not so plain figuring about everything from working space to cost remained to be done. Cost loomed the largest. In keeping the necessary economics in view, only one advance trip west was feasible. Accordingly, I, as Administrative Director, traveled cross-country in the dead of winter by coach. I collected the essential facts along with a major cold in the head which made me as a visitor from the East less than an impressive emissary. The President of Mills received me cordially but at a discreet distance. Economy forsaken, I returned in better accommodations. [Martha Hill also traveled out to Mills prior to the 1939 summer session, during her sabbatical from Bennington College in the academic year 1938–1939 as per her notes on Shelly's manuscript.]

Actually, by the same minor miracle by which the five previous budgets had been balanced, so did this one. Quotas of 140 resident and, because of the metropolitan location, 10 non-resident students were set. When the session began, 170 enrolled, the greatest majority full-time. The population statistics proved a valuable point. Understandingly enough, the geographical base shifted — about half from the West, a quarter from the Middle West, and the rest from the East, South, and from outside the United States. As before, a number of students had come for one or more previous sessions. In age range, experience, and professional classification, the Mills session duplicated almost exactly previous recent sessions at Bennington. The School, independent of location, was continuing to meet the need for a short-term intensive study of dance led by recognized authorities.

The detailed 1939 plan, to be worked out at long distance, called for

Charles Weidman teaching at the Bennington School of the Dance at Mills College, 1939 (photographer unknown, courtesy Special Collections, F.W. Olin
Library, Mills College).

imaginative adaptation, the kind of challenge that always delighted Martha
Hill. A Festival must be sacrificed in favor of allocating funds to the transportation from one coast to the other of 26 faculty and staff members and
the addition of two more to the staff from Mills summer faculty. For any
type of Festival, a nucleus of at least four professional companies and additional technical staff and facilities would have been required. Partly to
compensate for this curtailment, but as much because it made sense, the
curriculum was consolidated into three major programs: one each in dance,
music, and stage design. In the first case, students would study for six
weeks the dance methods of only one artist, with appropriate supplementary courses. The study of music and stage design could, if the student
chose, be expanded by electing courses for a nominal additional fee from
the on-going regular Mills offerings.

Eliminating a Festival for one summer had unexpected consequences.
Suddenly, there was more leisure. Work went on only five instead of seven
days a week. Evenings were free. Partly because of time for it, a new rapport

developed among everyone in the community — a chance to meet, talk, compare experiences, and enjoy the lovely California setting. Then too, the session coincided with the Golden Gate International Exposition, halfway across San Francisco Bay. There were also short trips on across the Golden Gate Bridge into San Francisco itself, and, on weekends, down the peninsula to Carmel, Monterey, and the Big Sur Country. A very different summer indeed, and a rewarding interval between the highly concentrated activity of the Bennington summers.

The necessity to forgo a festival failed to suppress the drive to produce some lesser equivalent. Whether as the result of the greatly increased number of daily visitors to watch work going on, or the subtle promotion of Esther Rosenblatt, a staff member borrowed from Mills and a born pro-

Hanya Holm teaching at the Bennington School of the Dance at Mills College, 1939 (photographer unknown, courtesy Special Collections, F.W. Olin Library, Mills College).

moter, an audience was generated for what were called demonstrations. Three events took place. The first, a concert of Modern American Percussion Music, suddenly drew over a hundred listeners. Somewhat later, a totally unexpected capacity gathering of over five hundred appeared for a performance by four young professionals, resident as teaching assistants: Ethel Butler from the Graham Company, Louise Kloepper from the Holm Company, and José Limón and Katherine Manning from the Humphrey-Weidman Company. The audience's evening was not wasted. The performance electrified the small hall where it happened.

Finally, announced only as student demonstrations, Martha Graham, Hanya Holm, Doris Humphrey, and Charles Weidman, each making the most unostentatious of introductions, turned loose the students they had been teaching in what was officially described as exercises in dance technique. Again, a capacity audience from miles around saw unforgettable dancing. Veterans of other summers set to beating their heels on the floor.

Ethel Butler (dark dress at left) teaching at the Bennington School of the Dance in the amphitheatre at Mills College, 1939. Merce Cunningham is on top row at left (photographer unknown, courtesy Special Collections, F.W. Olin Library, Mills College).

145

The one and only session of the Bennington School of the Dance at Mills College ended, as it deserved to, in a wall-shaking burst of applause. [Hill noted in the margins of Shelly's manuscript that the film *Young America Dances* about the Bennington School of the Dance was filmed during the summer of 1939 at Mills.]

Anna Halprin's Recollection

Elizabeth McPherson interviewed Anna Halprin, by telephone on June 23, 2009. McPherson transcribed and edited the interview with edits and approval given by Halprin in February of 2011.

HALPRIN'S BIOGRAPHY

Anna Halprin (b. 1920), birth name Ann Schuman, attended the Bennington School of the Dance in the summers of 1938 and 1939. A graduate of the University of Wisconsin, Halprin founded the groundbreaking San Francisco Dancer's Workshop in 1955, and the Tamalpa Institute with her daughter Daria Halprin in 1978. Included among her students are Trisha Brown, Sherwood Chen, Ruth Emmerson, Simone Forti, Sally Gross, Shinichi Momo Iova-Koga, Meredith Monk, and Yvonne Rainer. Halprin has forever reached to new directions and has inspired those around her to do the same, leading to a major redefinition of the art of dance in the 1970s. She has received many honors and awards including a lifetime achievement award in choreography from the American Dance Festival. She has created over 150 dance theatre works, is the author of three books, and the subject of several books including *Anna Halprin: Experience as Dance*. She has released numerous videotapes about her work, and a comprehensive documentary on her life and career, *Breath Made Visible* was released in 2009. She continues to perform, travel and teach.

HALPRIN'S ACCOUNT[4]

I went to the Bennington School of the Dance because I was enthusiastic about dance, and there weren't at that time places like Jacob's Pillow [not yet a school] and all the different summer festivals we have today. It was one of the only places I knew of to go and spend the summer dancing. It was the original American Dance Festival.

146

Anna Halprin, early 1940s (photographer unknown, courtesy Anna Halprin).

I was there for the summer of 1938 in Vermont and then in 1939 at Mills College in California. I was a teenager, but I was quite advanced. I was a natural so I kind of sailed through it. And was absolutely delighted while I was there. I was so stimulated by the whole atmosphere. Everything was just so new and the leadership was innovative. There was a great sense of excitement in the whole place. It was for me just a dream world.

147

I remember Martha Graham vividly because she was the most dynamic faculty member, dynamic in every way: how she looked, how she talked, how she walked. I was very overwhelmed by her, and truly I didn't find her a particularly likable person. She frightened me. And I felt that her approach to movement was extremely dogmatic. It really was a little too authoritarian for me to relate to the technique whereas I found Doris Humphrey a lot easier to be with, and not so overwhelming, and self-absorbed. And so I gravitated more toward Doris personality-wise. And in terms of the technique, Martha Graham's body build was very different from mine in that she was flexible in the hip joints. All the movement that she did on the floor required flexibility in the hip joints, which I never had. If you had to have such a patterned style, I felt that Doris' was a little more adaptable to my body. She used fall and recovery whereas Martha was all contraction and release, and that didn't feel good to me. In my second summer, I studied more with Doris Humphrey who then invited me into her company. But by the time I had graduated from the University of Wisconsin and then got to New York, the company had disbanded.

I found Charles Weidman amusing, but the person who really had the most affect on me was Louis Horst. And the reason was that he generated my creativity, which none of the others really did. They taught in a very dogmatic way, even though Doris wasn't like that in terms of her personality. Still it was a very set routine, and I didn't see the difference in that philosophically from ballet. But I was very impressed with Louis, and I think he is the only person who had any lasting influence on me. He gave us assignments in every class to bring back a dance. That was very challenging, interesting, and creative. And I did very well in that kind of a setting. He loved each dance I did. I got "first prize" every time I brought a composition in.

I danced in Eleanor King's *Ode to Freedom*, and that was a highlight for me to be able to perform. It was a fun dance. You see the things that I related to there were more creative, and gave me an opportunity to use my imagination. I don't think I've ever been attracted to the kind of experiences in dance where I am told what to do and how to do it.

I made a good friend who was staying across the hall from me in my dorm — Jeanne Beaman — that's her name now. She became a professor of dance in a university on the East Coast [University of Pittsburgh], but she came from Berkeley, California. She had been a ballet dancer, and she was

Louis Horst at Bennington School of the Dance, circa 1934 (photographer unknown, courtesy Bennington College).

always nursing her feet, and I was always going across the hall to help her massage her feet. We've remained best friends all these years. I remember they had kind of an honor system for getting ice cream cones. Jeanne and I didn't use the honor system too well — and we would gorge ourselves on

Merce Cunningham and Dorothy Weston at the Bennington School of the Dance at Mills College, 1939 (photographer unknown, courtesy Special Collections, F.W. Olin Library, Mills College).

ice cream! The other student I remember was Merce Cunningham at the Mills summer session. He was magnificent.

It was inspiring for a young person my age to be able to dance all day, with these great personalities in the field of modern dance. It was a great opportunity. The faculty was definitely on the cutting edge. And the campuses were beautiful, both Mills and Bennington. It was just wonderful.

Facts and Figures, 1939

Total Enrollment of Students: 170

Select Students

Major Course in Dance: Mercier (Merce) Cunningham, Helen Knight, Claudia Moore (Read), Alwin Nikolais, Helen Priest (Rogers), Ann Schuman (Anna Halprin), Nona Schurman, Betty Lynd Thompson, Theodora Wiesner, Martha Wilcox

Major Course in Music: Neva Aubin, Georg Dawson, Lucine Marcoux, Adelia Spangenberg, Helen Strain, Zoe Williams

Major Course in Stage Design: Molly Howe, Nathan Krevitsky, Patricia Moyer, Bette Orvis, Margaret Thomson

Faculty and Curriculum

Martha Hill, Director

Mary Josephine Shelly, Administrative Director

Rosalind Cassidy, Director of the Mills College Summer Session

Major Course in Dance (Students chose one section with Graham, Holm, Humphrey, or Weidman. Each section was conducted for 6 weeks with the major artist teaching for 3 weeks and their assistant for 3 weeks)

Taught by Martha Graham July 24–August 11
Assistant — Ethel Butler July 3–July 22
Accompanist — Ralph Gilbert

Taught by Hanya Holm July 24–August 11
Assistant — Louise Kloepper July 3–July 22
Accompanist — Freda Miller

Taught by Doris Humphrey July 24–August 11
Assistant — Katherine Manning July 3–July 22
Accompanist — Lionel Nowak

Taught by Charles Weidman July 24–August 11
Assistant — José Limón July 3–July 22
Accompanist — Pauline Lawrence

Major Course in Music for the Dance (for Accompanists/Composers)
Directed by Franziska Boas, Louis Horst, Norman Lloyd

Major Course in Stage Design for the Dance (Students studied design
   for dance)
Directed by Arch Lauterer
Assistant — Henry Seymour

Survey Course in Dance (Students studied 4 artists' techniques for two
   weeks each — one week taught by the artist and the other week taught
   by an assistant.)

Taught by Martha Graham
Assistant — Ethel Butler
Accompanist — Ralph Gilbert

Taught by Hanya Holm
Assistant — Louise Kloepper
Accompanist — Freda Miller

Taught by Doris Humphrey
Assistant — Katherine Manning
Accompanist — Lionel Nowak

Taught by Charles Weidman
Assistant — José Limón
Accompanist — Pauline Lawrence

Other Courses

Techniques of Dance Movement
Taught by Martha Hill and Bessie Schönberg
Assistant — Hortense Lieberthal (Zera)
Accompanists — Ruth Lloyd and Esther Williamson

Composition of Pre-Classic and Modern Forms
Taught by Louis Horst
Assistant — Mildred Wile

Dance Composition
Taught by Martha Hill and Bessie Schönberg
Assistant — Hortense Lieberthal (Zera)
Accompanists — Esther Williamson and Ruth Lloyd

Experimental Production
Taught by Ben Belitt, Martha Hill, Arch Lauterer, Norman Lloyd, and
    Bessie Schönberg
Assistants — Hortense Lieberthal (Zera) and Henry Seymour

Rhythmic Basis of Dance
Taught by Norman Lloyd

Percussion Accompaniment
Taught by Franziska Boas

Select Concerts, Demonstrations, and Events

July 13 Ethel Moore Hall	Lecture — "Thalamic Communication" by Dr. Douglas Campbell, University of Chicago
July 18 Science Building	Dance Notation Lecture — "Dance Writing" by Mr. Sol Babitz
July 20 Gymnasium	Methods of teaching social dancing Edith Ballwebber, University of Chicago
July 24–August 5 Student Union	Exhibition of Pictures Barbara Morgan, New York City
July 24 Lisser Hall	Workshop Evening: student work in Experimental Production Discussion led by Arch Lauterer
July 26 Ethel Moore Hall	Reception for Benny Goodman and the Budapest String Quartet
July 27 Lisser Hall	Percussion Concert Under the direction of John Cage Compositions by Lou Harrison, William Russell, and others

153

July 30 Ethel Moore Hall	Piano Recital, Albert Hirsch
July 31 Lisser Hall	Workshop Evening; student work in Pre-Classic and Modern Forms
August 1,2,3 Gymnasium	Sessions in American Country Dancing Mr. Lloyd Shaw, Cheyenne Mountain School, Colorado
August 3	Discussion in American Country Dancing by Mr. Lloyd Shaw
August 3–6	Filming of Documentary Movie, *Young America Dances* by American Pictures, Incorporated, under direction of Ralph Jester
August 4 Lisser Hall	A Concert of Modern Dance by Ethel Butler, Louise Kloepper, José Limón, Katherine Manning

Danza
Choreographed and Performed by José Limón
Music by Sergei Prokofiev

Romantic Theme
Choreographed and Performed by Louise Kloepper
Music by Harvey Pollins

Ceremonial Dance
Choreographed and Performed by Ethel Butler
Music by Ralph Gilbert

Danzas Mexicanas
Choreographed and Performed by José Limón
Music by Lionel Nowak
> *Indio*
> *Conquistadore*
> *Peon*
> *Caballero*
> *Revolucionario*

Statement of Dissent
Choreographed and Performed by Louise Kloepper
Music by Gregory Tucker

Canción y Danza
Choreographed and Performed by José Limón
Music by Federico Mompou

The Spirit of the Land Moves in the Blood
Choreographed and Performed by Ethel Butler
Music by Carlos Chavez

Suite in B Minor
Choreographed by José Limón
Performed by José Limón and Katherine Manning
Music by J.S. Bach
> *Polonaise*
> *Rondo*
> *Badinerie*

Pianists: Ralph Gilbert, Freda Miller, Lionel Nowak

August 7
Gymnasium

Lesson taught by José Limón and Demonstration by Boys Dance Group of Hayward (California) Union High School

August 9
Student Union

Exhibition of pictures of the Bennington School of the Dance by Victor Haveman

August 11
Lisser Hall

Final Demonstration of Student Work in Dance Composition, Music and Percussion Composition, and Stage Design

Pre-Classic and Modern Dance Forms under the direction of Louis Horst, assisted by Mildred Wile; compositions by: Norma Anderson, Karen Burt, Mercier (Merce) Cunningham, Meli Davis, Mildred Eberle, Ruth Hatfield, Josephine Ketcik, Marjorie Muehl, Dorothy Ohata, Joyce Palmer, Elaine Scanlan, Ann Schuman (Anna Halprin), Nona Schurman, Mary Tiffany, Eva Trofimov, Martha Wilcox, Julianne Wilson

Experimental Production, Advanced Composition, and Music and Percussion Groups under the direction of Ben Belitt, Franziska Boas, Martha Hill, Arch Lauterer, Norman Lloyd, and Bessie Schönberg;

155

compositions by: Jean Brownlee, Theodora Burch, Karen Burt, Lorraine Delara, Aileen Fisk, Gertrude Green, Laura Hammann, Sylvia Hirshowitz, Molly Howe, Ita Hoxsie, Margaret Kessing, Josephine Ketcik, Helen Knight, Nathan Krevitsky, Hildegarde Lewis, Hortense Lieberthal (Zera), Marjorie Lucas, Marjorie Muehl, Janet Nash, Adele Novotny, Dorothy Ohata, Joyce Palmer, Esther Pease, Helen Priest (Rogers), Lois Rathburn, Hildegard Spreen, Marian Stewart, Ruth Stone, Frances Streeter, Eva Trofimov, and Minerva Wootton; stage setting and lighting by: Molly Howe, Bette Orvis, Henry Seymour, Margaret Thomson

August 11
Gymnasium

Demonstration of dance techniques from the Major Course in Dance under Martha Graham, Hanya Holm, Doris Humphrey, Charles Weidman

Summer of 1940: First Summer of the School of the Arts

"In a way it was a logical move, and you can't go on repeating a formula forever."[1]— *Norman Lloyd*

Dates: June 29–August 17, 1940
Location: Bennington College, Bennington, Vermont

In the summer of 1940, the Bennington School of the Dance evolved into the Bennington School of the Arts. Reasons for this transition are not clear, but Mary Josephine Shelly indicates that she and Martha Hill were interested in fostering collaborations between the arts, and that the School of the Arts seemed like the right step at the time. The school had hit a peak in 1938 with the festival that included new works by each of the four choreographers. After the summer at Mills in 1939, perhaps a different slant or new expansion of the school seemed necessary to keep it vital. In addition, some individuals indicated that because the Bennington School of the Dance had been a resounding success, Bennington College faculty from differing disciplines wished to be part of it. The Bennington School of the Arts incorporated dance, drama, music, and theatrical design.

New additions to the dance curriculum for this summer included Ballet taught by Erick Hawkins and Dance Notation taught by Helen Priest (Rogers).

Mary Josephine Shelly's writings from the 1970s about the Bennington School of the Dance end with the year 1939. However, she compiled a Director's Report shortly after the conclusion of the 1940 and 1941 sessions that are included in this book, by permission of Bennington College.

Director's Report[2] by Mary Josephine Shelly

The reports submitted annually from 1934 through 1939 on the Bennington School of the Dance were useful primarily in planning the next

157

session. Each report contained specific recommendations for next steps. This report on the first session of the School of the Arts cannot serve the same purpose. The School of the Dance faced no special emergencies in the world at large in its six-year history; it succeeded in being self-supporting; and for these and more directly educational reasons, pursued a consistent plan elaborated but not radically changed from the one with which it began. All this is in direct contrast to the situation of the School of the Arts which must plan next year under a definite emergency; must eliminate the deficit authorized last summer on the understanding that it would not recur; and must in general experiment before it finds the ideal arrangement for a four-sided scheme involving both teaching and production and emphasizing collaboration.

Therefore, changes of almost any extent are in order if they promise to fit the emergency, balance the budget, or strengthen the scheme of work. The Executive Committee of the School approaches the question of plans for 1941 with this attitude. All that is attempted here is a brief summary for the record. Details of schedule, use of the plant, and similar facts about last summer's operations (1940) are already on record in the school's files.

The first session of the School actually worked out much as anticipated when this Committee of the Trustees met in June with the enrollment already nearly complete. The difference between what was anticipated and what happened was in the intensive activity and the daily events of the fifty-day period, which escape between the lines of a factual report.

THE COMMUNITY

The community numbered 198 persons: 54 faculty and staff, 34 fellows, 110 students of whom 88 paid full tuition. The distribution of fellows, apprentices, and student by division was: dance 68 percent, drama 14 percent, music 12 percent, theatre design 6 percent. Twenty-nine states and, for the first time in seven years, no foreign countries were represented. The geographical distribution was: East 60 percent, Middle West 20 percent, South 15 percent, Far West 5 percent. This was the smallest Far Western group in several summers. The age range was as in each preceding summer, three generations: 16 to 47 years, average age 24. There was a large group of young students, about 45 who were 21 years or younger. There were 42 men, the largest number enrolled in any summer. The proportion of teachers was noticeably less, the proportion of professional performers or young people planning on careers other than teaching correspondingly greater. Both this change and the increase in number of men can be accounted for principally by the increased grants for the fellowships (living usually provided), apprentices (paying little or no tuition) and scholarship students as well as by the inclusion of new divisions of work.

THE CURRICULUM

Coursework in each field as outlined in the bulletin went on daily for six weeks. Parallel to this, rehearsals for the Festival were held. The main departure from the curriculum agreed upon in June was the necessity for restoring to the music offerings piano and voice technique, the faculty for which had been dropped in May in the interests of economy. Student demand not only in the Music Division but by students of other divisions, principally dance, created the necessity and the two faculty members were therefore re-engaged although their salaries were much lower than their original appointments.

No other formal changes were made in the planned curriculum although all manner of internal adjustments to kinds and distribution of students were made after students arrived and made their programs.

The Divisions operated in the following general way:

• The Dance Division followed the plan developed in the School of the Dance and thus relatively standardized to meet current needs in the field. It had the most elaborate array of courses; courses were sectioned to conform to levels of ability; and the students were free to make individual choice of programs of work. A tendency noted this summer was increase pressure for the chance to perform. The field of dance has developed, students come with much more background; and they look to the summer to give them what their working situations usually do not afford — actual dancing, at as professional a level as possible. The plan for last summer did not fully meet this need.

• In The Drama Division, the curriculum was designed as an apprentice system and the whole group of faculty, fellows, apprentices and students was intended to function as an ensemble. The basic techniques of drama were offered and a continuous series of performances in scenes, special projects and workshop were provided. The extreme heterogeneity of ability

159

and background within a very small group handicapped the operation of this plan. It was necessary to compensate for this at the expense of an ensemble, and some provision for a larger nucleus to make the drama more nearly fit this plan is indicated.

• The Music Division enrolled no beginners, and the group was more nearly homogeneous. It functioned consistently as an ensemble and carried the bulk of its work in this form. Technical study was provided, but the main effort of the summer was directed toward composition, of which an extraordinary amount was done, and toward the study of a wide variety of vocal and instrumental works including student compositions, through performance in three weekly seminars, in connection with projects in the other divisions and in workshops.

• The Division of Theatre Design worked with students both individually on projects of their own choice, and as a group in crews serving the course in Experimental Production, the project of other divisions, and workshops. Design students aided in preparations for the Festival and some of them served on the Festival stage crew. They had the practical, if trying, experience of handling throughout the summer a small stage in constant use for all sorts of purposes, almost always working under pressure.

PROVISIONS FOR COLLABORATION

The special business of the School, collaboration between the performing arts, occurred in every possible form with varying results. Almost all students carried at least one course outside their own field. This made numbers in classes unpredictable until programs had been made, but the demands were met. A whole series of projects involving collaborators were undertaken. Students learned something about the practical business of planning as well as something about exchanging resources. Again at this point, a scale of developments not foreseen had to be met on an emergency basis, and more provision for projects falling outside class work needs to be made. For example, the most ambitious and one of the most successful projects of the summer — the fifth act of Purcell's *The Fairy Queen*, staged in workshop — called for a cast of singers, and dancers, a small orchestra with conductor, a dramatic director, a choreographer, a designer, a wardrobe mistress, and a stage crew. These projects, which have all the elements of a full production, are obviously valuable and appropriate in such a School.

160

At least in number and scale, they were a new development of this last summer.

The workshops provided another kind of exchange. One morning each week for six weeks the whole School was interchangeably audience and performers in at least three hours of work on stage. Each division was involved. Faculty as well as student body performed. Work ranged from simple exercises, through material in progress of development, to finished projects. The occasion took on inevitably the character of a public performance and had less of the laboratory aspect than had been anticipated. Discussion, for example, provoked small interest. It was evident that a supplementary level of performance such as music seminars is needed to place those workshops in proper relationship to a whole scheme which extends from elementary class work to a professional Festival. The six sessions were, however, undoubtedly productive. At the very least they unified the School and made concrete exposition of the four fields of study.

THE FESTIVAL

The Festival followed the six weeks of study and rehearsal. The whole School remained in residence for the first cycle of performance, after which the performing groups and the public audience occupied the campus. The attached program is the best indication that can be given within the limits of this report of the kind of production undertaken.

The audience for the twelve performances, including the whole School, the press and other complimentary admissions, numbered about 3600. The capacity of the theatre was 304 seats, and an equivalent number of seats was arranged in the Recreation Building in which the four afternoons of music were held. This change of location for music, decided on at the last minute, made it possible to manage the almost unmanageable schedule of rehearsals and performances. A substantial addition to the audience, at least two full houses, was turned away for the dance performances.

The Festival received usually complete press coverage from Boston and New York papers — the dance critics being given the whole assignment in almost every case — from several Mid-West correspondents, and from periodicals including *Time*, *Newsweek*, the *Nation*, and *Theatre Arts Monthly*. Criticism was extremely varied, in many cases unfavorable, and in all cases prejudiced by the discomforts of the College Theatre. It should be noted that press coverage was mainly for the Festival and not the School as a whole. Two excellent picture spreads (the *New York Times* Sunday rotogravure section[3] and *PM*[4]) were secured on the School, but no critical discussion of the whole project of the School of the Arts materialized.

Without attempting any final summary, a few observations may be made for future reference. These are made from the administrative point of view. The most active single group in the student body was the fellows. They were also the greatest problem because, being young professionals, they had large ambitions which not only exceeded in many cases their own abilities, but which taxed the time, energy, and space at the School's disposal. Moreover, they cost money instead of earning it. But their value to the School is unmistakable. They were experienced enough to be useful as performers and interesting as students. A solution to the problem of having fellows and taking care of them is certainly indicated.

An ensemble arrangement of working groups made up of faculty, fellows, apprentices and students appears ideal for a school engaged in study and production. It was most effective in music this last summer. It is the basic scheme for drama. Dance can probably make use of a less unified organization but needs an ensemble as part of its plan.

The plan followed last summer was at a maximum in its demands on the College plant, on time and energy, and in complexity of offerings. Only by an extravagant expenditure of effort on everyone's part was it possible to manage the summer. Some kind of simplification and some reduction of the load are imperative.

The idea of carrying on four related arts side by side was certainly shown to be productive. However, the School at this date is seriously imbalanced on the side of dance, which was expected, but which is not entirely good either for dance or for the other arts. It is important to recognize, that in the first session of the School of the Arts, the Dance Division accounted for 83 percent of the whole tuition income and 43 percent of the Festival income, without allowing for the influence of the dance performances in creating audience for the play and the music. Administratively, it seems likely that no marked change in this balance of earning power can be hoped for immediately, certainly not next summer, for all of the undoubted success of the new divisions. This fact must, in all common sense, be taken into account in planning a next session.

Ann Hutchinson Guest's Recollection

Elizabeth McPherson corresponded with Ann Hutchinson Guest by email on August 25 and September 8, 2008, and spoke by telephone on July 13, 2011. McPherson edited the responses to her emailed questions and telephone discussion and developed a narrative story that was then edited and approved by Guest on July 16, 2011.

GUEST'S BIOGRAPHY

Ann Hutchinson Guest (born 1918) attended the Bennington School of the Arts Summer Session in 1940. Born in New York City, Guest was educated in England, and learned the Laban system of movement notation early in her dance career. A founder of the Dance Notation Bureau in New York, she is the author of the definitive textbooks on Labanotation. She has staged numerous dances from historical dance notation systems as well as more contemporary notated choreographies, for performance by professional companies as well as for degree studies in colleges and universities. As a professional dancer or as a notator, she has worked with leading choreographers such as Agnes de Mille, Jerome Robbins, George Balanchine and Antony Tudor. For Guest's contributions to dance education she has been awarded two honorary doctoral degrees as well as a special citation from the National Dance Education Organization.

GUEST'S ACCOUNT[5]

I trained at the Laban-based Jooss-Leeder School from 1936 to 1939. In the summer of 1940, Helen Priest was to teach Labanotation at the Bennington School of the Arts. She got me interested in going. Each week there was a special introductory offering to modern dance techniques: Holm technique one week, Humphrey the next, Graham the next and so on. At that time there was a "Them and Us" attitude among the dancers in the different companies. There was a definite taking sides, but I was too new to have any preferences for one company over the other.

At first I enrolled in Hanya Holm's course for more advanced students. I took it as I wanted her more advanced work, but there were too many "weak sisters," and so it got "dumbed down" as the expression goes. We had good experience in walking circles with 10 steps, or 19 steps, developing

Ann Hutchinson Guest, circa 1940 (photographer unknown, courtesy Ann Hutchinson Guest).

our sense of proportion without counting. Hanya's movements had a linked quality; they developed from a simple, natural source. In that way, she was working much as the teachers at the Jooss-Leeder School had. Although personally I found her to lack humor and be quite tense, she was an enjoyable teacher in that she was not very demanding. She allowed students to do the movements very much in their own way. Indeed, it was this lack of specificity, of technical detail that allowed her students to develop their personal styles. But for me it was disappointing. I needed, and hence related to, much stricter technical teaching. This I found in Graham technique. This was also why I came to prefer the Cecchetti method of classical ballet instead of the Russian style.

After the week with Hanya, I had a week of Graham technique from Ethel Butler. Ethel had a forthright personality and a strapping, more peasant-like body (at that time the Graham dancers were more substantially built). Starting sitting on the floor she said "All right girls, get your legs apart, you are going to have to sooner or later!" Very earthy! It was the resistance to the floor, the counter energy — upward and downward and the focus on the sense of the spine — all of which I badly needed. The technique that I had had at the Jooss-Leeder School was based very much on swings, giving in to gravity — it lacked a resisting energy. Graham technique gave me a sense of being physically powerful. So for me, the big revelation that summer was encountering the Graham technique and falling in love with it.

Also at Bennington, there was a class for acting that I took. I remember one episode where we had to improvise that we were bringing gifts to someone who was getting married. We had to describe the gift somehow without saying for instance: "This is a can opener." We also studied the Greek comedy *Lysistrata*. I still have my part somewhere.

Another class was a composition class conducted by Martha Hill and Arch Lauterer. Lauterer would set a simple stage design we were to make use of. One was a rope dividing the stage diagonally, high enough to get under but creating two separate stage areas. We worked in small groups (not solos); Martha Hill gave comments on our individual efforts. This was how I first met Martha. She soon recognized that I was coming from European modern dance, my efforts being of the "waves breaking on the shore" variety, a big contrast to the staccato, isolation-like movements of the other students, a style that I thought very robotic. But these jerky movements were what the other students were using in their compositions. I wouldn't say I did not like those movements, it's that I was stunned that these were considered dance. To me dance was more flowing, more harmonious. I had to broaden my horizon!

I was in a piece that George Bockman choreographed, called *Johnny Get Your Gun*, about a quadruple paraplegic. Bockman was a member of the Humphrey-Weidman group, already an experienced dancer. He asked a few of us to take part in his piece that did not require technique. It had an anti-war theme and used text. We performed it on stage at the theatre in the Commons that was very well-equipped. But the big performance that summer was Graham's *Letter to the World*. I found it very impressive, and Martha quite stunning. I was fascinated by the combination of speech and dance. At the Bennington performances of 1940, the speaker was Margaret Meredith, very statuesque and clear. The costumes were period and well done. One little detail struck me — the dancers wore soft ballet shoes. But Graham dancers, particularly the men, weren't used to shoes, and their feet were a little floppy because you have to point harder in shoes!

After I left Bennington, I immediately started studying with Graham in September of that year. My experience was very positive from the moment I went to speak with Graham about studying at her school. In the States at that time, the attitude was that the European training was "old hat." When Graham asked about my previous training, and I told her about my studies at the Jooss-Leeder School, she said, "That is a very good start for wherever you want to go." What a relief to have such a positive response! In class, she was very encouraging. She would say, for instance, "That's it. You are getting the idea." She told wonderful stories, as in the one about an old bedraggled parrot who still lifted its head majestically thus commanding attention and respect. Graham opened doors for us students. She told us we must go and see Carmen Amaya who was appearing in a nightclub. This amazing gypsy dancer had wonderful abandon — she tore space to shreds. In January of 1942, I was in a concert at the 92nd Street Y with Welland Lathrop, a modern dancer from the West Coast. When next I saw Graham she complimented me on my performance, and said she would like me to be in the company when there was an opening. This did not eventually work out as my life took me in other directions.

Some of the students from Bennington I later met again in other classes or in connection with notation, and also, in time, as fellow performers in Broadway shows. My connection with Martha Hill continued to develop through my teaching at New York City's High School of Performing Arts when the dance division opened in September 1948, and later when I taught at Juilliard, both positions being the result of Martha Hill's belief in dance notation and belief in me.

Facts and Figures, 1940

Total Enrollment of Students: 110 (does not include company members)

Select Students and Apprentice Company Members

Helen Alkire, Margaret Erlanger, Nina Fonaroff, Joseph Gorbein (Gifford), Ann Hutchinson, Hazel Johnson, Carl Miller, Betty Lynd Thompson

Faculty and Curriculum

Administrative Director, Mary Josephine Shelly

Dance

Director of Dance, Martha Hill
Director of Festival Production in Dance, Martha Graham
Visiting Lecturer, Lincoln Kirstein
Accompanists not listed below: Ruth Lloyd and Zoe Williams
Charles Weidman and Doris Humphrey on leave this year.

Dance Technique
Taught by artists' associates. Students picked one technique to study
  intensively.

Graham Technique
Taught by Ethel Butler
Accompanist — Ralph Gilbert

Holm Technique
Taught by Harriet Roeder
Accompanist — Freda Miller

Humphrey Technique
Taught by Katherine Manning

Weidman Technique
Taught by Claudia Moore (Read)

Survey of Dance Technique (each of the four techniques is studied for 2 weeks each)
Same teachers as above.

Master Course in Dance (Hanya Holm taught this advanced course for selected students)

General Techniques of Movement
Taught by Bessie Schönberg
Assistant — Hortense Lieberthal

Pre-Classic and Modern Forms
Taught by Louis Horst and Mildred Wile

Dance Composition
Taught by Martha Hill and Bessie Schönberg
Assistant — Hortense Lieberthal (Zera)

Ballet (for limited number of advanced students)
Taught by Erick Hawkins

Experimental Production (including the use of design and speech)
Directed by Martha Hill, Arch Lauterer, Norman Lloyd

Rhythmic Basis of Dance
Taught by Norman Lloyd

Accompaniment for the Dance
Louis Horst and Norman Lloyd

Music Composition for the Dance
Louis Horst and Norman Lloyd

Dance Notation
Taught by Helen Priest (Rogers)

Dance Workshop (weekly showings of work)

Drama

Director of Theatre, Francis Fergusson
Fellows: Barbara Deming, Mac Dixon, Emily Sweetser, Edward Thommen, Elizabeth Waters

Acting
Taught by Marion Fergusson
Assistants — Elizabeth James and Edward Thommen

Speech for the Stage
Taught by Hope Miller

Makeup
Taught by Edward Thommen

Dramatic Form for Directors and Playwrights
Taught by Francis Fergusson
Assistant — Barbara Deming

Dramatic Literature
Taught by Wallace Fowlie

Body Training
Taught by Martha Hill

Playwriting
Taught by Francis Fergusson

Music

Otto Luening, Director of Music
Piano
Groups were formed in piano technique and repertoire under Carlos
Buhler.

Voice
(Vocal Technique as well as American, German, French, and Italian Song
Literature)
Taught by Ethel Luening and Hope Miller

Instrumental Ensemble
Taught by Otto Luening and Robert McBride

17th and 18th Century Music
Group studies in open rehearsal
Conducted by Ralph Kirkpatrick

Composition (Intermediate, Advanced, Free Counterpoint, Orchestration,
Modern Harmonic Devices)
Taught by Louis Horst, Norman Lloyd, Otto Luening, and Robert
McBride

History and Analysis
A series of group meetings throughout the session

Conducting
Taught by Otto Luening

Accompanying
Directed by Norman Lloyd

Music Workshop
Weekly showing of work

Theatre Design

Arch Lauterer, Director of Theatre Design
There were no pre-arranged courses in this area. The main work was actual
design and construction in dance, drama, and music.

Select Concerts, Demonstrations, and Events

July 6 College Theatre	Workshop (Dance Division) *Experimental Production* Directed by Martha Hill, Arch Lauterer, Norman Lloyd Choreography by students: Nik Krevitsky and Lois Rathburn *Pre-Classic Dance Forms* directed by Louis Horst Choreography by students: Miriam Bleamaster and Margaret Erlanger *Modern Forms* directed by Louis Horst Choreography by students: Jean Erdman, Harriet Garrett, George Hall, Frances Sunstein
July 6 College Theatre	Workshop (Drama Division) Improvisations Group participating: Barbara Coffin, Barbara Deming, Elizabeth James, Hal Jamison, Honora Kemmerer, Dorothy McWilliams, Will Parker, Shirley Stanwood, Emily Sweetser, Edward Thommen
July 6 College Theatre	Workshop (Music Division) *String Quartet, 3rd Movement* by Roger Goeb Chorale with Variations Claire Harper, 1st Violin Theodore Russell, 2nd Violin

170

Carol Welch, Viola
Aaron Bodenhorn, Cello

Birds Songs by Ernst Bacon
Barbara Coffin, accompanied by Lionel Nowak

July 11
College Theatre

Workshop (Special Drama Workshop)
Marcella Cisney and Dorothy McWilliams,
Directors
Liliom by Ferenc Molnar
Women Beware Women by Thomas Middleton
Romeo and Juliet, Act II, 5 by William Shakespeare
Our Town by Thornton Wilder

July 13
College Theatre

Workshop (Dance Division)
Experimental Production directed by Martha Hill,
Arch Lauterer, and Norman Lloyd
Choreography by students: Meli Davis and Nik
Krevitsky

Advanced Composition directed by Martha Hill and
Norman Lloyd
Choreography by students: Minea Craig and David
Zellmer

Pre-Classic Dance Forms directed by Louis Horst
Choreography by students: Elizabeth Coolidge,
Louise Greuel, Annabelle Ranslem, Carmen
Rocker, Frances Sunstein

Modern Forms directed by Louis Horst
Choreography by students: Nelle Fisher, Nina
Fonaroff, Lois Rathburn, Frances Sunstein

July 13
College Theatre

Workshop (Special Drama Workshop)
Marcella Cisney and Dorothy McWilliams,
Directors
Women Beware Women by Thomas Middleton
Robert Penn Warren's play (one scene)

July 13
College Theatre

Workshop (Music)
Compositions by Beatrice MacLaughlin, Frank
Wigglesworth, Ann Wolfson, Paul Hindemith

Played by Aaron Bodenhorn, Beatrice
    MacLaughlin, William Newman, Lionel Nowak,
    Ann Wolfson

July 13
College Theatre

Erick Hawkins in a Program of Dances
All works choreographed and performed by Erick
    Hawkins

Liberty Tree—A Set of Four Dances
    Patriot—Massachusetts
    Trail Breaker—Kentucky
    Free Stater—Kansas
    Nomad Harvester—California
Music by Ralph Gilbert
Set by Carlos Dyer
Costumes by Edythe Gilfond

Insubstantial Pageant—A Dance of Experience
Music by Lehman Engel
Set by Carlos Dyer

Yankee Bluebritches—A Vermont Fantasy
Music by Hunter Johnson
Set by Charlotte Trowbridge

July 20
College Theatre

Workshop (Dance and Drama)
Dance—Experimental Production directed by
    Martha Hill, Arch Lauterer, Norman Lloyd
Choreography by students: Minea Craig, Lois
    Rathburn, and Peter Wisher

Drama—Excerpts from Skakespeare's *Romeo and
    Juliet* and Wilder's *Our Town*; directed by
    Dorothy McWilliams

Discussion of lighting for dance and drama by Arch
    Lauterer

Pre-Classic Dance Forms directed by Louis Horst
Choreography by students Minea Craig, Harriet
    Garrett, Joseph Gornbein (Gifford)

Modern Forms directed by Louis Horst
Choreography by students May Atherton, Jane
    Dudley, Truda Kaschmann, Sophie Maslow

Compositions from the Master Course directed by
    Hanya Holm
Choreography by students Genevieve Lindeman
    and Annabelle Ranslem

General Discussion on Dance and Drama

July 20 College Theatre	Workshop (Music) Compositions by Charles Ives, Reba Marcus, Freda Miller, Theodore Russell; performed by Aaron Bodenhorn, Richard Chamberlain, Barbara Coffin, Claire Harper, Naomah Maise, Reba Marcus, Freda Miller, Lionel Nowak, Theodore Russell, Carol Welch

General discussion on music

July 27 College Theatre	Workshop (Drama) *The Farewell Supper* by Arthur Schnitzler Directed by Barbara Deming

Workshop (Music)
Compositions by Carlos Chavez, Barbara Coffin,
    Ann McDougle, Karol Szymanowski; performed
    by Claire Harper, Reba Marcus, Ann McDougle,
    Lionel Nowak, Theodore Russell

Workshop (Dance)
Experimental Production directed by Martha Hill,
    Arch Lauterer, Norman Lloyd
Choreography by students May Atherton, George
    Bockman, Katherine Litz, Betty Lynd
    Thompson, Elizabeth Whitney

Pre-Classic Dance Forms directed by Louis Horst
Choreography by students: Nik Krevitsky, Jeanne
    Michaels, and Ruth Parmet

Modern Forms directed by Louis Horst
Choreography by students: Jane Dudley, Lois
    Rathburn, Frances Sunstein, Betty Lynd
    Thompson, and Elizabeth Whitney

August 3
College Theatre

Workshop (Drama)
Johnny Get Your Gun
by Dalton Trumbo — Adapted from novel
Directed by Michael Cisney
Choreography by George Bockman
Music composed and directed by Mimi Wallner
Verse Choir directed by George Wilson

Pygmalion (Tea Party Scene)
by George Bernard Shaw
Directed by Dorothy McWilliams

Savonarola (Washerwoman Scene)
by William Van Wyck
Directed by Dorothy McWilliams

August 3
College Theatre

Workshop (Dance)
Experimental Production Directed by Martha Hill,
    Arch Lauterer, Norman Lloyd
Choreography by students: George Bockman,
    Molly Howe, Katherine Litz, Peter Wisher

Advanced Rhythmic Basis Class directed by
    Norman Lloyd
Choreography by students: George Bockman,
    Ethel Butler, David Campbell, Katherine Litz,
    Marjorie Mazia

Pre-Classic Dance Forms directed by Louis Horst;
Choreography by students: Miriam Bleamaster,
    Shirley Broughton, Margaret Erlanger,
    Genevieve Pais

Modern Forms directed by Louis Horst
Choreography by students: May Atherton, Sophie
    Maslow, Betty Lynd Thompson

174

August 3 College Theatre	Workshop (Drama) *The Fairy Queen* Music by Henry Purcell Dramatic Director — George Wilson Singers directed by Ethel Luening Dances by Claudia Moore (Read)
August 9 College Theatre	Workshop (Dance) *Pre-Classic Dance Forms* directed by Louis Horst Choreography by students including Louise Greuel, Eleanor Olden, Frances Sunstein *Modern Forms* directed by Louis Horst Choreography by students: Harriet Garrett, Lois Rathburn, Betty Lynd Thompson, Elizabeth Whitney
August 10, 12, 14, 16 College Theatre	*The King and the Duke*— A Melodramatic Farce from *Huckleberry Finn* Play devised and directed by Francis Ferguson Dances composed and staged by Martha Hill Music composed and conducted by Gregory Tucker Setting and lighting design by Arch Lauterer Costumes by Helen Bottomly
August 11, 13, 15, 17 College Theatre	Martha Graham Dance Group *El Penitente* Choreography by Martha Graham Music by Louis Horst Costumes by Edythe Gilfond Setting and Lighting by Arch Lauterer Danced by Merce Cunningham, Martha Graham, Erick Hawkins *Every Soul is a Circus* Choreography by Martha Graham Music by Paul Nordoff Costumes by Edythe Gilfond Setting and Lighting by Arch Lauterer

Danced by Martha Graham, Ethel Butler, Merce Cunningham, Jean Erdman, Nelle Fisher, Frieda Flier, Erick Hawkins, Sophie Maslow, Marjorie Mazia

Letter to the World
Choreography by Martha Graham
Arch Lauterer, Artistic Collaborator
Music by Hunter Johnson
Costumes by Edythe Gilfond
Setting and Lighting designed by Arch Lauterer
Assistant to Mr. Lauterer, Elizabeth Reitell
Danced by Martha Graham, Ethel Butler, David Campbell, Merce Cunningham, Jane Dudley, Jean Erdman, Nelle Fisher, Frieda Flier, Nina Fonaroff, George Hall, Elizabeth Halpern, Erick Hawkins, Marjorie Mazia, Sophie Maslow, David Zellmer
Speaker: Margaret Meredith

August 11 and 16
Recreation Building

Concert of Contemporary Music, Directed by Otto Luening
Music by Ernst Bacon, Samuel Barber, Marc Blitzstein, Paul Bowles, Theodore Chanler, Mary Howe, Charles Ives, Otto Luening, Reba Marcus, Robert McBride, Ann McDougle, Lionel Nowak, Quincy Porter, Karol Szymanowski, Emerson Whitborne
Performed by Aaron Bodehorn, Richard Chamberlain, Barbara Coffin, Claire Harper, Ruth Ives, Ethel Luening, Otto Luening, Naomah Maise, Reba Marcus, Robert McBride, Lionel Nowak, Theodore Russell, Carol Welch

August 14 and 17
Recreation Building

Concert of 17th and 18th Century Music, Directed by Ralph Kirkpatrick
Music by J.S. Bach, G.F. Handel, J.C. de Mondonville, Henry Purcell, Johannes Rosenmüller

Performed by Aaron Bodenhorn, Richard Chamberlain, Claire Harper, Ruth Ives, Ethel Luening, Otto Luening, Naomah Maise, Robert McBride, Theodore Russell, Carol Welch

10

Summer of 1941: Last Summer of the School of the Arts

"School of the Arts became fragmenting whereas before this, you had dance as the matrix art, to which everything else contributed."[1]— Norman Lloyd

Dates: July 5–August 17, 1941
Location: Bennington College, Bennington, Vermont

After the first summer of the Bennington School of the Arts, Mary Josephine Shelly indicates that there were major issues: the size of the school became unwieldy and taxed all personnel as well as the physical plant; the school ran at a deficit for the first time; and dance had far more students than the other disciplines, creating an imbalance. In addition, the school became more dispersed and less centralized by extending the focus to other disciplines, with leading faculty such as Hanya Holm, Norman Lloyd, and Bessie Schönberg, to indicate a sense of decline at least for dance. These problems were not fully corrected for the summer of 1941, and the school ran in much the same manner as in 1940 only with some reduction in staffing to reduce costs. There were, in addition, growing tensions between Arch Lauterer and Francis Fergusson, both of the Drama Division at Bennington College and on faculty at the Bennington School of the Arts. And there was an escalating difference of opinion between Louis Horst and members of the Music Division at Bennington College over the best ways to teach music composition. It seems Louis Horst's ideas were less traditional than those of the Bennington College music faculty. Despite all of these issues, students such as Joseph Gifford, whose story appears in this chapter, had a very positive experience.

One quite interesting development in the student population in dance at the School of the Arts is that they began enrolling more students looking toward professional performance careers and fewer dance teachers — the opposite of the

178

School of the Dance years. This was in part because the administration greatly increased the number of scholarships offered, but it also reflects the expansion of the field of modern dance to include more possibilities for performance and therefore performers. And the economy had improved somewhat from the worst of the Great Depression years. The performance and workshop schedule for the School of the Arts years was enlarged to include weekly showings that Shelly indicates was at the request of students who were interested in as many performing opportunities as possible.

In 1941, members of the school performed outside Bennington for the first time (besides the summer at Mills), at the Green Mountain Festival of the Arts in Middlebury, Vermont and at The General Stark Theatre, a movie theatre in the town of Bennington. This was in addition to the festival performances of 1941 that were held at the Bennington College Theatre as they were in 1940, not the Armory.

Director's Report[2] by Mary Josephine Shelly

In place of the annual report on the summer school, this occasion is taken to draw up a summary of the years from 1934 to the present in terms mainly of administrative factors. There is attached an appendix of facts and figures about personnel and finances [see p. 294]. This bare skeleton is in its own way revealing and some of the information about trends, or at least about ups and downs, may be useful in the future.

The eight years divide themselves into three unequal periods: 1934–1938, the launching of the School of the Dance and the five closely connected first years; 1939, the migration of the school to Mills; 1940–1941, the life, to date, of the School of the Arts.

THE SCHOOL OF THE DANCE: THE FIRST FIVE YEARS, 1934–1938

In the fall of 1933, Dr. Leigh had been commissioned by the Trustees of the College to devise an enterprise that would use the plant and occupy the employees and be suitable to Bennington's general character as an educational institution. An academic summer session seemed neither possible nor any particular contribution to American education, already rife with academic summer sessions. Concentration on some one field was the likeliest choice, and of the several possible fields, the arts were chosen. In the end, this narrowed down to the dance because Dr. Leigh believed what Martha Hill had already done with dance at Bennington to be singularly good education, and from this and other encounters with dance while organizing the College, had become interested in its possibilities, and because this art in contrast with other arts had no center elsewhere.

By putting its resources at the disposal of the dance almost a decade ago, the College through Dr. Leigh and the Trustees is in no small degree responsible for the existence intact at this moment of an American dance art. Through six years of Depression and the coming of war, a base such as that at Bennington has been nearly indispensable. Surely no other college could have lent itself as well to what proved to be an intensely alive and far-reaching undertaking.

The School began in a somewhat awkward relationship to the College. The normal public relations with College administration, faculty, and to a lesser extent Trustees, were difficult to keep clear because the School operated almost autonomously. It collected its own income and dispensed it under its own budget, with all the inevitable irregularities of handling a six-weeks population from all over the land and engaging in the putting on of shows. It had a non-resident administrative staff with only Martha Hill as go-between for the New York office of the College, where the School discharged its business from September to June, and the College itself.

However awkwardly set up at the beginning, the School was a huge success. Dr. Leigh calculated in November 1933, that 45 students would, if need be, pay the bills. Actually 103 were admitted to the first session.

The first influx of students had been induced to enroll by an eight-page bulletin announcing, in addition to the ambiguous premiere, that "classes will take place also in the garden and the orchard," the names of the people who would teach and little else. The dancers — Graham, Holm, Humphrey, Weidman — were called "visiting artists," as indeed they were, each of them teaching just one week. Louis Horst, Norman Lloyd (just beginning his career in this field), John Martin and Bessie Schönberg (still a student and assistant at Bennington), with Martha Hill and Gregory Tucker and few helpers and accompanists, made up the rest of the faculty.

Statistically pictured, the first session looks this way: 103 students (chosen from among a much larger number which applied), from 26 states (about half East, a quarter Midwest, the rest South and Far West), from at least 35 different universities and colleges and almost as many different elementary and secondary schools, ranging in age from 15 to 49 years, averaging 27 years, all of them women and two thirds of them teachers; a faculty and staff of 23; making a community of 126 persons. One public lecture by John Martin, solo concerts by Graham and Humphrey-Weidman, and a demonstration by Hanya Holm, who had arrived from Germany about two years before, were presented that year on a bare stage with black velvet curtains as décor to a total of 437 people from what is described in the first annual report as "Bennington, Old Bennington, North Bennington, Arlington, Saratoga Springs, Pittsfield, Williamstown, Putney, and other nearby communities." This first public effort, progenitor of the Festival, netted $373. The School lived in four houses, used seven pianos, earned $17,684 and spent $17,002, for a profit of $683. It spent the $17,000 in roughly these proportions: to the College, it paid about 20 percent of its income as return at 4 percent on the investment represented by the use of the plant; 40 percent more of its income to house and feed students; 30 percent for salaries; and the other 10 percent for administrative costs, including publishing a bulletin, reimbursing the Comptroller's office for services rendered, and buying $444 worth of lamps for the dwelling houses, which had been unhandily built without bedroom lights and hence were left in darkness by the departure of the College students with their personal property. The facts and figures are given in this detail for the opening year as a basis of comparison for what follow.

What followed was four years of building up on all counts. Admissions rose from 103 to 150, still oversubscribed; the faculty and staff to 52; the men students from 0 to a high of 11; public performances to a high of 9, the audience to 3800 in 1938, a total of about 10,000 in the five years with the Armory as well as the College Theatre in use; all states but Arkansas checked in; the School finally moved into all twelve houses and got around to needing twenty-two pianos. In the make-up of the community, there was a remarkable consistency from year to year: always about the same geographical spread, age distribution, institutional representation, and classification of interests and occupations.

The financial record corresponds: income rose to more than $41,000 in 1938, with the school earning between 1934 and 1938 a total of $150,000 and spending all but about $3,000 which accumulated as surplus, a little

181

Students at the Bennington School of the Dance, 1934 (photographer unknown, courtesy Bennington College).

each year. The largest surplus was in 1935 when $1,296 was left over from costs. About $7,500 or 5 percent of the total income was from box office. No more than a one dollar admission was ever charged and people were always turned away. The tuition and residence fee edged up a little each year, from $190 in 1934 to $255 in 1938 with students' work costumes, an item now payable in addition to tuition, covered. The money was spent as follows: about 30 percent for salaries, 30 percent for students' room and board, 16 percent for rental of the plant, 3 percent for part support of the New York office of the College, 1 percent for publishing the bulletin and carrying paid advertising (which totaled $173 in five years), 1 percent for repairs and maintenance of the plant and equipment of the College, including $1,000 paid on the cost of the famous tent in 1938, 5 percent for special costs of production, 1 percent for rental of the Armory and bus transportation back and forth, 4 percent for general administrative costs including hospitality, travel, and the outside lecturers and special events brought into the School in earlier summers, the balance for comptroller's office and library services which were not then covered by rental, and miscellaneous costs.

The School was in these years clearly two things: a teacher-training center influencing, in its field, literally the whole country; and a small-scale but unique theatre enterprise. Practice in the dance was affected in places as remote as possible from Bennington. The School was the incubator for the New York dance season. The Russian ballet had not yet moved on in the United States. Theatrical dancing in those winters consisted of Sol Hurok's earlier European importations, the musical comedies, and the winter concerts of Graham, Humphrey-Weidman and Holm, for which the pièces de resistance had been done at Bennington the previous summer.

These things — to alter radically the teaching of an activity, any activity, in any really large number of American schools, actually to plant that activity in new places, and to make a mark of any size on the metropolitan theatre, are exceptional consequences of a college's efforts at using its plant in the summer.

THE SCHOOL OF THE DANCE
AT MILLS COLLEGE, 1939

In 1939, the School picked up and went to California for a summer. The summer was confined to teaching because production, to which Bennington had become used, would have strained the resources of Mills, to say nothing of unbalancing the budget. The Mills session originated in the efforts of Rosalind Cassidy, Convenor of the School of Education at Mills, whose persistence made the session possible. Mills must have viewed with some alarm this venture. But all came out well. Practically every application was accepted and 170 students were admitted. The session earned a comfortable 3 percent surplus of $2,373, Bennington bringing home 40 percent of it, or $949, and leaving Mills 60 percent, or $1,424.

The session at Mills followed the pattern of the summer 3000 miles away back home in Bennington. The caliber of the student body was below the level reached in the East by 1938 because the West Coast had had less development. That was one reason we went west. The population shifted, exchanging 50 percent easterners for 50 percent from beyond the Rockies, although 30 out of the 170 students followed the School from the Eastern Seaboard and 40 more came from the Middle West. Otherwise the picture was closely identical to that of other summers, and by adding this sixth summer to the others, the facts and figures were upped proportionately, bringing total income close to $200,000 (the Mills session earned over $38,000), raising the accumulated surplus as indicated above, and enlarg-

Katherine Manning teaching at the Bennington School of the Dance at Mills College (photographer unknown, courtesy Special Collections, F.W. Olin Library, Mills College).

ing the total number of different students who passed through the School to 850 (in each summer from 15 percent to 20 percent were repeats).

This was the last session of the Bennington School of the Dance. The die had already been cast, at Martha Hill's and my instigation, for incorporation of the School into the School of the Arts. All the reasons for this step are difficult to recall, but predominant among them was a genuine belief in the rightness of the step and a genuine enthusiasm for the animating principle of the new venture, collaboration.

THE SCHOOL OF THE ARTS, 1940–1941

Enthusiasm for the School of the Arts plan was shared by the Trustees and made it easier to face the discovery in May 1940, after approval in

January of a preliminary budget, which confidently predicted a $60,000 income, that Bennington's summer venture was for the first time about to lose money. Actually, it lost no money, but it paid no return to the College after paying the College a total of almost $25,000 in rent alone up to the time it went to Mills. It scraped through with the highest fee in its history, $275, paid by only 88 students. The scraping took place in individual salaries, January commitments being out all along the line, and by other painful contractions at a dozen points, including retreat to the College Theatre from the town location where we had hoped to perform.

The causes of this abrupt change in drawing power were many, among which not only the coming of the war that fall but the particularly dreadful spring of 1940 were certainly major ones. We had counted on an unlimited dance population as security until we got a toehold among the countless competing enterprises in drama and music. That dance population shrank in half overnight. The sound of the new project, we now know, scared away many old customers and potential customers; we suddenly put our fee up $275; it was a summer of the most extensive competition we had ever had in dance, most of our competitors being our own step-children; and we had been going strong in a relatively small field for six years. At any rate, 88 full-paying students 74 of them in dance, did come at the high fee, which was doubtless remarkable, and it was a good summer in almost all ways once it got started.

This last summer we repeated the same sequence of events, only on a smaller scale. In January we cut down our estimates to the actualities of 1940, but put the fee back to normal. And despite this, again in May faced closing shop. Both years it was the Trustees Committee for the School of the Arts, which, with Mr. Page this last year, stood by and made the final decision to go ahead. Fortunately this year we recouped some of our anticipated losses and have now restored the salaries surrendered in May, and the session of 1941 was in many ways the best we have ever carried out.

But there are, apart from all the other considerations which this report leaves out, a few facts to look at, When the full-paying population dropped in 1940 from an average of 141 to a total of 83, the income, because of the sharply increased fee, remained almost exactly at the average of the preceding six years: the gross income in 1940 was $30,509, the 1934–1939 average was $31,890. The real difference shows up in the amount spent for salaries, not individual salaries, but number of persons to be paid by those paying; we spent over $18,000 in salaries in 1940 when we had never before spent more than about $14,000. In other words, the ratio had been about four persons paying to one paid. Suddenly it changed to one person paying to about one and a quarter to be paid. In 1941, the salaries went down to $14,600, but still only 90 students paid full fee and they paid only $250, and there was still a large faculty to be paid.

In addition to salaries, other important costs went up: production, administrative costs, and the like. The community was much bigger, the School much more complex on every score. After six years of giving no reductions in fees, we suddenly admitted 30 or more students for little or no tuition, this in order to have a population representative enough to work with. The faculty and staff jumped from an average of 35 (previous high of 52) to 65 in 1940, 59 in 1941. Some of these were fellows or assistants needed as performers in the music and drama units, but they all had to be paid at least the equivalent of living.

The population changed in another way, although the effect of this change on income is difficult to evaluate conclusively: after six years of enrolling an average of 65 percent teachers, the proportion in 1940 was 32 percent teachers, and this was almost exactly repeated in 1941. The geographical distribution changed very little, a few less Middle Westerners and a few more Easterners coming in 1940 and 1941. And Arkansas finally turned up [in 1941]. The number of men jumped from a high of 11 before 1940, to 32 in 1940, back to 17 in 1941 due to the draft. The average age dropped three years with the range still 15 to almost 50.

Details could be added, but this much analysis is sufficient to permit a conclusion: on the financial side, the income base of the School is too narrow for its expanded superstructure of costs; and on the personal side, the market for the School has shifted from teachers primarily, to primarily a younger, more professional group. How to read the two facts for the future depends upon the nature of that future. Certainly any financial plan must be curtailed even over the rock-bottom budget drawn up in the emergency of May 1941. Last summer's actualities do not serve as a safe minimum. Too many of the factors causing the loss of income in 1940 and 1941 are still at work, and those not offset by sufficiently strong new inducements to students, to allow any but very conservative expectations.

Obviously the story of the School is not written here. This report errs deliberately on the side of practical emphasis and even tiresome insistence on dollars, cents and noses counted. However, this report makes available one aspect of the story to which reference must of necessity be made, both in evaluating the past and planning the future. The rest of the story would, in any case, escape in the telling.

Joseph Gifford's Recollections

Elizabeth McPherson interviewed Joseph Gifford by telephone on July 14, 2008. McPherson transcribed and edited the interview, developing a narrative that was then edited and approved by Gifford in February of 2011.

GIFFORD'S BIOGRAPHY

Joseph Gifford (born 1920) attended the Bennington School of the Arts in the summers of 1940 and 1941 under the name Joseph Gornbein. He began his professional career in New York City as a member of the dance company of Doris Humphrey and Charles Weidman. In the early 1950s, he formed his own company, the Joseph Gifford Dance Theater, which performed annually in NYC and on tours throughout the United States. During his years in NYC, he assisted Doris Humphrey in her teaching, appeared in several musicals on Broadway, and was on faculty for 20 years at the New Dance Group. He joined the faculty of the School of Theatre Arts, Boston University, to establish a curriculum in movement training for the actor in 1961, and taught there for 24 years. In 1985, Mr. Gifford joined the faculty of the American Symphony Orchestra League's workshops for conductors. He taught annually for the ASOL, until 2006. He has also worked privately with prominent American conductors, including Christopher Wilkins, Neal Stulberg, and Joe Illick. Mr. Gifford continues to give seminars and private classes for conductors and instrumentalists throughout the United States and in Europe.

GIFFORD'S ACCOUNT[3]

Music was my first love before I discovered dance, and I have been collecting art for years and years, as well as photography. But when you dance, nothing gets in the way. There's no violin there; there is no conductor's baton; there's no paintbrush. The dancer's instrument is it.

187

Joseph Gifford, circa 1950s (photographer unknown, courtesy Joe Gifford).

And when you see dance in its most beautiful supreme way, it is extraordinary.

I danced through college at Wayne University which is now Wayne State University, and then transferred to University of Michigan at Ann Arbor. We didn't have a dance department. We had dance as part of physical education. Ruth Bloomer was the director, and she later became head of dance, for a year or two, at Connecticut College School of the Dance summer program. She was very encouraging to me. While at the University of Michigan, I heard about the Bennington School of the Dance. I went there on scholarship for the summers of 1940 and 1941. There was an absence of men, so I just asked for a scholarship and got it. Incidentally, I was still using my birth name Joseph Gornbein then. I didn't change my name to Gifford until my first year in New York with Doris Humphrey and Charles Weidman.

Bennington was thrilling. Having been in the Midwest all of my life, I remember my first view of the green in front of the Commons where we ate and where the little theatre was. The physical plant itself was so charming, and so New England. I was just thrilled to be in the midst of all of this extraordinary dance energy. After lunch, we would all sit on the green — the Graham Company, the Humphrey-Weidman people. From that marvelous view, looking toward the Green Mountains, we'd watch Martha Graham with her parasol and her funny little walk going down to her house where she was staying. I remember watching the Graham dancers do phrases across the green, for photographs probably. I was in love with dance and the Green Mountain air. It was a very special time.

And it wasn't just the dance, it was also the musical and theatrical things going on. Starting in 1940, the summer program had become the Bennington School of the Arts, incorporating the School of the Dance. I got to meet Hunter Johnson, the composer, and Ralph Kirkpatrick, the harpsichordist who was a guest artist there, and some of the actors and so forth and so on even though I was mostly involved in dance.

At Bennington, there was a pattern, and whoever was the main focus that year, gave a master workshop. Martha Graham was the person in 1940, so I did the Graham workshop. (Doris and Charles weren't there at all that year.) All the Graham classes were given by Ethel Butler who was in the company at the time. And I remember Merce Cunningham was in the classes, having just come into the Graham Company. I remember how he would lead the group across the diagonal — his high, easy spring. So that was very exciting, although I think when I got on the floor and started to do contractions with my legs wide, I knew that the Graham technique was not for me.

I tried taking a ballet class taught by Erick Hawkins, and he kicked me out and said, "You are not ready for this class." Of course, he was so right!

I also studied with Bessie Schönberg, and her class was really interesting. It was the only class at Bennington, as far as I know, that wasn't technique or composition. It was explorative. She would set up themes, and we would take a theme and kind of improvise on it. It was very, very charming and whimsical, going into the unknown all the time. She was a lovely teacher. Little did I know how important she was to become later on.

I took Louis Horst's composition classes, his Pre-Classic Forms, and I think I took his Modern Forms the second year in 1941. He liked me — I was one of the favorites because I had a good sense of form and structure. I found Louis's work very, very influential for me, and I think for lots of other people too although he could be vicious with the young girls. Some would start crying and run out of the room. I may be exaggerating, but I don't think I am exaggerating by much. He was tough. He'd sit there with his big paunch, and with one eyebrow look over from his right eye or left eye and grumble something at you. But he was important. He was a rock for modern dance. Of course he was musical director for Martha Graham, and I guess a lover for her at one point before Erick Hawkins came along.

And then there were the directors: Martha Hill and Mary Jo Shelly. I remember Martha Hill vividly, and Mary Jo. Martha was always the smiley one, always upbeat. Mary Jo was the no-nonsense, grounded one.

Those summers were loaded with physical education teachers from high schools and colleges. I was thinking earlier today that it was a godsend for the modern dance companies, because that's where they got their gigs, through the PE teachers throughout the country. The PE teachers would go back home to their communities and bring the companies out to perform.

We used to have a collaborative showing once a week where work was shown — dance compositions and theatrical scenes. There was a tiny stage space on the second floor of the Commons that had been made into a theatre by Arch Lauterer, the scenic designer, who was also in residence. (The Armory wasn't used when I was there.) I opened up one of the programs with a dance called *Fanfare*. It was to music by my friend Carl Miller who went to Bennington in 1940 to study music for dance with Norman Lloyd and Louis Horst. Carl actually took me to my first dance class back in Detroit a few years earlier.

I remember seeing Martha Graham perform in the summer of 1940 — a dress rehearsal of her Emily Dickinson dance, *Letter to the World*, before she went on tour. I was remembering the other day that John Martin, the dance critic, originally blasted it. Graham re-did it and brought it back in 1941, and I remember reading Martin saying in regards to his prior negative review: "It is a pleasure this morning to eat those words."[4] The first year, an actress [Margaret Meredith] from a theatre down in Charleston, South Carolina came to do the speaking. The second year, Jean Erdman was the speaker. Eventually, I knew all these dancers over the years — like Jane Dudley, and Sophie Maslow.

In 1941, Charles and Doris were there as well as Martha Graham. Hanya Holm wasn't around any more by that time. She had gone to run her dance program in Colorado by then. I took the Humphrey-Weidman master workshop in '41 and a woman named Claudia Moore Read who was in the company at the time, taught the technique classes. (The choreographers would assign members of their companies to do the teaching, mostly.) I had begun to feel I was a Humphrey-Weidman person by then.

There was a rivalry going on between the Graham people and the Humphrey-Weidman people which was unfortunate, but that's how it was. I must say, that the Graham dancers thought they were the cat's meow. They really thought they were the best. And although the most apparent rivalry was amongst the students, I think Doris and Martha didn't see eye to eye as well. They were such different personalities. John Martin once said in one of his books — a very interesting analysis — that Martha Graham was kind off balance naturally and fought to come on balance, whereas Doris was naturally balanced and willed herself to go off-balance.[5] Interesting. Of course Doris' technique was fall and recovery, and Martha's was contraction and release. But going back, they were such different personalities. And I suppose there was a built-in rivalry because they were the main players on the stage at that time, and there were limited resources to go around.

There was also Hanya Holm, but by that time she had lost her company. I studied for a year with Hanya when I started dancing with Doris and Charles in New York because I felt like I needed to find another technique. Hanya Holm wasn't a happy camper at that time.

Graham did *Punch and the Judy* the summer of 1941, and also *Every*

191

Soul is a Circus. I think it was one of the first times Hawkins performed the repertory. There was actually a group of men for the first time: Merce Cunningham, David Campbell, and David Zellmer.

Doris did a dance called *Decade* in 1941. It wasn't very successful. I think it was too literal. It was about the difficulty in having a dance company. And there was a speaker. It was like modern dance against business. But what it did was it gave us excerpts of the dances that Doris and Charles had done the previous 10 years. She revived certain things. There was Charles doing his beautiful *The Sunken Cathedral* to Debussy. And he and Doris did *Duo-Drama* to music by Roy Harris. And there were other sections of dances, so it was kind of a retrospective of the previous ten years threaded and woven together. She may have done it once more in the 16th Street studio in New York.

Some of the dancers I remember were Marjorie Mazia and Freda Flier. Marjorie was married of course to Woody Guthrie. Later on, Marjorie used to get me jobs teaching children to make a living in New York.

So, by 1941, I knew I was going to be a dancer. A short while after my summer at Bennington, the Humphrey-Weidman people put out a notice saying that if you sent them $1000, you could send anyone you wanted for a year's scholarship. I was from Michigan, and the Michigan Dance Council at the time had auditions. I don't think there was too much competition, and I got it, and went on to get the scholarship with Doris and Charles. And then I joined the company. I have a program where I've written "My first professional performance." I don't know where it was. I've got the feeling I must have been the victim in *Lynchtown*. I wasn't really in the company then, but they drag a person across the stage. I have a feeling I was the person being dragged across the stage. I actually did perform in *Lynchtown* and other works that Doris and Charles did of course for about 4 years before Doris stopped performing. And when Doris left/stopped, I didn't stay with Charles. I felt my heart was with her.

I think one of the best things I got from Bennington was that it presented a kind of a tapestry, an overview of American modern dance. In a sense, it was a tasting menu: Bessie's work, Louis,' and Martha's, and Doris' and Charles.' It became a springboard to go from that broader aspect to shape it into a more narrow channel with Doris and Charles to whom I

Doris Humphrey and dancers at the Bennington School of the Arts, 1941 (photograph by Hans Knopf, collection of Charles H. Woodford).

gave everything. And it was national, all these people from all over the country. It was a great gift that I received.

I went back to Bennington College a few years ago, sixty years since I had been there for the summer workshops. I was visiting a friend in Vermont, and when he heard that I'd been to the school, he said "Let's go to Bennington College. Let's drive there. It's only an hour away." There was nobody around. I saw that little place where I used to stay, the small dormitories. And I stood in front of the Commons there. It was interesting, but I was a little bit detached at the same time. You move on, but I stood there all those years later. I thought wow this is still as it was before. Amazing.

Facts and Figures, 1941

[*Some specific information was unattainable for this year. The advance bulletin was much less detailed, and Shelly's Final Report was an overall review of the school from 1934 to 1941 instead of particular to the year 1941.*]

Total Enrollment of Students: 126 (does not include company members)

Select Students

Fannie Aronson, Joseph Gornbein (Gifford), Ita Hoxsie, Iris Mabry, Virginia Moomaw, Virginia Tanner, Theodora Wiesner, Frank Wigglesworth

Faculty and Curriculum

Administrative Director, Mary Josephine Shelly

Dance Division

Director, Martha Hill
Accompanists included Ralph Gilbert, Pauline Lawrence, Ruth Lloyd,
    Yolanda Lorenz, Zoe Williams

Dance Courses Offered

Technique
Graham Technique (Introductory and Advanced)
Taught by Martha Graham and Ethel Butler

Holm Technique (Introductory and Advanced)
Taught by Harriet Roeder, Associate for Hanya Holm

Humphrey-Weidman Technique (Introductory)
Taught by Marie Maginnis and Claudia Moore (Read)

Humphrey-Weidman Master Course
For advanced students
Taught by Doris Humphrey and Charles Weidman
Claudia Moore (Read), Associate

Repertory — Humphrey-Weidman
Students learned Weidman's *Lynch Town* (later called *Lynchtown*) and
Humphrey's *The Shakers*

Techniques of Modern Dance
Taught by Bessie Schönberg
Assistant — Hortense Lieberthal (Zera)

Ballet
Taught by Erick Hawkins

Tap
Taught by William Bales

Pre-Classic and Modern Forms
Taught by Louis Horst

American Country Dance
Listed in advance materials, but may not have run

Dance Composition
Taught by Martha Hill
Assistant — Hortense Lieberthal (Zera)

Experimental Production
Directed by Martha Hill, Arch Lauterer, Norman Lloyd

Rhythmic Basis for Movement
Taught by Norman Lloyd

Improvisation and Speech for Dancers
Taught by Marion Fergusson and Mary-Averett Seelye

Make-up
Taught by Edward Thommen

Drama Division

Director, Francis Fergusson

Instructors/fellows not listed below included: Barbara Deming, Elisabeth
James, Dorothy McWilliams, Will Parker, Mary-Averett Seelye

Drama Courses Offered

Acting
Taught by Marion Fergusson

Dramatic Literature
Taught by Francis Fergusson

Body Training through Dance
Probably taught by Martha Hill

Speech and Voice for the Stage

Make-up
Taught by Edward Thommen

An Acting Company was planned to tour in the vicinity of Bennington.

Music Division

Director, Otto Luening

Instructor, Ethel Luening

Visiting Artist and Lecturer, Ralph Kirkpatrick

Music Courses Offered (instructors unknown other than above)

*Technique and Repertoire of Piano, String Wind Instruments, and Voice
(Group Instruction)*

Composition

Orchestration

Conducting

Accompanying

Choral Singing

Instrumental Ensemble
Directed by Otto Luening

Theatre Design Division

Director, Arch Lauterer

Other faculty/fellows: Charlotte Trowbridge

There were no set classes as each student's program was arranged individually, with experienced students given the opportunity to work with the professional groups.

Select Concerts, Demonstrations, and Events

July 12 College Theatre	Workshop (Dance)

July 12
College Theatre

Workshop (Dance)
Experimental Production directed by Martha Hill, Arch Lauterer, and Norman Lloyd
Compositions by Stanton Benjamin, Margaret DeHaan, Dorothy Kendall, Nik Krevitsky, Charles McCraw, Joyce Peloubet, Sidney Stambaugh, Theodora Wiesner, Delphine Zasloff

Advanced Composition directed by Martha Hill
Compositions by Mary-Averett Seelye, Ethel Tison, Charlotte York

Modern Forms directed by Louis Horst
Compositions by Jane Dudley, Nina Fonaroff, Gertrude Green, Alix Tairoff

July 19
College Theatre

Workshop (Dance)
Experimental Production directed by Martha Hill, Arch Lauterer, Norman Lloyd
Compositions by Madge Friedman and Virginia Tanner

Advanced Composition directed by Martha Hill
Compositions by Cynthia Barrett, Margaret Livingston, Gladys Ryland, and Alix Tairoff

Pre-Classic Forms Directed by Louis Horst
Compositions by Ruth Ellis, Cynthia Gano, Carol Kobin, and Sidney Stambaugh

Modern Forms directed by Louis Horst
Composition by Nina Fonaroff

July 19
College Theatre

Erick Hawkins with Jane Dudley and Jean Erdman

Trailbreaker—Kentucky
Choreographed and danced by Erick Hawkins
Music by Ralph Gilbert

The Ballad of Molly Pitcher
Choreographed and danced by Jane Dudley
Music by Earl Robinson

Trickster Coyote
Choreographed and danced by Erick Hawkins
Music by James W. Harker

Chaconne: The Pilgrim's Progress
Choreographed and Danced by Erick Hawkins
Music by Wallingford Riegger

Yankee Bluebritches—A Green Mountain Dance
Choreographed and danced by Erick Hawkins
Music by Hunter Johnson

Harmonica Breakdown
Choreographed and danced by Jane Dudley
Music by Sonny Terry and Oh Red

In the Time of Armament
Choreographed by Erick Hawkins and danced by
   Jean Erdman and Erick Hawkins
Music by Hunter Johnson

July 24   Green Mountain Festival of the Arts, Middlebury,
          Vermont
        The School for Wives by Molière
        Music by Jean-Baptiste Lully
        Translation by Emily Sweetser
        Directed by Francis Ferguson
        Ballets composed and directed by Martha Hill
        Screens designed by Edwin Avery Park
        Musical Director — Otto Luening
        Cast: Muriel Brenner, Joan Cheeseman, Joseph M.
          Dixon, Ita Hoxsie, Elisabeth James, Ray Malon,
          Will Parker, Paul Rockwell, Mary-Averett Seelye,

Shirley Stanwood, Sidney Stambaugh, Edward
Thommen
Members of the Vermont Symphony Orchestra

The Impressario by W.A. Mozart
Scenario by Eric Blom
Staged by Francis Fergusson
Screens designed by Edwin Avery Park
Musical Director — Otto Luening
Cast: Richard Chamberlain, Ruth Ives, Ethel
Luening
Members of the Vermont Symphony Orchestra

July 25

Green Mountain Festival of the Arts, Middlebury,
Vermont
Lecture on Modern Dance by John Martin

Vermont State Symphony Orchestra with Martha
Graham, Doris Humphrey, Charles Weidman
Alan Carter — Musical Director and conductor
Robert McBride, Associate Conductor
Zlatko Balokovich, Violin Soloist

Concerto Grosso, Op. 6, No. 6 for Strings by George
Frideric Handel
Symphony No. 4, "The Italian" in A Major, Op. 90
by Felix Mendelssohn
Concerto in D Major for Violin, Op. 77 by Johannes
Brahms

Alcina Suite
Choreography by Charles Weidman
Music by George Frideric Handel
Danced by Charles Weidman and Doris
Humphrey

Atavisms: Bargain Counter and Lynch Town
Choreography by Charles Weidman
Music by Lehman Engel
Danced by Beatrice Seckler, Charles Weidman, and
members of the Company

199

The Shakers
Choreography by Doris Humphrey
Music — Traditional
Danced by Doris Humphrey, Charles Weidman,
and members of the Company

Humphrey-Weidman Company: Molly Davenport,
Gloria Garcia, Charles Hamilton, Katherine Litz,
Marie Maginnis, Claudia Moore (Read), Beatrice
Seckler, Nona Schurman

Every Soul is a Circus
Choreographed by Martha Graham
Music by Paul Nordhoff
Musical Direction by Louis Horst
Costumes by Edythe Gilfond
Setting by Arch Lauterer
Danced by Martha Graham, Ethel Butler, Merce
Cunningham, Jane Dudley, Jean Erdman, Nina
Fonaroff, Erick Hawkins, Pearl Lack (Lang),
Marion Scott

July 26
College Theatre

Workshop — Dance
Experimental Production directed by Martha Hill,
Arch Lauterer, Norman Lloyd
Compositions by Carol Kobin, Nik Krevitsky, Joan
Lesser, and Theodora Wiesner

Pre-Classic Forms directed by Louis Horst
Compositions by Flora Blumenthal, Ita Hoxsie,
Carol Kobin, Sidney Stambaugh, Carolyn
Wilson

Modern Forms directed by Louis Horst
Compositions by Iris Mabry, Schilli Maier, Barbara
Thomas

Repertory Class directed by Charles Weidman
Lynch Town
Choreography by Charles Weidman
Music by Lehman Engel

Danced by Cherry Balaban, Deborah Barron, Flora Blumenthal, Jean Brownlee, Eileen Cassidy, Evans Davis, Ruth Ellis, Catherine Fredericks, Nancy Gerhan, Joseph Gornbein (Gifford), Charles McCraw, Virginia Moomaw, Annabelle Ranslem, Sidney Stambaugh, Virginia Tanner, Barbara Thomas, Helen Waggoner, Charlotte York

August 2 College Theatre	Workshop — Dance *Pre-Classic Forms* directed by Louis Horst Compositions by Ruth Ellis, Cynthia Gano, Schilli Maier *Modern Forms* directed by Louis Horst Compositions by Shirley Broughton, Gertrude Green, Pearl Lack (Lang), Schilli Maier, Iris Mabry *Experimental Production* directed by Martha Hill, Arch Lauterer, and Norman Lloyd Compositions by Jennie Grainger, Nik Krevitsky, Marjorie Mann, Teru Osato, Ethel Tison
August 3 and 4 The General Stark Theatre (movie theatre)	Molière's *The School for Wives* and Mozart's *The Impressario* See program notes from July 24
August 9	Workshop — Dance *Pre-Classic Forms* directed by Louis Horst Compositions by Jane Arrowsmith, Flora Blumenthal, Carolyn Wilson, Delphine Zasloff *Modern Forms* directed by Louis Horst Compositions by David Campbell and Alix Tairoff *Advanced Composition* directed by Martha Hill and *Experimental Production* directed by Martha Hill, Arch Lauterer, and Norman Lloyd Compositions by Fannie Aronson, Cherry Balaban, Margaret DeHaan, Cynthia Gano, Jennie

Grainger, Carol Kobin, Joan Lesser, Barbara
Livingston, Charlotte Livingston, Margaret
Livingston, Joyce Peloubet, Elizabeth Ray,
Gladys Ryland, Virginia Tanner, Frances
Sunstein, Theodora Wiesner, and Charlotte
York

Advanced Tap Dancing directed by Bill Bales
Patrick's Day Parade
Choreography by Bill Bales
Danced by Eileen Cassidy, Nancy Gerhan, Muriel
Gold, Gertrude Green, Dorothy Kendall,
Virginia Moomaw, Annabelle Ranslem, Elizabeth
Ray, Jean Thomas

August 9 and 16 Carriage Barn	Bennington Festival — Music Concert Harpsichord Recital by Ralph Kirkpatrick Works by J.S. Bach, Jacques Champion de Chambonnières, François Dandrieu, Giles Farnaby, Orlando Gibbons, Thomas Morley, Bernardo Pasquini, Alessandra Poglietti, Jean Philippe Rameau, Domenico Scarlatti
August 10 and 11 The General Stark Theatre (movie theatre)	*The Barker: A Play of Carnival Life in Three Acts* Written by Kenyon Nicholson Directed by Francis Fergusson Set designed by Ben Hudelson Costumes designed by Edward Thommen Performed by Carol Bacher, Joan Brockway, David Crowell, Natalie Disston, Joseph Dixon, Edith Engelson, Marion Fergusson, Claire Field, Richard Golden, Stewart Graham, Mary Hobson, Ben Hudelson, Robert Hunt, Elizabeth James, Hortense Lieberthal (Zera), William Loomis, Virginia Lunsford, Marillyn Lush, Anne Luskin, Ray Malon, Lillian Marks, Lucille Murray, Will Parker, Faith Richardson, Paul Rockwell, Shirley Stanwood, Edward Thommen, Virginia Van Dyke

August 9, 11, 13 College Theatre	Doris Humphrey — Charles Weidman and Company

Decade
Choreography by Doris Humphrey
Musical Director and pianist — Lionel Nowak
Setting and Lighting by Arch Lauterer
Script by Alex Kahn
Costumes by Pauline Lawrence
Danced by Doris Humphrey, Charles Weidman,
and Company

Members of the Company: Molly Davenport,
Gloria Garcia, Charles Hamilton, Katherine
Litz, Marie Maginnis, Claudia Moore (Read),
Nona Schurman, Beatrice Seckler, Allen
Waine

Apprentices: Patricia Balz, Evans Davis, Joseph
Gornbein (Gifford), Ruth Parmet, Ida Reese, and
Jeanne Thompson

August 10 and 17 Carriage Barn	Concert of Contemporary Music with Henry Cowell, assisted by Ethel Luening, Otto Luening, Ruth Ives, Lionel Nowak

Works by John Barrows, John Becker, John Alden
Carpenter, Henry Cowell, Herbert Elwell, Edwin
Gerschefski, Richard Franko Goldman, Lou
Harrison, Louis Horst, Walter Piston, David Van
Vector

August 10, 12, 14, 16 College Theatre	Martha Graham and Dance Company *El Penitente* Choreographed by Martha Graham Music by Louis Horst Costumes by Edythe Gilfond Setting and Lighting by Arch Lauterer Mask by Isamu Noguchi Danced by Merce Cunningham, Martha Graham, and Erick Hawkins

Letter to the World
Choreographed by Martha Graham
Arch Lauterer, Artistic Collaborator
Music by Hunter Johnson
Costumes by Edythe Gilfond
Settings and Lighting by Arch Lauterer
Danced by Ethel Butler, David Campbell, Merce
    Cunningham, Jane Dudley, Nina Fonaroff,
    Madge Friedman, Harriet Garrett, Martha
    Graham, Erick Hawkins, Pearl Lack (Lang),
    Sasha Liebich, Barbara Livingston, Iris Mabry,
    Marion Scott, Frances Sunstein, David Zellmer
Narrator (One Who Speaks): Jean Erdman

Punch and the Judy
Choreographed by Martha Graham
Arch Lauterer, Artistic Collaborator
Music by Robert McBride
Costumes designed by Charlotte Trowbridge
Setting and Lighting by Arch Lauterer
Danced by Ethel Butler, David Campbell, Merce
    Cunningham, Jane Dudley, Jean Erdman, Nina
    Fonaroff, Martha Graham, Erick Hawkins, Pearl
    Lack (Lang), Sasha Liebich, and David Zellmer

Members of the Company: Ethel Butler, David
    Campbell, Merce Cunningham, Jane Dudley,
    Jean Erdman, Nina Fonaroff, Erick Hawkins,
    Sasha Liebich, David Zellmer
Apprentices: Madge Friedman, Harriet Garrett,
    Pearl Lack (Lang), Barbara Livingston, Iris
    Mabry, Marion Scott, Frances Sunstein

August 13 and 15   A Program of Dance Projects
College Theatre   I. (Wednesday only) directed by Louis Horst

Fanfare
Choreographed by Joseph Gornbein (Gifford)
Music by Carl Miller

Dilemma
Choreographed by Iris Mabry
Music by Federico Mompou

Three Sarabandes
Choreographed by Ethel Butler, David Campbell,
Iris Mabry
Music by Ralph Gilbert

II. *Mississippi Sketches* directed by Bessie
Schönberg
Choreographed by Bessie Schönberg
Music by Norman Lloyd
Lighting by Stanton Benjamin
Performed by Babette Fishel, Joan Harrison, Ita
Hoxsie, Helen Laurila, Marjorie Mann,
Suzanne Sage, Kee Spruyt, Ethel Tison,
Theodora Wiesner
Singers: Margaret Boegeheld, Richard
Chamberlain, Ruth Lloyd, Reba Marcus

III. (Friday only) directed by Louis Horst
Night Suite
Music by Darius Milhaud
Composed by Cynthia Barrett, Shirley Broughton,
Schilli Maier, Alix Tairoff under the direction
of Fannie Aronson, Gertrude Green, Nik
Krevitsky

Yankee Doodle Greets Columbus, 1492
Choreography by Nina Fonaroff
Music by Louis Horst

IV. *Today's Stepchild*
Composed and Directed by Zoe Williams
Music by Zoe Williams
Performed by Jane Arrowsmith, Marjorie Dorwarth,
Susan Frank, Charlotte Hofmann, Julia Schaefer,
Nancy Seamster, Jacqueline Welch

205

V. *Es Mujer*
Composed and Directed by William Bales
Music — traditional, arranged by Louis Sandi and
    Geronimo Baquerio Foster
Performed by William Bales, Joan Cheeseman,
    Cynthia Gano, Carol Kobin, Joan Lesser,
    Hortense Lieberthal (Zera), Teru Osato, Joyce
    Peloubet, Rosabel Robbins, Jean Thomas

VI. From *The Swallow-Book* by Ernst Toller,
    English version by Ashley Dukes
Directed by Martha Hill, Arch Lauterer, Norman
    Lloyd
Production Scheme — Arch Lauterer
Movement and Dance — Martha Hill
Music and Speech — Norman Lloyd
Scene Construction — Edward Glass, assisted by
    Halbert Frank
Cast: Stanton Benjamin, Muriel Brenner, Margaret
    DeHaan, Eunice Gitlow, Jennie Granger, Helen
    Hurd, Margaret Livingston, Harriet Noble,
    Rebecca Prout, Elizabeth Ray, Gladys Ryland,
    Cleota Spotts, Joseph Stokes, Winifred Valentine,
    Katherine Weber, Delphine Zasloff

August 16
College Theatre

Workshop–Dance
Experimental Production directed by Martha Hill,
    Arch Lauterer, and Norman Lloyd
Compositions by Cynthia Gano, Joseph Gornbein
    (Gifford), Jennie Granger, Nik Krevitsky, Cleota
    Spotts, Sidney Stambaugh

Advanced Composition directed by Martha Hill
Compositions by Jennie Grainger, Virginia Tanner,
    Ethel Tison, and Charlotte York

Pre-Classic Forms directed by Louis Horst
Compositions by Jane Arrowsmith, Flora
    Blumenthal, Cynthia Gano, Charlotte Hofmann,
    Ita Hoxsie, Carol Kobin, Joan Lesser, Charles

McCraw, Schilli Maier, Suzanne Sage, Jeanne Thompson, Delphine Zasloff

Modern Forms directed by Louis Horst

Compositions by Gertrude Green and Barbara Thomas

Repertory directed by Charles Weidman

Choreography by Doris Humphrey

Danced by Deborah Barron, Flora Blumenthal, Jean Brownlee, Eileen Cassidy, Evans Davis, Ruth Ellis, Ruth Fiske, Joseph Gornbein (Gifford), Charles McCraw, Virginia Moomaw, Annabelle Ranslem, Virginia Tanner, Barbara Thomas, Helen Waggoner, Charlotte York

11

Summer of 1942: Bennington College Summer Session

"It was a total Bennington College summer session that last summer of 1942. So that it never occurred to us that we would be asked not to continue."[1]— Martha Hill

Dates: July 6–August 15, 1942
Location: Bennington College, Bennington, Vermont

Bennington College ran yet a different type of summer session in 1942. Instead of a School of the Dance or School of the Arts, they offered courses in the fields of dance, music, graphic arts, plastic arts, government, economics, and science in the Bennington College Summer Session. In February of 1942, Doris Humphrey wrote in a letter to her former company member Eva Desca Garnet that Bennington College "has reorganized its summer session to include science, agriculture, and so forth, and has re-organized the dance center almost out of existence."[2] The plan had been for the Martha Graham Dance Company and the Humphrey-Weidman Dance Company to be in residence, but the new president of Bennington College Lewis Jones would not support the costs of a festival or salaries for the choreographers. Only the choreographers' expenses would be paid. Humphrey and Weidman chose not to accept the offer—a company member (Nona Schurman) would teach in their place.

Even with the change of name and focus, because the dance courses were run very much as they had been, with the same types of courses and faculty, 1942 is still considered the last year of the Bennington School of the Dance. Although there was no festival performance scheduled, the Martha Graham Dance Company performed American Document, *and dancers William Bales, Jane Dudley, Jean Erdman, Nina Fonaroff, Henrietta Greenhood (Eve Gentry), Sophie Maslow, and Nona Schurman presented work. In addition, Merce Cunningham and John Cage presented their first collaboration (co-choreographerd by Jean Erdman).*

The United States had entered World War II in December of 1941, and it was very much on the minds of Americans. The summer session offered lectures on "War and the Future" that appear to have addressed growing concerns of faculty and students. There were courses offered in American Country Dancing in the summers of 1941 and 1942, and there were evening events of Square Dancing in 1942. This was perhaps because of a growing nationalism related to the politics and social issues surrounding World War II.

1942 would be the last summer of the Bennington School of the Dance for a variety of reasons. The overriding one related to the war. To control fuel costs and respond to fuel rationing, the college, under the leadership of their new president Lewis Jones, decided to close during the bitterly cold Vermont winter months beginning in the academic year of 1942–1943, and start the second semester in the spring which meant running long into the summer. There literally was no time for a full summer program. In addition, the Vermont State Armory was now needed for military efforts, and no longer available as a theatre, leaving the College Theatre as a less than satisfactory performance venue for a dance festival. Other contributing issues were that the summer program was no longer making money, and that there was tension amongst the music and drama faculty. From the new president's viewpoint, the solution to all of these problems probably seemed quite simple — end the summer dance program. Nevertheless, there were some important dance activities at Bennington in the following years, which are discussed in Chapter 14.

No Director's Report has been located for this last summer session, however dance critic John Martin wrote an article about it that was published in the New York Times *on August 23, 1942.*

John Martin's Recollection

MARTIN'S BIOGRAPHY

John Martin (1893–1985) was born in Kentucky. He held various jobs as an actor, publicist, and editor before serving in the Aviation section of the Army Corps during World War I. In 1927, he was appointed the first dance critic for the *New York Times*. A leading force in bringing public recognition to modern dance, Martin helped to establish it as a major art form. He wrote several books including *The Modern Dance* (1933) and *The Dance* (1945). After retiring from the *New York Times* in 1962, Martin

209

taught at the University of California at Los Angeles for several years. He received many awards and honors including the Capezio Award in 1969.

MARTIN'S REPORT[3]

One of the most important institutions that have developed within the field of American dance, the dance project at Bennington College, last week completed its ninth Summer session. Since this year was, for obvious reasons, its most difficult, the record of its accomplishment is of particular interest.

For the first time in the history of the project (and in the history of the college itself, as well), the Summer session included other subjects besides dance. Inasmuch as previous years have always found the time and available space too limited to carry out all the ideas with which the place fairly vibrated when the dance alone occupied both premises and program, it is easy to see that problems might be difficult when such an exuberant topic was required to share its quarters with other topics, artistic, social and agricultural.

According to a racy and informal report by Mary Josephine Shelly, who with Martha Hill founded the project in 1934, there were no disasters, but quite the reverse. At those points here the various interests of the summer crossed paths, as in the weekly forums on the general subject "The War and the Future," lively discussions developed about the relative merits of the sciences and the arts. Furthermore, some of the dancers turned to sculpture and painting with interesting results, and all of them enjoyed the food grown on the college farm. Since the festival, which had been an annual event for a number of years, was abandoned, teaching became the central activity and functioned at an extremely high level. "In short," says Miss Shelly, "it was amiable, active and productive, and even without a festival nobody really wanted to go home" when it was over.

Concert Schedule

In spite of the omission of any program of performances from the Summer schedule, there were actually no less than four concerts, besides the weekly "Dance Workshops," in which students showed their compositions to their colleagues assembled. One of those concerts was by Martha Graham and her company, who were in residence throughout the term.

Miss Graham had made a revival (and a somewhat revised version) of her *American Document* for a special outdoors series in Washington early this month, and upon her return to the college she presented the work in the college theatre.

Another concert found Jane Dudley, Sophie Maslow and William Bales repeating with slight alterations the brilliant program they gave here last season at the Humphrey-Weidman Studio Theatre. A third event had Jean Erdman, Nina Fonaroff and Merce Cunningham doing solos and Miss Erdman and Mr. Cunningham twosomes on their first joint program. The fourth concert was a joint one by Henrietta Greenhood [Eve Gentry], who represented Hanya Holm in the Summer's teaching schedule and Nona Schurman, who performed a similar function for Doris Humphrey and Charles Weidman. Each of these young dancers had worked out a group composition during the summer as a special compositional project, and these numbers as well as solos made up their program. Such a series as this is just exactly what the American dance field needs, for it abounds in gifted young artists who are generally so busy working in other people's companies that they have no time to do their own creative work.

Martha Graham's Project

Miss Graham, besides her teaching, devoted herself to the composition (but not the presentation) of a new work [probably *Deaths and Entrances*] which she will probably show in New York in the coming season. It is as yet untitled and its subject is unrevealed, but its music will be by Hunter Johnson, who provided the music for *Letter to the World*.

During the six weeks of the session there were seven evenings of square dancing, led, with one exception, by Martha Hill. On the exceptional evening, Ralph Page came in as a caller, with Will E. Ayers as fiddler. Miss Hill also, working with Norman Lloyd as musical collaborator, presented a great deal of Latin-American dance material in such form that it can be used by the ordinary citizen and make him, perhaps, a bit more aware of his kinship with his good neighbors to the south.

All in all, it does not look as if the handicaps of the first war Summer had cramped the Bennington dance project too much. Always a fairly plastic institution, it seems to have adapted itself to the situation with admirable results and a spirit which can only be described as spunky. Says Miss Shelly: "We are in no better shape to plan for the future than is anyone else, but certainly no worse, and we are, after nine years, pretty tenacious." A hopeful and forward looking sentiment that could not be better expressed.

Hortense Lieberthal Zera's Recollection

Elizabeth McPherson interviewed Hortense Lieberthal Zera on July 6, 2008. McPherson transcribed and edited the interview to develop a narrative which was then approved by Zera in February of 2011.

ZERA'S BIOGRAPHY

Hortense Lieberthal Zera (b. 1916) graduated from New York University in 1936 with a degree in Health and Physical Education, having

Hortense Lieberthal (Zera), circa 1942 (photographer unknown, courtesy Hortense Zera).

212

focused her studies in Dance under the direction of Martha Hill. She assisted Hill and Bessie Schönberg at the Bennington School of the Dance from 1937 to 1941, and conducted her own classes in 1942. Zera was a faculty member at The New Dance Group, and taught dance, sports, and health education in the New York City public high schools until retirement. She currently explores her creativity through painting and sculpting, and is a Vice President of The Martha Hill Dance Fund.

ZERA'S ACCOUNT

In 1936, soon after I graduated from NYU where I met Martha Hill, she asked me if I would be her assistant at the Bennington School of the Dance. Would I be her assistant?!! I would have been anything for Martha. She was the greatest. What a person — she was so honest and real. I was her assistant and Bessie Schönberg's at the Bennington School of the Dance until 1941. Bessie and Martha taught technique and composition, and I would assist them by demonstrating and going around and helping people. They taught a general kind of movement. It's hard for me to specify. It wasn't a system, like you knew it was Graham, or you knew it was Hanya Holm. But Martha Hill did some of each, and invented her own movements as well, her own activities. Then, the last year I taught on my own because Bessie couldn't be there. Martha said "Will you cover?" I said, "Okay Martha. Whatever you say." I enjoyed it. By that time it was 6 years later. I had a little confidence.

And I got to take classes too. I guess I liked Charles Weidman and Doris Humphrey better than Martha Graham. She is threatening you know? I have respect for her. She did a tremendous job — she was talented, knowledgeable, a really strong person, but certainly not the kind of person I could have worked with as my life's work. But I could work with José Limón or Doris Humphrey and Charles Weidman. I worked with them a lot at their studio. José was a doll. And Hanya Holm, I loved her classes. I also really enjoyed my classes with Ruth and Norman Lloyd. I had known them since NYU. They became good friends of my husband's and mine, and I am still in touch with their sons. I was privileged to know all of these people.

There is talk sometimes about discord among the faculty, that there was some tension between the followers of Graham and Doris for instance. Well you know that happened, but I didn't pay so much attention. I felt like you're damn lucky you're here. The way I remember it, it was a lovely atmosphere overall. People were happy to be there. And the Bennington College campus is such a beautiful place.

These years were really the beginning of modern dance. I remember how everybody outside of modern dance reacted to me. Young men, or my family members would say, "Take off your shoes!" They thought I was nuts to dance around barefoot. In those days, if you were dancing at all, you were doing ballet, or tap, jazz, whatever, but take your shoes off and dance barefoot in just a leotard? I was teased like crazy. Everybody who knew about dance thought this is nuts—you take off your shoes and you dance barefoot?!

When I was growing up I had ballet, piano, and all that stuff that little Jewish girls had to take when they were growing up in Brooklyn. I also used to play tennis, ride horseback, play hockey in the park, all that stuff. Because when you grew up in Brooklyn in those days, you didn't have to have a trainer and a whole program. You wanted to play ball, you got out in the street. There wasn't that kind of traffic that we have today. You wanted to play field hockey, you went to Prospect Park. We rode horseback on Ocean Parkway and in the park. It was there, and it wasn't out of reach financially. You did what you wanted to do, what you could do. You know how I got to NYU? Well, I had a friend who lived on my block, Chris Shaffleton who was at NYU at the time, and I was getting ready to go to college. And she said, "Where are you going to go?" I said, "I don't know. I haven't even thought about it." She said, "You're a good athlete, why don't you come to NYU?" I said, "Thanks, I think I will." And I did. It wasn't any big deal getting accepted in those days. I was a health/physical education major, and dance was part of the physical education program. How could you not like it if you like physical stuff? I think all the physical activity is why I've lived this long. Honestly I do.

I did a fair amount of performing at NYU, and at Bennington I performed in a Bill Bales dance and an Anna Sokolow dance. And I did some of my own choreography. The year the Bennington School of the Dance was at Mills out in California, I was sitting in the library one day with Ben Belitt, and we were looking through Emily Post's *Book of Etiquette*. I was struck so much by some of the passages, and Ben said, "Why don't you make a dance? There haven't been many dances to words." That was true. And so I did it. My dance *Never Sign a Letter Mrs.* was filmed for the movie short *Young America Dances.*

That summer at Mills was just fantasyland. A group of us went out together by train, and on the way, we went to the Southwest, the Native American lands. What did I know about Native Americans? Martha [Hill] introduced me to all of that. She was very knowledgeable about it and very excited. I loved it. I still do.

I have often thought about how lucky I was. I was a Brooklyn girl and all the sudden I am up in Vermont having breakfast with Martha Hill, José Limón, Charles Weidman, Doris Humphrey, Louis Horst, Sophie Maslow, Jane Dudley, Norman and Ruthie Lloyd — all these wonderful people. It was social. It was friendly. It was relaxing. Nobody thought "Oh my God" because of the immensity of the situation. Well, I may have thought so, but not really because I had a good feeling with them always. They weren't full of bologna. It was easy. No great egos. Just all these wonderful people. A joy to know. And they were at the top of their business

Adults from left to right: unknown, Elizabeth Meyer, Hortense Lieberthal (Zera), Ruth Lloyd, Martha Hill; toddler — Jimmy Meyer; baby — David Lloyd. Bennington School of the Dance, 1940 (photographer unknown, courtesy Bennington College).

too. I loved it. Those were wonderful years, wonderful, wonderful. I was so privileged.

Facts and Figures, 1942

Total Enrollment[4]: approximately 70
(Some specific information was unattainable for this year as no Final Report has been located for this summer.)

Select Dance Students and Company Members

May Atherton, William Bales, Ethel Butler, David Campbell, Merce Cunningham, Jane Dudley, Nina Fonaroff, Henrietta Greenhood (Eve Gentry), Pearl Lack (Lang), Sophie Maslow, Nona Schurman, Theodora Wiesner, David Zellmer

Faculty and Curriculum

Dance Courses

Modern Dance (Introductory and Advanced sections in each dance method)

Graham Technique
Taught by Martha Graham and Assistant

Holm Technique
Taught by Henrietta Greenhood (Eve Gentry)

Humphrey-Weidman Technique
Taught by Nona Schurman

Technique of Modern Dance (Introductory and advanced sections)
Taught by Hortense Lieberthal (Zera)

Ballet Technique (Introductory and Advanced sections)
Taught by Erick Hawkins

Dance Composition (Introductory and advanced sections)
Taught by Martha Hill and Hortense Lieberthal (Zera)

Pre-Classic and Modern Forms
Taught by Louis Horst

Projects
Directed by various members of the faculty

216

Rhythmic Basis of Dance (Introductory and advanced sections)
Taught by Norman Lloyd

Music Accompaniment for the Dance
Taught by Norman Lloyd

Music Composition for the Dance
Taught by Louis Horst

Dance and Music Recreation
Taught by Martha Hill and Norman Lloyd

Recreational Course in Modern Dance
(This course was listed in the bulletin but may not have run.)
Taught by Hortense Lieberthal (Zera)

American Country Dancing
Taught by Martha Hill

Workshop
Weekly showings of student work

Music Courses

Composition
Taught by Otto Luening

Ensemble (Introductory and advanced)
Taught by Ethel Luening, Robert McBride, Gregory Tucker

Vocal Technique and Repertoire
Taught by Ethel Luening

Private Instruction in Voice or Instruments
By arrangement with faculty

Seminar
Twice a week sessions for the performance and criticism of works in
    progress

Workshop
Weekly showings of student work

Graphic and Plastic Arts Courses

Studio in Painting
Taught by Paul Feeley

Studio in Sculpture
Taught by Simon Moselsio

Graphic Arts: Wood Cutting, Wood Engraving, and Color Block Printing
Taught by Charles Smith

Architectural Drawing
Taught by Edwin Avery Park

Government, Economics, and Science Courses

Forum on the War and the Future
Taught by Faculty and Visiting Lecturers

Public Administration
Taught by James McCamy

Elementary Statistical Method
Taught by George Lundberg

Social Research
Taught by George Lundberg

The Economics of War
Taught by Horst Mendershausen

Philosophic Backgrounds of Certain Contemporary Attitudes
Taught by Margaret Patterson

Practical Agriculture
Supervised by Robert Woodworth

Fundamentals of Food Production
Taught by Robert Woodworth

Aerodynamics
Taught by M. Helen Polanyi

Bacteriology
Taught by Yvette Hardman

Biochemistry
Taught by Robert Meyers

Bacteriology and Chemistry Research
Taught by Robert Meyers

Photography Laboratory
Taught by Robert Meyers

Select Concerts, Demonstrations, and Events

July 8
Carriage Barn
Square Dancing with Martha Hill as caller

July 9
Lounge
Forum on War and the Future; Horst Mendershausen Statement; Social Studies Faculty, panel

July 9
Carriage Barn
Square Dancing with Martha Hill as caller

July 11
College Theatre
Dance Workshop
Advanced Composition class directed by Martha Hill, and Norman Lloyd, Music Director
Compositions by Cynthia Barrett, Theresa Bell, Mary Gardner, Billie Kirpich, Naomi Rodeheffer, Emily White

Pre-Classic and Modern Forms directed by Louis Horst
Compositions by May Atherton, Ethel Butler, Jane Dudley, Angela Kennedy

July 15
Lounge
Forum on War and the Future; George Lundberg Statement; Social Studies Faculty, panel

July 17
Carriage Barn
Square Dancing with Martha Hill as caller

July 18
College Theatre
Dance Workshop
Introductory Composition Class directed by Hortense Lieberthal (Zera)
Composition by Violet Warfield

Advanced Composition Class directed by Martha Hill and Norman Lloyd, Musical Director
Compositions by Billie Kirpich

Pre-Classic Forms directed by Louis Horst
Compositions by Diana Gellman, Kinch Horan, Ray Malon, Sonia Sperber

Modern Forms directed by Louis Horst
Compositions choreographed by May Atherton, Angela Kennedy, Suzanne Sage, Rose Serrao, Theodora Wiesner

July 25 Commons I	South American, Mexican, and Spanish phonograph recordings
July 25 Carriage Barn	Square Dancing with Martha Hill as caller
July 29 Lounge	Forum on Arts and the War Martha Graham — statement; Martha Hill, Louis Horst, Norman Lloyd, and Gregory Tucker — panel

August 1
College Theatre
	Dance Workshop
	Introductory Composition Class directed by Hortense
	   Lieberthal (Zera)
	Compositions by Joan Collingwood, Gladys Kirkwood,
	   Naomi Rodeheffer, Dorothea Stephan, Lois Stern

Advanced Composition Class directed by Martha Hill and
   Norman Lloyd, Musical Director
Compositions by Cynthia Barrett, Mary Gardner,
   Gladys Kirkwood, Suzanne Sage, Emily White,
   Kathryn Wolfe

Pre-Classic Forms directed by Louis Horst
Compositions by Mary Gardner, Diana Gellman,
   Sonia Sperber

Modern Forms directed by Louis Horst
Compositions by May Atherton, Cynthia Barrett,
   Evelyn Hurwitz, Theodora Wiesner

August 1 College Theatre	Dance Concert: Merce Cunningham, Jean Erdman, Nina Fonaroff

Seeds of Brightness
Choreographed and danced by Merce Cunningham
   and Jean Erdman
Music by Norman Lloyd

Theodolina, Queen of Amazons
Choreographed and danced by Nina Fonaroff
Music by Louis Horst

Credo in Us
Choreographed and danced by Merce Cunningham
and Jean Erdman
Music by John Cage

Renaissance Testimonials
Choreographed and danced by Merce Cunningham
Music by Maxwell Powers

Café Chantant— Five A.M.
Choreographed and danced by Nina Fonaroff
Music by Jacques Larmanjat

The Transformation of Medusa
Choreographed and danced by Jean Erdman
Music by Louis Horst

Hoofer on a Fiver
Choreographed and danced by Nina Fonaroff
Music by Alexander Tcherepnine

Ad Lib
Choreographed and danced by Merce Cunningham
and Jean Erdman
Music by Gregory Tucker

Accompanist: Helen Lanfer
Percussion Group: Nancy Calafati, Hazel Johnson,
Helen Lanfer, Ray Malon

August 2 Fairview	Music Concert with Robert McBride and Gregory Tucker playing compositions by Feruccio Busoni, Claude Debussy, Paul Hindemith, Robert McBride, Gregory Tucker, Heitor Villa-Lobos
August 2 Carriage Barn	Square Dancing with Martha Hill as caller
August 5 Social Lounge	Forum on War and the Future; Peter Drucker statement; Studies faculty, panel
August 6 Carriage Barn	Square Dancing with Ralph Page as caller

August 8 College Theatre	Dance Workshop *Introductory Composition Class* directed by Hortense Lieberthal (Zera) Compositions choreographed and danced by Elizabeth Marvin, and Jane Williams

Advanced Composition Class directed by Martha Hill and Norman Lloyd, Musical Director
Compositions choreographed and danced by Cynthia Barrett, Theresa Bell, Mary Gardner, Gladys Kirkwood, Billie Kirpich, Naomi Rodeheffer, Susanna Sage, Natalie Shepard, Emily White, Katheryn Wolfe

Pre-Classic Forms directed by Louis Horst
Compositions choreographed by Jane Bender, Billie Kirpich, Rose Serrao, Sonia Sperber, and Violet Warfield

Modern Forms directed by Louis Horst
Compositions choreographed by May Atherton, David Campbell, Angela Kennedy

Percussion Class directed by Norman Lloyd

August 8 Commons I	South American phonograph recordings
August 8 College Theatre	*Martha Graham and Dance Company* *American Document* Choreographed by Martha Graham Music by Ray Green (no program located for this performance)
August 12 Social Lounge	Forum on War and the Future; Peter Drucker statement; Studies faculty, panel
August 12 Lounge	Recorded compositions of Norman Lloyd for South American documentary film
August 13 College Theatre	Dance Concert: William Bales, Jane Dudley, Sophie Maslow with members of Martha Graham Dance company

222

Suite: Scherzo, Loure, Gigue
Choreographed and danced by Dudley, Maslow, and
     Bales
Music by J.S. Bach

*Two Dust Bowl Ballads: I Ain't Got No Home in This
     World Anymore* and *Dusty Old Hat*
Choreographed and danced by Sophie Maslow
Music by Woody Guthrie

Short Story
Choreographed by Jane Dudley and danced by Dudley,
     Elizabeth Halpern, Pearl Lack (Lang)
Music by Paul Creston

To a Green Mountain Boy
Music by Zoe Williams

Excerpts from *Folksay*
Choreographed by Sophie Maslow and danced by
     David Campbell, Joan Cheeseman, Pearl Lack
     (Lang), Sascha Liebich, Sophie Maslow, Margaret
     Starter, David Zellmer
Text by Carl Sandburg: "The People Yes"
Folk songs sung by Burl Ives

Black Tambourine
Choreographed and danced by Williams Bales
Music by Zoe Williams

Harmonica Breakdown
Choreographed and danced by Jane Dudley
Music by Sonny Terry

August 14 Commons	Square Dancing with Martha Hill as caller
August 14 College Theatre	Dance projects composed and directed by Henrietta Greenhood (Eve Gentry) and Nona Schurman

It's a Bargain at Any Price
Script and choreography by Henrietta Greenhood (Eve
     Gentry)

223

Danced by Theresa Bell, Eunice Carlston, Susanne
Ernst, Henrietta Greenhood (Eve Gentry), Billie
Kirpich, Ray Malon, Suzanne Sage, Sona Sperber
Music by Betty Jean Horner

Restless Song
Choreography by Nona Schurman
Danced by Eliza Dickinson, Dorothea Douglas, Mary
Gardner, Diana Gellman, Angela Kennedy, Nona
Schurman, Carol Senft, Rose Serrao

Tell Me of the Living
Choreographed by Nona Schurman
Text by Carl Sandburg, read by Williams Bales

Four Walls Blues
Choreographed by Henrietta Greenhood (Eve Gentry)
Music by Meade Lux Lewis

Running Laughter
Choreographed by Nona Schurman
Music by Irene Regine Poldowski

August 15   Dance Workshop
College Theatre   *Introductory Composition Class* directed by Hortense
Lieberthal (Zera)
Compositions choreographed and danced by Susanne
Ernst, Elizabeth Marvin, Adele Rogers, Judy
Underwood, Violet Warfield

Advanced Composition Class directed by Martha Hill and
Norman Lloyd
Compositions choreographed and danced by Evelyn
Hurwitz, Gladys Kirkwood, Naomi Rodeheffer,
Natalie Shepard, Kathyrn Wolfe

Pre-Classic Dance Forms directed by Louis Horst
Compositions choreographed and danced by Theresa
Bell, Mary Gardner, Diana Gellman, Billie Kirpich,
Carol Senft, Rose Serrao, Kathryn Wolfe

224

Modern Forms directed by Louis Horst
Compositions choreographed and danced by May
Atherton, Angela Kennedy, Rose Serrao, Theodora
Wiesner

Looking Back: Group Discussion on the Bennington School of the Dance, 1959

With Louis Horst, José Limón (joined halfway through), Pauline Lawrence Limón, Norman Lloyd, Ruth Lloyd, Bessie Schönberg

This group discussion on the Bennington School of the Dance involved important faculty members from the summer program and festival and was moderated by Martin Masters and Jeanette Schlottman. The discussion took place at Connecticut College School of the Dance/American Dance Festival in July of 1959. The version presented here has been excerpted and edited by Elizabeth McPherson from the transcription residing in the American Dance Festival Archives at Duke University. The excerpts have been re-ordered in some instances to facilitate readability. In many key ways, the discussion summarizes the school by exhibiting the camaraderie felt among the faculty and revealing highlights of the school for these faculty members. It also indicates the continuities from the Bennington School of the Dance to Connecticut College School of the Dance. Used by permission of the American Dance Festival Archives.

Biographies

MODERATORS

Martin Masters (n.d. available): press agent for Connecticut College.

Jeanette Schlottmann (later Roosevelt) (b. 1919–): Schlottmann was the Director of Connecticut College School of the Dance/American Dance Festival from 1959 to 1963, then served on its advisory committee until 1968. She was a faculty member in physical education at Connecticut

College from 1958 to 1963, and at Barnard College from 1951 to 1957 and 1964–1986. Schlottman authored several books on folk dancing, and was a founding member of the Congress on Research in Dance and the Society of Dance History Scholars.

PARTICIPANTS

Louis Horst (1884–1964): Born in Kansas City, Missouri, Horst was the musical director for Denishawn from 1916 to 1925. It was in this role that he met Martha Graham, whose life would be intertwined with his for years to come. Horst was Graham's musical director from 1926 to 1948. He accompanied concerts, composed music for her dances, advised her on music and dance composition, and was her lover. Horst also accompanied concerts for many of the early modern dancers including Doris Humphrey and Helen Tamiris. He was the foremost dance composition teacher of the time period, teaching at the Neighborhood Playhouse, the Bennington School of the Dance (1934–1942), the American Dance Festival, and Juilliard among other places. His methods of teaching dance composition are outlined in his two books: *Pre-Classic Dance Forms* and *Modern Dance Forms*. Horst was also the founding director and editor of the publication *Dance Observer.*

José Limón (1908–1972): Born in Culiacán, Sinaloa, Mexico, he immigrated to the United States with his family in 1915. After a year of studying art at the University of California at Los Angeles, he moved to New York to study at the New York School of Design. In 1929, he was deeply inspired by a dance performance by Harald Kreutzberg and Yvonne Georgi. He found his way to the Humphrey-Weidman School and within a year was performing with them. Limón would continue performing and studying with Doris Humphrey and Charles Weidman for the next 10 years, and during this time spent the summers of 1936–1939 at the Bennington School of the Dance. He began exploring choreography soon after he began studying dance, his first major work *Danzas Mexicanas* premiering at the Bennington School of the Dance at Mills College in 1939. He married Pauline Lawrence in 1941. With his mentor Doris Humphrey as artistic director, he founded the José Limón Dance Company in 1947. For more than two decades, Limón was in residence at the American Dance Festival as well as being a core Juilliard faculty member.

Pauline Lawrence Limón (1900–1971): Born in Los Angeles, California, Pauline Lawrence graduated from Hollywood High School in 1917, and joined the Denishawn Company as a pianist and danced minor roles. She joined the Humphrey-Weidman Company at its inception in 1928, serving in various capacities including pianist, business manager, and costume designer. She and José Limón married in 1941, and she became the costume designer and business manager for the José Limón Dance Company at its inception in 1947. She relinquished her role as business manager in the mid 1950s, but continued to design costumes until her death. She was on faculty at the Bennington School of the Dance from 1934 to 1941 or 1942.

Norman Lloyd (1909–1980): The composer received a B.S. in Music from New York University in 1932 and an M.S. in Music from NYU in 1936. While there he accompanied dance classes and become acquainted with Martha Hill. He was at the Bennington School of the Dance each summer 1934–1942, teaching "Music for Dancers," accompanying dance classes, composing for the major modern dance choreographers, and conducting and playing for the festival performances. During the academic year, he was on faculty at Sarah Lawrence where he stayed until 1945. He was a faculty member of The Juilliard School from 1949 to 1963, served as dean of the Oberlin Conservatory in the 1960s, and in 1965, was director of arts programming for the Rockefeller Foundation. Important modern dances for which he composed music include *La Malinche* (Limón), *Lament for Ignacio Sanchez Mejias* (Humphrey), *Panorama* (Graham), and *Quest* (Weidman).

Ruth Rohrbacher Lloyd (1910–2002): see page 52

Bessie Schönberg (1906–1997): Born in Hanover, Germany, Bessie Schönberg was one of the foremost dance educators of the 20th century and was highly influential in contemporary dance in the United States. Schönberg joined her American mother in Oregon as a young woman, and began studying at the University of Oregon where she met Martha Hill, fresh from her studies with Martha Graham. They would become friends and soon colleagues. Hill and Schönberg moved to NYC in 1929 immediately joining Martha Graham's dance group. Following an injury, Schönberg turned her attention to teaching. She taught at the Bennington School of the Dance from 1934 to 1941, and joined the Sarah Lawrence College faculty in 1936 where she created and directed one of the earliest stand-alone dance departments, shepherding growth and development of the program and her students until 1975. Some of her former students became well-known professional choreographers and dancers, including Carolyn Adams, Elizabeth Keen, Meredith Monk, Lucinda Childs and Victoria Marks. After her retirement from Sarah Lawrence, she continued to teach choreography, influencing such artists as Robert Battle while she was on faculty at Juilliard.

The Discussion[1]

N. Lloyd: You know nobody has ever done the story of the impact of this school — not the full impact. John Martin has touched on it when he talks about the Bennington group, but this was a whole art movement, which actually got its impetus from this six-week summer program because it gave the dance a home, which it never had except in studios. It touched a lot of people all over the country.

Schönberg: And beyond. The Bennington School of the Dance put Bennington College on the map internationally. You could hear about the School of the Dance in Europe.

Horst: Robert Leigh [the first president of Bennington College] was very smart because nothing could have put a young college on the map as well as something like this. In those days Bennington was the dance center of the world. The poet Ben Belitt called it OberBennington, you know like Oberammergau.

N. Lloyd: What was important about this Bennington project was that the leading modern dancers came together with the potential audience. Wouldn't you say that Louis? The course of study was set up really to be a kind of survey for college teachers of what dance was all about. A lot of them had read about it, but never had seen any. And there weren't any big tours of companies at that time.

Schönberg: Most of the students were teachers of physical education who wanted to put dance into their college programs. And the situation was somewhat interesting in that most of the teachers were much, much younger than the students. I was the youngest of the classes I taught, and I think that was fairly general during the first years.

N. Lloyd: The whole thing started with Martha Hill and Mary Jo Shelly who is now public relations director of the Girl Scouts.

Schönberg: Dr. Leigh said to Martha [Hill], "We ought to use the plant more during the summer, Martha. We ought to have a dance school."

N. Lloyd: Bennington College had just begun. [Started in 1932.] The buildings weren't all built.

P. Limón: Oh, no.

N. Lloyd: And the trees on the campus were very little things — only about a foot tall.

P. Limón: They weren't really ready to have a dance school.

N. Lloyd: The student body was composed mostly of teachers who had more money than the Bennington School of the Dance faculty as we were mostly all struggling. Bennington was the first time we had all eaten regularly for a long time. But these Bennington School of the Dance students got to know Graham and Doris and Charles, and then they would have them out to their colleges. The first dancers danced on what Louis [Horst] called the Physical Education circuit. Practically none of the dancers danced in theatres, but rather gymnasiums.

Schönberg: Do you remember those remarkable first contracts we received which said, "If there are 60 students you will get a salary of this and this. If there are only 40 students, you will get this and this, and if there are only 20 students, will you come anyhoo?" We were guaranteed room and board no matter what. Then we would get bulletins — enrollment has now reached 60. Then it got up to 70 and then it was over 90 finally wasn't it? Those contracts were wonderful.

N. Lloyd: And then at the end of the session, we all got a bonus!

Oh, and the big scandal that first summer — all the girls had to wear flesh colored leotards. Well in that area of Vermont, there are all these little hills. Bennington College is on one of them, and there were farms on other hills. From a distance, you could see that there were groups of people with opera glasses trained on the campus. So because of those flesh-colored leotards, rumors went around that we were a nudist colony.

Schönberg: The leotards were carefully designed because Martha Graham and some of the other artists felt that they had to see the movement, and they didn't want to see black leotards. Soaring suits or fleshings, that is what they were called. Berta Ochsner and Marian Van Tuyl were there that first year.

N. Lloyd: And Sybil Shearer was there. We had these young artist dancers in addition to the physical education teachers. The first summer Sybil was there, everyone advised her to drop this idea of dancing.

Schönberg: Her mother was along too.

N. Lloyd: But she just kept on working and working by herself, and eventually she ended up in Doris' company.

Schönberg: Every time you opened any studio door, there was Sybil on the floor working.

R. Lloyd: John Martin was there for three days at the beginning, or was it a week? And he gave these lectures in the lounge.

N. Lloyd: On "What Is Dance?" The first time he talked on "How Not to Look at a Dance," and things like that. He just gave these lectures.

Schönberg: Then it was decided that he should be there for the whole six weeks.

N. Lloyd: Then the next year, everyone went to sleep.

P. Limón: That was because it was so early in the morning.

Schönberg: He really was good, but it was impossible for moving bodies to sit still that long and listen.

N. Lloyd: We were trying all sorts of things. We tried outdoor dancing, and all the redheads like Rusty [Ruth] Bloomer and Marian [Knighton] Bryan hated us, with their fair skin out on the lawn under the sun.

Louis Horst: As I like to say, the first year we ran Bennington and after that Bennington ran us. The first year, every evening there was a party in some house and we were either at the Tuckers or Martha Hill would give a party. [Gregory Tucker was on the Bennington College music faculty. He was a pianist, teacher, and composer.]

I remember that first year that Martha [Graham] came back up to get me at the end of the session, and I was giving a party and didn't get any liquor because the store was closed. Martha and the two Birds — Dorothy and Bonnie, motored back to some place and picked up a lot of liquor, and then I had a party.

Schönberg: You remember there wasn't any liquor in Bennington. You had to go across the line to that place.

P. Limón: Hoosick.

N. Lloyd: Hoosick Falls. [The two towns are minutes from each other, just across the Vermont state border into New York State.]

P. Limón: Remember those nocturnal dances we used to have? Some of

Martha Hill holding wine carafe; Gregory Tucker far left; others unknown at the Bennington School of the Dance, about 1934 (photographer unknown, courtesy Bennington College).

us would go to one house after another — parties — and dance like mad.

N. Lloyd: Oh those first year parties.

P. Limón: We were terribly gay.

Schönberg: I remember dancing like mad.

N. Lloyd: At 12 o'clock the faculty would start running across the campus — jumping and screaming — to the horror of the students. We wouldn't think of it up here at Connecticut College.

Horst: Every night somebody on the faculty gave a party.

N. Lloyd: Well it was different atmosphere. We had just come out of prohibition.

P. Limón: And we knew we could sober up and go back and do great things any moment. But then we all got more responsible or something in the following years — not that we weren't responsible then.

N. Lloyd: Nobody on the faculty had any children.

P. Limón: Oh Doris [Humphrey] had a baby. Charles was born in 1933.

Because I can remember the first time I saw her, and everyone kept saying, "How's the baby?" But then you see this was a time before World
War II and then there were some years in between Connecticut and
Bennington. The Bennington School of the Dance lasted 6 years [not
including the School of the Arts years or the last summer of 1942]. I
remember, in the years after it ended, I used to go to Martha Hill and
say, "Well isn't there a plan for something?" "Well, not just now," she'd
say, but wait awhile and I think there will be something."

N. Lloyd: I remember Martha Hill talking about Connecticut. She went
down from Bennington to look it over, and she came back and said,
"They have a wonderful theatre, and you should see the number of
places they have to eat in town."

Horst: In 1939, we were at Mills. They wanted us out there, so that the
people from the West could come without paying so much for railway
fare. So they invited us to the campus at Mills. It was known as the
Bennington School of the Dance at Mills College, and we gave no major
performances there. The only performance there was of the Assistant
Teachers. José [Limón] danced.

P. Limón: He did his Mexican sketch [*Danzas Mexicanas*].

Horst: Katherine Manning and Ethel Butler danced. The three of them
gave a concert.

N. Lloyd: We went to Mills College in 1939, and then were back at Bennington for '40, '41, and '42.

Horst: The School of the Dance became part of what was called the School
of the Arts.

N. Lloyd: And after '42, they stopped having the summer session on
account of the having no fuel. They had to have a long winter vacation
to conserve fuel, which meant they had to run the spring semester into
the summer. There was no time for the School of the Dance.

Horst: In '43, '44, and '45, Martha [Graham] and I went up and taught
the last month of regular school. Martha was a guest artist, and I was
called Visiting Lecturer in the Music Department. That was my title to
get me in.

Martin Masters: What happened when you came to Connecticut College
in 1948? Was that a continuation of the same sort of program you had
at Bennington?

N. Lloyd: Connecticut College School of Dance started in 1948, and it was pretty much a continuation, but there are differences. At Bennington, we all lived on the campus. The faculty ate together and the students ate together — two dining rooms.

Schönberg: People seemed to like it that way. Maybe it was just me. I thought it was wonderful.

Horst: And we had a lot of sociability among the faculty. We had parties all the time. Every night somebody gave a party.

P. Limón: Remember the time we tried to get the piano through the door?

N. Lloyd: We got it through! Well, Marty, it was a different atmosphere. Life was different in 1934. Don't you remember? It was the Depression — not one person in my graduating class got a job — not one.

Schönberg: But there was a tremendous dedication to this ideal.

N. Lloyd: I remember at meals at Bennington, every meal was a kind of aesthetic discussion too. We were getting to know each other. We were exploring. And Martha [Graham] was quoting Mary Austin a lot.

Horst: Well we lived near Mary Austin in 1933. We rented an adobe house up on the hill in the back of Sante Fe and at six o'clock in the morning all the church bells would start ringing — you know like in Latin American countries, and we could look right over Mary Austin's.

N. Lloyd: In those years, you had nothing to gain, therefore you gave your whole self and all your time — and people were open to new things — anything. There was the whole Rooseveltian optimism among the artists and dancers particularly.

P. Limón: They used to give a demonstration of work done in the classes, in the gym.

Schönberg: They did wonderfully. You see, techniques at that time were important.

Horst: If you think of the first concerts in modern dance in '26, '27, and '28 — well in '34, there was still a vibrancy of going ahead. I think that there are not really any people to take Doris and Martha's place now. José is doing it, but he is really part of the original group.

N. Lloyd: But 25 or 30 years is a very long span of time for a revolutionary art movement. Usually by that time it's taken over by the main stream. And ballet, you see, is not the same as before modern dance. They've taken what they want from modern dance.

Louis, do you remember that we turned down Lennie Bernstein (which never appears in his biography)? He wanted to come up to Bennington. We were looking for someone to be a music director for Doris Humphrey, and Lennie was just finishing his junior year at Harvard, and he decided that the thing he wanted to do most in the world was to work with dancers so he came down and played an audition — he played a Ravel concerto on our old upright.

Schönberg: Well he really came to Martha Hill and asked her for a job, and Martha —

Horst: Martha turned him over to us to audit him. And he was terrific, but he was rough.

Schönberg: And over his head, Norman and I would look at each other and —

N. Lloyd: Well, obviously we knew that this kid was so talented that he should go on with music. Truth be told, I had an audition too before being invited to Bennington.

Horst: I put a thing before him to play and he played it.

R. Lloyd: And Louis said "All right" and Norman said "Is that all?"

N. Lloyd: Ruth and I were just married and I decided (I knew they needed another accompanist) to have Ruth there, so I sent Ruth the most difficult modern music I could find and said "Learn this."

R. Lloyd: He said that if I could do something, I could come along. I might not get paid, but I could live free.

N. Lloyd: So Ruth became the other accompanist.

Horst: But I know Martha Hill came over with you to my place and I had to examine you.

Schönberg: Listen, that first concert of Martha's [Graham] that first year — wasn't that interrupted by a thunderstorm?

N. Lloyd: In the tiny theatre in the Commons.

Schönberg: Martha didn't like thunderstorms. She did a solo concert that night, and there was such a bad storm that the lights went out.

Horst: And in 1938 we built that tent for the performances and then the windstorm came and knocked it down.

Schönberg: I remember Ted Glass, Hank Seymour, and Arch Lauterer hung on those ropes during the night like sailors in a storm. Costumes got soaking wet, and the floor was so wet it couldn't be used.

Horst: I'll never forget the first night of *El Penitente.* It was the hottest night in the world. It was the premier of *Letter to the World* but before *Letter* we did *Penitente.* Robert McBride was playing the clarinet. Otto Luening was playing the flute, and it was so hot in that corner that Otto was sweating so much he couldn't see the notes.

N. Lloyd: We did all this — everything was done "in spite of." And composers were interested because they knew they couldn't be played by a full orchestra anyhow. Nobody would play an American composer. [In music concerts, Americans were favoring European composers at that time.]

Horst: There was a marvelous atmosphere after the performances at the Armory in town when people just walked through the streets without using the sidewalks. You know, we always used to go to the Putnam Hotel afterwards and when Martha came in they all got up and cheered, and when Doris had her night, same thing.

R. Lloyd: Coming into this whole enterprise cold, my first contact with the dance was that they had a series of lectures by the choreographers, and this apparently may have been a new thing at that point. It meant meeting a public and having to articulate their feelings. The way this articulation took place, it made me think — well I mean there is a difference now — between then and now in the way that Doris [Humphrey] and Martha [Graham] have learned to talk about what they are doing. It's quite different from those early lectures. We used to have the lectures/discussions out in the quadrangle at the barn and the air was thick with great loyalties and you were tremendously loyal — you were a Graham girl or you were a Humphrey girl, and never the twain shall meet. And they tried to trick each other — I mean there was a lot of exciting exchange between audience and speaker. And this sort of thing is quite different — I mean, if you *were* a Graham technician, that's what you were. And you just didn't do the other things. Now, everybody does everything.

N. Lloyd: And ballet was certainly looked down on. There wasn't any good ballet in this country at that point. It was at its low point.

P. Limón: You see, all the leading dancers, having had it a Denishawn, were so eager to get on about their business and what they wanted to do that they couldn't be bothered with ballet. They themselves had it, and they knew where to put their feet. You know what I mean. They did it naturally, and they didn't want to bother. They had to develop a very substantial technique to make the dances that they wanted so that they could deliver the thing they wanted in the dances.

Lincoln Kirstein was the editor of the *Hound and Horn*. And he would try to persuade Charles and José and a lot of other people to go into ballet. He was very much interested in what they were doing, but something about it —

Schönberg: Well it wasn't balletic enough. And that's when he started Ballet Caravan, which came up to Bennington in 1936. This later grew into Ballet Society and then City Ballet.

> *José Limón enters.*

Horst: When was your first summer at Bennington José?

J. Limón: 1936 [Records indicate that he was also there in 1935 as an assistant to Charles Weidman]. And then the fellows program began in 1937. [Esther Junger, Anna Sokolow and Limón were the fellows.]

Horst: I know when John Martin [dance critic for the *New York Times*], and I met you to arrange the program, Esther Junger came first alphabetically, and she complained that she didn't want to open even though the idea was to go in order of last names. John Martin said, "Why don't you spell your name with a "Y"?

J. Limón: Oh how perfectly grand. How wonderful.

Horst: You did *Pavane for the Living* and *Pavane for the Dead* and *Sarabande for the Living* and *Sarabande for the Dead*, and in between were sandwiched pieces of music. [sections from *Danza de la Muerte*]

N. Lloyd: Which were supposed to be about a half minute long and each of them was at least 10 minutes long.

J. Limón: Anna's piece was really terrific. She did *Phantasmagoria*. [*Phantasmagoria* was a section of *Façade-Exposizione Italiana*]

P. Limón: I loved the way they walked up the wall.

N. Lloyd: Well Alex North was at Bennington then. Alex came up in '35 to do my orchestrating and instead he played tennis with Ruth.

R. Lloyd: That's the way it was.

Horst: And I used to get mad at Alex because I always wore a sport coat to dinner, and he came in a sport shirt.

N. Lloyd: Alex and I would run up to the store and get a bottle of orange pop and run like mad back to our place and then pour it and mix gin and orange pop. No ice.

J. Limón: You know, in those days I must confess, I wasn't drinking. I didn't know the first thing about drinking. And the gin tasted awful. I

Louis Horst and Hanya Holm with their pets at the Bennington School of the Dance, 1938 (© Barbara Morgan, Barbara Morgan Archive).

238

came upon this delicious pleasure very much later. And I said to myself, "You fool. What you are missing!"

Louis, I remember your strolls about campus.

N. Lloyd: With the dog.

J. Limón: With Max

N. Lloyd: The dachshunds all over the place.

J. Limón: Martha and Louis had —

Schönberg: Max and Stonewall Jackson.

Horst: And Max ran away one night and the whole campus was looking for him. And one time, I was walking across campus and someone said, "There goes Louis and the dog Maxie." And Doris [Humphrey] said, "No, that's Max and his man Louis."

N. Lloyd: Well Martha's dachshunds were trained so that at the end of class, Dini [de Remer] played a little trill and the dogs came out of the dressing room and ran across the floor.

J. Limón: I used to laugh at [the accompaniment for] the Graham classes. I used to listen, and Dini would play the bass keys on the piano by the hour. Apparently it worked.

N. Lloyd: When Dini comes up we should have her do a demonstration.

J. Limón: She only played with the one finger. I never heard the other one.

N. Lloyd: She always played with two.

J. Limón: I listened in the keyhole by the hour, and it was one.

But of course the most fantastic story of any — the most delicious one was when Doris gave the *Trilogy* with *With My Red Fires* and *New Dance* and everything else — and there were the little Graham girls — everyone was terribly partisan in those days — and Martha heard one of them say, "I don't understand how she does it. She never took a lesson from Louis."

N. Lloyd: I wish we had a tape recording of Louis trying to teach the oboe player to play in a meter of five up at Bennington.

Horst: Yes, because Hugo [Bergamasco, a flautist] used to get those musicians who couldn't play in five.

N. Lloyd: And you screamed at them. You called them every name in the book.

Horst: The early days.

13

Recollections and Anecdotes

In the 1970s, Bennington College received a grant from the National Endowment for the Humanities for a book on the Bennington School of the Dance, working in conjunction with Martha Hill. Over 70 interviews were conducted by Theresa Bowers of the Columbia University Oral History Research Office from 1978 to 1980, as part of the book project. Most of the selections that make up this chapter are excerpts from interviews that were part of the project. A few selections are from other interview projects, and some were written by the authors themselves. The reader is asked to take into account that many selections come from oral interviews and that speech, when written down, can seem less fluid. Very limited editing was possible on interviews excerpted in this chapter because there were restrictions placed on their use and most of the interviewees have passed away so there could be no confirmation after editing. A variety of topics are covered, and a variety of opinions presented. Sometimes the information is contradictory for reasons that include the unreliability of human memory as well as that the memories come from different years and from different points of view. My intention is that the stories presented provide a collage that fleshes out and adds detail to elements of the school not fully addressed in other parts of the book. Biographies of contributors can be found in the appendix.

On Arriving

DAVID ZELLMER

It is mid-day, July 1, 1940, as I step down from the bus while it hesitates at the curb of a downtown street, its engine still running. The driver assures me this is, indeed, Bennington, Vermont, my destination. He retrieves my heavy, leather suitcase from the luggage compartment. (It contains all my worldly possessions, except the Corona typewriter, which I hand-carry.)

The bus departs with an explosive snarl. I am left alone on the sidewalk of this unfamiliar town. A factory whistle stirs the summer heat with its noontime blast.

I am armed only with a letter assuring me I am expected and will be met here at the bus stop and driven to the college. And congratulating me for having won a dance scholarship. Still, I wonder and worry, waiting, clutching the stub of a one-way bus ticket that has stranded me here.[1]

ALWIN NIKOLAIS

One of the first things was very delightful. When I arrived, I went to Mary Jo's and Martha's [Mary Jo Shelly's and Martha Hill's] Office. Martha was having a martini at the time, and I remember she asked, "Nik, would you like a martini?" For persons of this stature to call me Nik, which was endearing, and then secondly to offer me a martini—. I was a student, but the feeling of welcome and maturity made me fall in love with Martha and Mary Jo and Bennington right away.[2]

The Atmosphere and Campus

Bennington's idyllic setting and physical plant influenced the overall feel of the summer program enormously. The rural locale, and the proximity of the buildings to each other played a major part in the experience for many of the participants.

HELEN PRIEST ROGERS

My first impression of being here [at the Bennington School of the Dance] was of buildings that stood way up in this hill with these huge views. Because at the beginning, the buildings were very large and trees were very small and there were hardly any bushes [because they had been newly planted]. You had this row of stark houses in a line and this big Commons that overlooked everything. It was a very beautiful setting. I enjoyed that part of it very much.[3]

Dancers outside the Commons at the Bennington School of the Dance, 1938 (photograph by Lionel Green, courtesy Bennington College).

One of the lighter moments of the early years at Bennington was the memory of gatherings that happened spontaneously on the marble under the balcony in Commons; the porch below was marble. There was a piano out there and the Lloyds [Norman and Ruth] used to sit and play duets, everything under the sun, wonderful, wonderful pieces — some popular pieces, and some improvisations. That was a wonderful thing after meals to gather there and hear them. It's a memory you don't forget.[4]

THEODORA WIESNER

The Commons building was the center. Most of the studios were there. A lot of the studios were there. The dining rooms were there. There was a faculty dining room and a student dining room, and then at the top of the building there was the theater. Everything — then the first floor when you came in was the post office and a little store where you could buy necessities. And there was a lounge. There would be lectures in the lounge at one end, and so on and so forth. And so that was the hub of everything. And then we'd live in these little houses, and they were fairly close together. It wasn't a long walk to go across from one house

On the porch outside the Commons at the Bennington School of the Dance, circa 1938. Charles Weidman is in center in light trousers, with William (Bill) Bales next to him (© Barbara Morgan, Barbara Morgan Archive).

to another. So we were fairly compactly housed. And each house had a bath, showers and tubs and washbasins on each floor, each wing. And after rehearsals, we'd gather there, to soak our feet and so on and so forth, quite a sight.[5]

Well, you would have friends that you saw more of than the majority but it was a very fluid kind of social situation because the dining rooms were in the Commons Building. After meals, everyone just came down and sat on the green there and everybody mixed together. Louis, Martha, Doris, and the dogs, and so on. I know that in Connecticut [at Connecticut School of the Dance/American Dance Festival] after the war, the people that had been at Bennington, that was what they missed the most, this gathering together on the green in front of the Commons Building.[6]

243

NORMAN LLOYD

About the 4th of July at Bennington

Well, after all, Bennington should have fireworks, but there was no money. This might not have been the first summer, but certainly the second and for a couple of summers. So Mary Jo Shelly would give me something like five dollars to go down to Bennington, on the Fourth of July, and hang around the place that sold fireworks and buy up whatever I could with five dollars, which didn't buy much. But I discovered that there were certain fireworks — also my father had been in the business briefly so I knew a little bit — if the instructions were torn off or you didn't know exactly what you were buying, like buying a can of something with no label, you could get it for very little. So I bought a lot of stuff like that, some of which worked and some of which didn't work. There'd be a Niagara Falls that went upside down and chased people all over the fields. The best thing I did was buy sparklers so that each person had a sparkler. That was our big Fourth of July celebration at Bennington.[7]

Dancers' Attire: Early Leotards

There were no stores where one could buy a leotard in those days. Dancers made their own generally, but the Bennington School of the Dance had uniform leotards made by a sporting goods company called Wright and Ditson. Apparently, there was a learning curve in developing a leotard that was wearable after washing.

RUTH LOVELL MURRAY

Then the other thing which was a particular difficulty for everybody were the leotards we had to wear.[8]

They stretched so that they were twice as big the first time you washed them.[9] Of course we had to wash these things, and then try to dry them so they would shrink a little, we hoped. So we would hang them over the trees and out the windows, and so on. One of these particular times the Board of Trustees appeared, and wondered what was going on in this place. I don't know really what we did with the leotards. We

Martha Hill (in dress) with students at the Bennington School of the Dance, circa 1934 (photographer unknown, courtesy Bennington College).

had to sew them up the sides to make them tighter, turning them inside out.[10]

HERMINE SAUTHOFF DAVIDSON

Remembering a different version of the leotards from another year that created the opposite problem.

We had these mud colored leotards which were heavy knit cotton. They had short sleeves, and you just pulled them on in one piece — no zippers. I think we were issued, I don't know, two or three of these a week, and we could buy extras if we wanted to, but the laundry went into Bennington and came back, and they shrunk, and they shrunk, and they shrunk. So we ended up having to make them two piece, because we just couldn't stand it. They were too tight in the crotch, and you couldn't stand up straight in them after a couple of weeks. So we ended up having to cut them apart and put elastic in both parts.[11]

245

Competition Between the Choreographers and Their Students

DOROTHY BIRD (VILLARD)

About the summer of 1935...

Bonnie [Bird] and I were together so much at Bennington that summer that John Martin affectionately christened us Boatie and Doatie.

Martha Graham (left) and Doris Humphrey at the Bennington School of the Dance at Mills College, 1939 (photographer unknown, courtesy Special Collections, F.W. Olin Library, Mills College).

246

Unlike Bonnie, I took Martha's stern commands to heart, remaining detached from the other dancers. Perhaps I secretly welcomed the excuse to steer clear of everyone outside of Martha's group. I never once spoke to Doris Humphrey, Hanya Holm, or Charles Weidman, or to the members of their respective companies, although I had seen them dance and knew all of them by sight. I always carefully lowered my eyes if Doris looked my way, but I did watch her from a distance. With her cloud of curly red-gold hair, cornflower blue eyes, and delicate feminine bearing, Doris presented the total contrast to Martha, whose dark straight hair would always remind me of a wild horse's mane, and whose eyes were veiled by lashes that grew straight down. Doris appeared to me to be a porcelain figure — exquisite, fragile, almost breakable, a Nordic ice maiden. Underneath Martha's puritan exterior, I knew that red-hot coals were always smoldering, ready to explode into flames.[12]

CHARLES WEIDMAN

About how the artists got along with each other in the summer of 1938, when the companies of Martha Graham, Hanya Holm, Doris Humphrey, and Charles Weidman were all at Bennington working and performing:

I got along fine except with Martha [Graham]. She pulled one on me ... Martha, she insisted that I share the program with her. And before, Doris and I would share programs, and you talked the thing over with balance. That made me very, very mad. Martha didn't want to be associated with another female or something like that for some reason. When you share a program, then you talk the things over so you know you're not going to step on the other's toes or something like that. I went to Martha [Graham] and told her, "You make me feel like I'm a stud horse" or something like that. But [she said] it was her manager. Her manager insisted... That was the only thing that was that sort of kind of tension... [However] one of Doris' favorite sayings was that an artist is like an oyster — it must be irritated in order to create a pearl.[13]

VIVIAN FINE

It was a funny thing, Doris never mentioned Martha's name to me in all the years that they were there. It was an avoidance thing. I didn't have the feeling of enmity. But they were both developing their own things which are really quite different, really quite different. There must have been some sense of rivalry. I think Graham was probably attracting more followers than Doris, but she was more radical in her movement, Martha. I felt that. I thought of her as a more radical dancer—Graham, than Humphrey. Just because the Humphrey dance was more curved, just in a very simple level. I though of it as more traditional. And it all seemed all perfectly natural to me — every bit of it.[14]

Doris was a very beautiful dancer, but whether she had that element of greatness that Graham had at that time I don't know; it would be hard for me to say. But Graham was so — she was so stark, so unrelenting and so powerful in what she did; while Doris was — her things were more in the realm of beautiful, and dramatic, and people recognized her work had value. But Graham had more the feeling of a cause, and people are attracted to a cause.[15]

MARTHA HILL

There was competition between the young followers — not the company members—but I mean the young students. They used to laugh about there being a Graham tree and a Humphrey-Weidman tree and a Holm tree where people congregated after dinner. But the leaders, the artists, were not clannish at all.[16]

Intersections Between Physical Education and Professional Dance

Students at the Bennington School of the Dance are often categorized as being physical education teachers or students looking towards professional careers. In actuality, these categories often overlapped, and some who had started in one category ended up in another. Yet I have used those categories in the selections that follow in order to help orient the reader to the speaker's perspective.

THEODORA WIESNER

From the point of view of a graduate of University of Wisconsin (in physical education) who would later direct Connecticut College School of the Dance and the Brooklyn College Dance Program.

And of course the people from Wisconsin were more interested in Hanya than they were in Martha Graham, because Marge H'Doubler

Gatherings after meals at the Bennington School of the Dance, 1938 (© Barbara Morgan, Barbara Morgan Archive).

[taught dance at the University of Wisconsin] had never liked Martha Graham, really, and she had always suggested that her students if they wanted to study, go and study with Mary Wigman in Germany, you see, and so a lot of them did. Now Louise Kloepper went to Germany because she wanted to study dance, and she didn't know where to go, and she had some relatives in Germany, so her mother decided that that would be the place to go, so that the relatives could look after her. So she went to Germany. And an awful lot of Wisconsin graduates went to study with Mary Wigman, and then when they came to New York after Hanya was here, this was the place that they went because this was the technique with which they were more familiar.[17]

HERMINE SAUTHOFF DAVIDSON

From the point of view of a graduate of the University of Wisconsin (in physical education) who then taught at New York University with Martha Hill

249

Well, the summer before I went to New York, the summer of 1935, I went to Bennington, and this was kind of my introduction to what would be available in New York, and much as my earlier enthusiasm had been directed toward Wisconsin [University of Wisconsin where Margaret H'Doubler was teaching dance], I realized that there would be some conflict, and this was at first hard to accept — the idea that there wasn't complete harmony between what Wisconsin was doing and what New York was doing, particularly in the person of Martha Hill and the growing Bennington School idea, which was to bring the concert dancer into contact with the collegiate programs. Martha Hill, I think, had an extremely good and sensitive perception of the need for the concert dancers to be able to get out of New York, have a circuit which they could pursue, and have some audiences who were ready to receive them. At the same time, the educational institutions — the collegiate group — needed to see in what direction American choreography was going, other than ballet, other than theater dance, which at that time was musical comedy.[18]

ELEANOR LAUER

From the point of view of a professional dancer who would go on to be a leading force in dance in higher education

They [the physical education teachers] were intelligent and sensitive and they could see the possibility, and they did not hesitate to come and try to learn, and I thought, that's okay by me. And for many of them it was putting themselves in a very vulnerable position because you were always there with youngsters who were gung ho and thought the older people were just for the birds anyway. And these women believed in it enough that they were willing to come and put themselves out in public, in class, without hesitation, in order to help their own students, and I think that had an effect.[19]

GERTRUDE SHURR

From the point of view of a professional dancer who had come up through physical education.

We had to explain over and over and over again the theory of contraction and release [to the physical education teachers]. At first it seemed

Dancing on the lawn at the Bennington School of the Dance, circa 1934 (photographer unknown, courtesy Bennington College).

to be such a mystery; it was such a mystic. So I really learned how to explain it in terms that this physical-education person could understand. I did it skeletally with the bones — what happened. I did it with the muscles — what happened to the muscles. I did it from — Martha's first impulse was the breathing — what happened to the body when the breath's out of the body? What happens when the breath's in the body? Then I gave them also the dramatic thing behind it. So I had all these explanations and, let me tell you, I had to dig deep down to find out how to make these people understand this. Now Martha couldn't do that. She gave you the first inspirational thing of contraction and release, and her need of that kind of movement. But when you had to teach fifty people and tried to tell them what are contraction and release, you had to be so academic. And Martha did not like to be academic. Even now, it's very difficult for her [Graham] to sort of re-explain what this is.[20]

DOROTHY BIRD (VILLARD)

From the professional dancer's point of view

They [the physical education teachers] couldn't believe they had to sit on the floor to begin with. Then they couldn't believe that you would be so fussy about where the back was and what precision —. They were used to indicating; they were used to indicating movement, so you'd make a straight line or bent line — you'd go that and that — but no absolutely filling of movement with contained energy and no beauty involved. Just a position, position, position. And this was movement. So it was staggeringly hard for some of them, and some of them were frightfully excited.[21]

We wore these leotards we made ourselves and skirts. We didn't buy leotards; I don't think you could buy them. And we wore wrap-around wool skirts, but it was cold. We'd go in and we'd warm up. I would tell them all to space out and warm up. So one girl finished warming up and she said, "I warmed my spot. Would you mind saving it for me please?" She thought you warmed the spot on the floor. Didn't even know you were supposed to be warming up your muscles; the floor was so cold — hilarious. They were people from all over the country and they were nice. They were very, very friendly and very excited.[22]

But every group was excited in the early days with her [Martha Graham]. She was a phenomenal teacher! She was out of this world! She could just energize anybody.[23]

HANYA HOLM

From the master teacher's point of view

It was really a thing where the people came from all over the country to inform themselves. Of course you know that you can't learn how to dance in 4 weeks or 2 weeks or 1 week. It is simply impossible. But these were people who had some kind of training.... There was something happening which was quite remarkable that these people out of physical education were really the first ones who took the glove up and started fighting for the modern dance, not the arts, but the physical education people. And they have really done the job of bringing the awareness throughout the country in action. They really started that whole ball rolling, and as good as they could, introduced the modern dance within their curriculum.

But that of course was limited because mainly they were physical education and had to have sports and what not....[24]

Remembering the Faculty: Martha Graham

ETHEL BUTLER

About working on Panorama *as a member of the workshop group of the Graham Company*

All I can remember is going to the Armory with masses of people and working, and Martha doing, sometimes, some involved things and rhythmic patterns. And the augmented company sitting up all night trying to memorize it, coming back the next day only to find that Martha scrapped the whole thing and decided she wasn't going to do that.[25]

THEODORA WIESNER

Well, she [Martha Graham] was very intense. She always was very intense. She was working hard to get it done. And if things didn't go right, she'd get very angry, and there's nothing more exciting than to see Martha Graham angry. She is just fabulous.[26]

SOPHIE MASLOW

About Martha Graham's teaching of technique

She [Martha Graham] worked on what she was interested in, at the time, and you might do class after class and not do any kind of jumps or anything across the floor. It was what she was interested in at that time in developing, and that's what you did.[27]

Remembering the Faculty: Martha Hill

DORIS HUMPHREY

I first knew Martha Hill in the early 1930s when the modern dancers were young, headstrong, running like wild things through the streets of

tradition. With what patience and tact she persuaded us all to find common cause under the friendly wing of Bennington College, and how well she managed with Mary Jo Shelly, to bridle those rebels without sacrificing their individuality. The difficulties must have been more burdensome than we were aware of, yet I never saw any signs of irritation or impatience on the faces of the directors of the School of the Dance. Somehow they found solutions to all the problems, untied temperamental knots (well, almost all of them), found time and space for ambitious dances where none seemed to exist, secured scores, costumes, sets, made a wonderful stage out of an armory — in short, established a home and a producing center for modern dance. I remember Martha [Hill] after stormy sessions lasting well into the night, coming across the Bennington campus of a beautiful summer morning looking serene and fresh, with all the answers on a piece of paper held in her capable hands. Not only this, but she carried on a strenuous program of her own classes, claiming no glory for her considerable contribution to the training of young students.[28]

BESSIE SCHÖNBERG

Quite early on the morning of the opening day [1934], I was awake and went to the window and looked out. It must have been at least 6 o'clock, when I saw Martha Hill passing the road under my window. For the first time it came to my realization that she was nervous, that she was frightened about this project [the Bennington School of the Dance]. Martha Hill seemed to me always someone who couldn't know fear or apprehension of any sort and to have this single fact that she was up and about at this unholy hour all set was a very clear indication.[29]

HERMINE SAUTHOFF DAVIDSON

But Martha Hill was a very marvelous person in that job. I wondered what it was like to try and keep all those egos satisfied. It must have been hell, and there must have been times when she was at her wits' end, but she never showed it. And then there was a production going on, and trying to keep the townsfolk mollified and — Oh![30]

Opposite: **Martha Graham and Erick Hawkins at the Bennington School of the Dance, circa 1940 (photographer unknown, courtesy Bennington College).**

Martha Hill (left) and Bessie Schönberg at Bennington College, 1934 (photographer unknown, courtesy Bennington College).

Remembering the Faculty: Hanya Holm

CLAUDIA MOORE (READ)

About Holm's technique classes

Hanya's work was solidly grounded in German gymnastics, coming from Mary Wigman. Now nobody over there would admit that, because I went over and studied with Mary later. Certainly nobody would say this thing came from German gymnastics, but even [Rudolf von] Laban, [Emile Jacques] Dalcroze — they all were infused with gymnastics back in history, and her work was solidly based, educational, logical. She knew anatomy; she's the only one who really knew anatomy, I'm sure — I mean scientifically.[31]

[Hanya Holm] call[ed] muscles by names. You see, I had anatomy, kines[eology], and physiology in college, so when I heard words I knew, muscles I had studied, this meant something to me. So I felt like that was the thing to use on the educational level, even though I might prefer something else.[32]

Hanya's work, her space was the thing I loved. She had the best space work for me.[33]

NANCY MCKNIGHT HAUSER

About how Holm inspired devotion

Well, Sybil [Shearer] was still in college at that time, I think, and she came that first year. I think it was the first year. Anyway, Hanya and I, they

Hanya Holm, circa 1939 (photographer unknown, courtesy Special Collections, F.W. Olin Library, Mills College).

257

gave Hanya and me an apartment. And Sybil fell madly in love with Hanya. She just worshipped her, took classes and everything. And I hadn't even noticed that much but I came out of my bedroom in the morning and here would be Sybil, stretched, lying down in front of Hanya's door. So that when Hanya opened the door, she'd fall over her. I said, "Sybil, what are you doing?" "I'm waiting for Hanya" [she said].[34]

EVE GENTRY (HENRIETTA GREENHOOD)

About dancing in Hanya Holm's Trend...

We counted so much, to this day sometimes I find myself counting when I am beating an egg — yes. And it was very difficult, the music was difficult but exciting to work with. All of it was very exciting work on *Trend*— hard, very hard work.[35]

But then we were completely devoted. We would have gone to rehearsal any day, night, hour, that Hanya needed us. We would rehearse as long as she wanted us. We never said, "Are we going to be paid or aren't

Hanya Holm with leg extended teaching at the Bennington School of the Dance, 1937 (photograph by Edith Vail, courtesy Suzanne Brewer).

we going to be paid?" Or "I have a headache" or "my toe hurts." We just worked. And gave. And of course, because of that, we got something that you don't get, unless you are completely devoted.[36]

Remembering the Faculty: Louis Horst

ALWIN NIKOLAIS

About studying with Louis Horst

One of the courses that had a tremendous impact on me was Louis Horst's. He was an extraordinary person. He didn't like men very much and, also, he abhorred dilettantism. In his class, you had to work very carefully and hard. He had the most caustic tongue of any teacher I ever encountered and one was scared to death of him. However, if you survived that tongue, you really had a very dear friend and a very devoted teacher.

Louis Horst teaching dance composition, circa 1948 (photographer unknown, photograph first appeared in **Dance Magazine**).

But he insulted all the weak ones right out of the class. A class that started with thirty ended up with about twelve within two days.[37]

I think from Louis I got a very strong devotion towards the art. I believe I lost my egocentricity and narcissism and put it at the service of the art. I think Louis did this for me. Perhaps even more than the others.[38]

MARIAN VAN TUYL CAMPBELL

Remembering Horst's sometimes cutting comments...

Then you had teachers from all over the country who had been yearning to teach dance and keep up with the times, to become more — teachers are just really avid to become better teachers, there's no question about it. But these women would come and they were neither technically prepared nor were they choreographically sophisticated. And they would subject themselves to the most brutal experiences, embarrassing, I mean, for instance, in Louis' class, one got up, and he said, "What's the name of your dance?" And she said, "The Happy One." At the end of the dance, Louis said, "I'm glad someone was happy." That was the kind of thing that went on.[39]

HELEN KNIGHT

Experiencing Horst

For instance, there were people who considered themselves professional dancers, that would get up and do the scarf-waving technique, and Louis would just slay them. They were just romanticizing and having a glorious time; it was nothing to do with what he was teaching at all. He would just crucify some of them. But they needed to be crucified because they were hanging on to the same old thing, and these were people that were dancing, as I say, semi-professionally and did concerts.[40]

Remembering the Faculty: Doris Humphrey and Charles Weidman

CLAUDIA MOORE (READ)

About Weidman and Humphrey's technique classes

He [Charles Weidman] also had a great deal more barre work only without the barre; we had the boxes, the big boxes, the collapsible boxes that they put up to make architectural structures for the dances. They would put them up, and we would hold onto them for a barre and do pliés and relevés. One of the hardest was to put your foot up on that box and lift it fifty times. We did legs at the barre because later I wrote them up.[41]

He [Weidman] never analyzed anything. He never — he couldn't explain anything. You just did eight this and eight that and do it this way, and he showed you or somebody showed you and that was the end of it. Doris, you see, was the analytical one.[42]

[*continuing*]

Doris came into class with the phrase of movement in her mind, usually one she was going to use in a dance — maybe. And she started with something very simple and stretchy and bending or something, warmed you up, added to it; stood up, added to it, moved it across to the next spot, then across the floor; then with people, and when you finished the class you were doing a phrase of movement.[43]

MARY SHAW SCHLIVEK

About Humphrey's technique class

The one I liked best of the technique teachers was Doris Humphrey. She always gave a challenge to the imagination. You never knew what she would do each class, but you knew it would make you think.[44]

ELEANOR LAUER

About Weidman's technique class

Charles was a riot. At that time he was working on a sequence of exercises that you kept adding to. You start out and then you'd add to it, you'd add to it, you'd add to it, and by the time the term was over you had a whole thing that would last about 50 minutes. You'd start at the beginning and just keep going.[45]

Each day you'd start at the beginning. At first it only took you about five minutes to get through, and then you'd add two minutes and then it would be seven minutes the next day.[46]

But anyway, he [Charles] would stand out there and just shout the whole time you know. And he had José [Limón] as his assistant. And José would demonstrate and shout at us. And Pauline Lawrence was at the piano and she was playing and shouting at us. You know, "Come on there,

Doris Humphrey at the Bennington School of the Dance, 1941 (photograph by Hans Knopf, collection of Charles H. Woodford).

get that leg going. Get in there. Get on the beat." And José is doing all this stuff and yelling, "Charles." It was just a rare scene. It was called Body Mechanics, but it was not basic movement at all. It was a sequence of things he liked to do, I think.[47]

262

Remembering the Faculty: Arch Lauterer

ALWIN NIKOLAIS

Other very interesting classes I think that left a strong impression on me were those that Martha Hill and Arch Lauterer conducted in Experimental Production.[48]

These classes really opened up my vision to other dance potentials. For instance, we did projects in theater-in-the-round. We did projects using the voice. In several of my later choreographies, I made extensive use of the voice. Some of these stimulations came from that class. I remember one [exercise] that Arch did that was very interesting, and I think made me think of lighting as a possible kinetic influence. The class had quite a few in it. He had set up a lighting circumstance in which a spotlight came from the front, at an angle, on stage. Then he had somebody just walk through it from upstage to downstage. I remember his asking, "What did you see? What did you see?" And

we looked and looked, and he had it done over and over and over again. Then he said, "You must look at it very carefully and give me a reaction to what you saw." None of us came up with the expected reaction. Then he pointed out what we had failed to see. We were so engrossed, I guess, in just watching the figure, that we didn't see the figure in relation to the light. What happened was that the trajectory of the light was such that the dancer walked into the light slowly and went out quickly. But it was an illusion. The dancer did not actually change his physical speed. It

Charles Weidman, circa 1939 (photographer unknown, courtesy Special Collections, F.W. Olin Library, Mills College).

263

was a perceptive demonstration of the speed that light values could give to the dancer. This device I've used a thousand times since then.[49]

Thoughts on the Relationship of Music and Dance

NORMAN LLOYD

Dance at that time was coming through the period of declaring its independence from music. Martha [Graham] felt that she needed music, but the music should be secondary. She'd gone through the period of composing to [Alexander] Scriabin, to Edgard [Varèse], to whatever. It was very much in the discussion: how independent can dance be? The only way you can assert your independence is to make dance number one and make everything else subservient to that, even to the point where costuming was played down; no sets. You see, everything contributory to dance. I don't know whether it was Joe Campbell or somebody else who said, "Obviously the ultimate would be to dance with no music and no costume." No light, probably, or just a bare — enough light to be seen. And this would have been the ultimate. But instead, you place the emphasis on dance by doing the dance first. You don't necessarily get good musical results, and I'm not sure whether you get good dance results. Occasionally the things would click.[50]

OTTO LUENING

[Louis] Horst was a very strong supporter of the dance anyhow. He pulled things into a shape that almost no other musician did. Because he had the idea of what he called an "accompaniment composer" in which the music must not be too strongly identified so that it detracts from the main object of dance which is the movement or at least the total effect.[51]

Experiencing the Bennington School of the Dance from a Child's Perspective

CHARLES HUMPHREY WOODFORD

"I am an artist first, and afterwards a woman," my mother Doris Humphrey wrote. Mother and wife were in second and third place, not

264

that she thought of herself as negligent in these areas. As long as I was cared for — although often by other people — and wife and husband could write to each other, their correspondence now stored in the New York Public Library, she was fulfilling her responsibilities as she saw them.

Norman Lloyd says in Chapter 12 that were no children at Bennington, and I suppose that was true in the early years. In 1934 and 1935, I was left behind in the charge of a German governess, who should not be confused with the contemporary "nanny." A governess in those days was in strict control of every element of a child's upbringing. Her Nazi sympathies were discovered after a photo of Hitler appeared in my bedroom. As I grew older we became good friends and I continued to keep in touch until her death.

In 1936, my grandmother, affectionately known as "Mamasan" from her travels in Japan as a guest of my mother on the Far Eastern Denishawn tour, was invited to Bennington to be my babysitter. I enjoyed the chance to play on the open lawns and developed a love for the countryside that continues to this day. The most memorable event was my birthday party to which Humphrey-Weidman company members wore silly paper hats.

In 1937 and 1938, some Humphrey-Weidman dancers were enrolled as babysitters both at Bennington and in New York, particularly Nona Schurman. But Pauline Lawrence had, by that time, become a second parent. I would sometimes be brought to the costume room at Bennington where she would be having fittings. Betty Joiner was assisting her and also became a babysitter, writing down and illustrating a story I dictated about a farm that was blown to the top of the Empire State Building. Later, her mother, Inez who I called Iney, came to live with us and babysit in New York while the Humphrey-Weidman Company was on tour. Iney, who was studying children's literature at NYU, compiled a book of poetry for me and taught me how to recite them with the right inflection and enunciation. This won me a scholarship to the King-Coit School where the dance teacher, Michael Mordkin, pronounced me hopeless in ballet.

At Bennington, I was brought to the dining room to say goodnight to my mother, a ritual that was repeated in New York when I would go to her bedroom for a few minutes before going to bed. It was an era when parents with other concerns were content to have children less seen and less heard, except when called upon or when convenient.

I was a child who loved the outdoors, but was often put into overly long naps. One annoying one was when my mother was repeatedly listening to the same phrases from *Passacaglia* over and over again while I was confined to bed. I was taken to the Bennington Armory once, probably for a rehearsal. But the performance I remember the most was of *With My Red Fires* at the Hippodrome in New York. The circus had just been there and there was still an animal smell. Straw was on the floor from the elephants. When I saw the scary figure of the Matriarch, I had to be told that it was my mother.

The sounds of cocktail parties at Bennington could be heard while I was

Charles Humphrey Woodford at Charles Weidman's farm in Blairstown, New Jersey, 1939 (photographer unknown, collection of Charles H. Woodford).

going to sleep. One morning, after one of these I went to where the party had been and ate the martini olives and Manhattan cherries left in the glasses.

I traveled with Pauline to Mills College in 1939, sharing a berth with her on the cross-country train and also staying in her apartment there. Mills was different because there were other children, including those of the Budapest String Quartet, and there was a summer camp where I learned to swim. The campus had many flowerbeds, so a friend and I decided to pick some and sell them for pennies to students in the dorms, once right under the nose of Martha Hill, who looked on disapprovingly. I remember watching rehearsals at the outdoor Greek Theater, but again it was for the lack of a babysitter that I had to be there and quite boring for one so young.

Many of the adults I met at Bennington became friends. More than that, Pauline and José Limón became surrogate parents. Others were Eleanor Frampton, known as "Frampy," Charles Weidman's first teacher in Lincoln, Nebraska; Martha Hill; Theodora ("Teddy") Wiesner; Pauline Chellis; Lionel Nowak; Eleanor King; and Katherine Manning. They were part of my extended dance family, who I fondly remember for their kindnesses to me, a boy whose parents could not always be parenting.[52]

Performance and Post-performance Stories

BESSIE SCHÖNBERG

About Martha Graham preparing for performance

I was asked to go backstage and remind Martha [Graham] of curtain time on the night of an opening of a new program that she was doing in the Bennington College Theatre. I recall that I was wondering what state I would find her in because her nervousness and her hating to start a new performance was proverbial, even then. But I don't think I would ever have expected to find what I did. I opened the door and found her standing in the middle of the dressing room, facing a mirror, with her mouth full of pins, and a barely-begun costume slightly draped over her into which she would insert a pin here and there. Fitting it while she looked at herself in the mirror. Well, I must have stood there rather aghast telling her there was only ten minutes or something. But she managed a little smile and wryly took the pins out of her mouth and explained that this is what kept her from being too nervous; that she liked to do something like that shortly before performance time. It made perfect good sense the way she said it. I was convinced she was right. This was another one of those strange little pieces of the mosaic that comes a way of knowing a person, and the circumstances.[53]

HELEN PRIEST (ROGERS)

One of my memories is that after the performance — after all performances that were done in the Armory — we tended to gather as groups

267

for discussion and reminiscences and everything of the performance, at the Hotel Putnam pharmacy which was next door or close to the Armory. I was in the pharmacy with a group of dancers, and Martha [Graham] was there quite in the back. In the door of the pharmacy and down the whole length of it, in quite a sweep, came Miss Ruth St. Denis. She went right to the very end where Martha Graham was — Martha was standing up — and she embraced her. We were all so awed by this meeting of these two great ladies because we had understood at the time that they hadn't spoken to each other for some time. But Miss Ruth had seen that performance and came and, in a sense, bowed to Martha at that point as if to say "this is wonderful." It was thrilling to be present at the time that that happened.[54]

(*Ruth St. Denis had been Martha Graham's teacher and mentor at Denishawn from 1916 up until 1923 when Graham broke away to develop her own artistic visions.*)

LIONEL NOWAK

About Doris Humphrey and Charles Weidman performing in the College Theatre while Nowak was accompanying them offstage

It [The College Theatre] was kind of square, in a way, but when you made that square operative, there was practically no off-stage space. These little flats at the side, you'd have to squeeze your way by them. I remember one time Doris had to make a quick entrance and Charles had to make a quick exit, and they got caught right at the same flat there, and that flat was shaking and they were each trying to push the other out of the way. In the meantime, time was passing on stage, and I was going crazy out there — what was going to happen?[55]

Lasting Impressions and Overall Legacy

CHARLES WEIDMAN

In this vicious world of competition and all and trying to get along, and production and everything, it was very pleasant. Probably like New London [Connecticut College School of the Dance] too. Given a place, with a company, all fed, with all the lovely extra time you needed to work

Charles Weidman at the Bennington School of the Dance at Mills College, 1939 (photographer unknown, courtesy Bennington College).

on one production. No rent to pay, no nothing... And of course the place was very, very pleasant, the countryside and all that.[56]

MARTHA GRAHAM

In 1934, I began to teach summers at Bennington College in Vermont, a wonderful place where we were given the freedom and possibility to make our dances. There were visiting artists there throughout the season, including Doris Humphrey, Charles Weidman, and Louis Horst... I would blissfully drive around the campus and town in a little model-T Ford with no license, and no fear. But Martha Hill, who founded the dance program at Bennington, lived in terror of my trips. When I took other teachers for a drive, she would say, "Pray! With Martha's driving, that could be the end of the history of modern dance."[57]

BEN BELITT

(Acclaimed poet who was a faculty member at Bennington College)
Martha Hill was always concerned with ways in which she could extend her faculty, open up the resources of the Summer Dance School and include all kinds of ancillary arts there. I think between them both [Hill and Arch Lauterer] they had secretly cooked up a scheme, at the end of spring, to invite me, free of charge, roundtrip, board and room, to Mills

Ben Belitt at the Bennington School of the Dance, 1938 (photographer unknown, courtesy Bennington College).

College — which was Bennington's first move from Vermont — "just to live with and look at dance." They wanted to minister to my literacy in dance and give me the opportunity of seeing this strange medium in all its various mutations. And that is exactly what happened — I was drenched in the dance. At Mills I had the unique opportunity, day after day, of seeing all these great artists in the process of teaching their classes. I very soon became a "literate" eavesdropper on Hanya Holm's exercises and discourses on circles and squares and assorted geometrical formations. Of course, there were the other artists, too. (Martha Graham least of all, at the time, because as I have pointed out, Arch was very Bauhuas, "echt Deutsch." He had alerted me specifically to Hanya Holm. He had said: *this* was the summit of modern dance. Graham was volatile and marvelous; but Arch had had little to do with her. In the first performance it was Hanya Holm that moved the earth and shook out its secrets.[58]

EUGENE LORING

(Ballet choreographer who performed at the Bennington School of the Dance as a member of Ballet Caravan.)

Oh, I am quite sure it [the Bennington School of the Dance] has influenced my life tremendously. I can't put my finger on specific things, but I know watching all those different moderns I'm sure has influenced my work, indirectly. I mean I couldn't say, well, I got that from Martha — I wouldn't do that — or I got that from Doris; I don't work that way.

I know for one thing the way their classes were run certainly has affected me. Because a traditional ballet class starts with pliés, right? Well, I always thought that was wrong. When I'd watch a modern class, I would see that they'd start by such simple things like breathing. When I started to teach, I devised a whole thing which I call pre-barre, and we do that here [University of California at Irvine], and I did it in my own school in Hollywood. That's a direct influence from the modern, that one would start in an easier manner; that's directly from the modern dance.[59]

JEAN ERDMAN

When I was a student, it was my first plunge into a professional atmosphere, because even though we had this wonderful instruction at Sarah Lawrence, still the atmosphere was still student, not professional student

271

either, though we were trying to get close to it. It was there that I knew, that I found out what a commitment to a dance career would mean, and I also found out there, because of the curriculum that was set up and the areas in which the work was being taught and done, that it was a very full and rich existence, even though it's highly specialized, you know. And the passion of opinions about works and so on was just — was inevitable — right? — when you are committed. I don't know how useful those were, but they were there, and they certainly shaped one's immediate future path.[60]

SOPHIE MASLOW

I thought it was great. It was a very stimulating experience. Aside from the dance part of it and all the benefits of being able to do a great deal of work in one summer, there were all the other stimulating things. Now I don't know if everybody took advantage of that and if they felt the same way. But meeting the people in other companies and having continual discussions about dance. And afterwards — I know that when Bill [Bales] and Jane [Dudley] and I worked there — we had a lot of things in our contact with the people who weren't dancers that was very stimulating. Ben Belitt would read us poetry. The first time I ever heard *Finnegan's Wake* or knew anything about it was when he read us sections of it. It was also his explanation of the different puns in various languages, and so on, that made it extremely enjoyable. And then other poets that I hadn't heard of that he read us and talked about. Alexander Schneider and Ralph Kirkpatrick were up there working on a program one summer — they were practicing — and occasionally they let us come in and listen to their rehearsals and that was a terrific experience. So that the general stimulating atmosphere was very exciting.[61]

ELEANOR LAUER

I always said when I went to Bennington for six weeks that you didn't really know until about December what you'd learned. I mean it was so intense and there was so much that you didn't try to sort it out at the time. It was sort of as though you put it all in a box or something, and then later took it out bit by bit and examined it to see what it was, and sometimes the things that you thought you really weren't getting much out of or weren't doing very much about turned out to have a lot more in them than you had thought at the time, and you suddenly realized that something you had learned back there really had made a difference, and at the time you were so busy just trying to get with it and get it done.[62]

GERTRUDE SHURR

I feel that it [teaching at the Bennington School of the Dance] forced the four powers [Martha Graham, Hanya Holm, Doris Humphrey, and Charles Weidman] to almost codify their technique because they had to teach it. In teaching you had to re-explain and re-explain and everything else, and I think it forced a very good structure in their technique. The thing that I think was the most important thing of that first summer was the fact that after the six weeks, we had to do an open-class demonstration. It was the first time we had ever seen any work from Hanya Holm; we had never seen her work. Also, it was the first time that we saw Doris' and Charles' work, and it was the first time they saw Martha's work.[63]

We had a fabulous demonstration, and I want this really as a historical thing: It was the first time anyone ever saw Martha's technique starting on the floor with the stretches, going into that open fourth position and moving on a stationary base, moving around, standing up and doing knee bends, brushes, prancing — all the things that we take for granted. Martha showed it for the first time there. And the running in place, the falls, the falls from the sitting position. All these movements that people take for granted now started, or were shown, at that time.[64]

MARTHA HILL

Well, and we learned much more from working intimately with these people in a six-week session there what would be best for them, therefore would be best for the art. And what was best for them was to get away from all the demands of the city, to have a group that was well-fed, well-housed, available twenty-four hours a day to create work for the next season. This was the most valuable thing. Then, added to that, if you could give the artists a composer to compose a new work. You could have a costume designer design costumes and have them actually constructed there on the campus. If you could give an out-of-town showing to the work. You see, this was what was invaluable.[65]

It was much more that we were a community of artists working

273

together and trying to do the best thing for the arts and, incidentally, for themselves; and maybe first of all for themselves but then secondarily for the art—whichever way. But it would be much more dreaming dreams among ourselves and then organizing them.[66]

I think that Bennington was no different from their round of activity [for the choreographers and dance company members], except that the moil and toil of the city was taken away. Everybody was assured of three meals a day and a roof over his head, and beautiful country air and landscape, so that the concentration of getting a work done—I think if you asked any of them, they would have said they worked much faster because everything was concentrated. Nobody had to take buses and subway trains; you were all there. Everybody ate in the Commons, and if you wanted to get word about changing a rehearsal—you weren't going to do the quintet tonight; you were going to work on—. There was a great energy saving. So that it was just like more of the same in one sense, but somebody else was paying for it, and it wasn't as much work.[67]

Martha Hill (in dark dress) with students, circa 1934 (photographer unknown, courtesy Bennington College).

Alwin Nikolais at the Bennington School of the Dance, 1937 (photographer unknown, courtesy the Alwin Nikolais and Murray Louis Dance Collection, Mahn Center for Archives and Special Collections, Ohio University Libraries).

There we had students from the first who were interested in a broader way in the whole of the dance. We had young students who were just out of high school, or college students; but we had a large group of older students who had taught and who were interested in extending the boundaries of what they knew.[68]

As an overarching thought on the school

It was the right time and the right place, and people felt the need for it.[69]

ALWIN NIKOLAIS

So Truda [Kaschmann] and I went to Bennington [in 1937]. It was probably one of the most extraordinary experiences of my life. I was imbedded in the idea of dance but I had no knowledge of the dynamics of it as an American art, as an indigenous art, as probably one of the most vital arts that America ever knew. So I was swept into this extraordinary American art venture.[70]

It was the historical time and the socio-dynamics of that time that made modern dance possible. Bringing together all these American dance forces was like an atomic energy plant; the dance passion for this new American modern dance was so high that if you'd studied belly dancing there you would have come out an artist. It was almost inevitable because the devotion was so strong. Here were extraordinary people and great teachers who steered you into a very powerful focus immediately, and one was projected into deep and passionate penetrating experiences.[71]

Epilogue

Postscript to the Bennington School of the Dance

Although the Bennington School of the Dance ended in 1942, reverberations followed through the World War II years at Bennington College, and later at Connecticut College and Duke University. Martha Graham, along with members of her dance company and Louis Horst were in residence for the regular school sessions in June and July from 1943 to 1945. Graham was a guest artist, and Horst was a visiting lecturer. On July 11, 1946, the newly established José Limón Dance Company premiered two works at Bennington College: *The Story of Mankind* and *Lament for Ignacio Sánchez Mejías*, both choreographed by Doris Humphrey.

After World War II ended, Martha Hill, with the support of New York University, began developing the idea for a new summer program, preferably outside the city. She visited several locations and eventually settled on Connecticut College, which would sponsor the new summer project along with New York University. The original name was New York University — Connecticut College School of the Dance. A special trial session with a small group of students was run in 1947, and in 1948 the school officially opened. Hill was the founding director, and Ruth Bloomer (who had attended the Bennington School of the Dance and was teaching dance at Connecticut College already) joined her as co-director in 1949.

New York University was the originating force behind the new summer program, and there was keen interest in it at the beginning. Jay B. Nash, head of the Physical Education Department at New York University, expressed his enthusiasm: "To be able to carry on the Bennington idea with the cooperation of Connecticut College with its rich background is a distinct privilege for those of us connected with New York University."[1] There was also support from the Chancellor at New York University who wrote in an NYU bulletin of 1949: "...we have conducted for the second year, in cooperation with Connecticut College, a six-week 'School of the Dance,' thus affording terpsichorean aspirants an opportunity to caper in a genial clime."[2] NYU's support did not continue however, and Connecticut College took over completely for the summer of 1951. Theodora Wiesner explained that the festival performance events of the first summer accrued substantial debt that Hill took on personally as Connecticut College and New York University only agreed to be financially responsible for the school. The following fall, Hill and some her colleagues and friends organized two benefit performances at the 92nd Street Y and made back what Hill had expended. The summer school and festival continued to run at a deficit in the early years, and Wiesner remembers the deficit issue as being why New York University withdrew their support after the summer of 1950.[3]

The public performance festival of New York University — Connecticut College School of the Dance was called the American Dance Festival with the first resident companies being: the Martha Graham Dance Company, the José Limón Dance Company, and the trio of Jane Dudley, Sophie Maslow, and Bill Bales. All of the choreographers had been participants as faculty or company members at the Bennington School of the Dance. Some of the seminal works that premiered during the early years of the festival were: Graham's *Diversion of Angels* (1948), Humphrey's *Invention* (1949), Limón's *The Moor's Pavane* (1949), Limón's *The Exiles* (1950), and Sophie Maslow's *The Village I Knew* (1950).

Hill directed or co-directed the new school and festival from 1948 to 1958, followed by Ruth Bloomer from 1949 to 1958, Jeanette Schlottman from 1959 to 1963 and Theodora Wiesner from 1963 to 1968. Charles Reinhart became director in 1968, and under his direction, the summer workshop and festival moved to Duke University in 1978. Stephanie Reinhart was co-director from 1993 to 2002, and Jodee Nimerichter was associate director from 2003 to 2007 and then co-director from 2007 to 2011. When Reinhart stepped down from being director in 2011 and became director emeritus, Nimerichter succeeded him as director. The summer program continues to thrive today as one of the most respected dance festivals with a vibrant school and performance series. Although run by different entities than the Bennington School of the Dance, Connecticut College School of the Dance and American Dance Festival are certainly follow-ups to the Bennington years, with much of the spirit and vision of Bennington intact.

Legacy

Bennington School of the Dance had extraordinary influence that was pervasive and long lasting in part because it facilitated the interweaving of fields such as music and dance and the professional dance field and education. The school had a lasting impact on those who were there as choreographers, teachers, students, staff, and audience members. It helped solidify modern dance as a distinct art form, through encouraging and nurturing choreographers and bringing them together to present modern dance as one genre instead of individuals working independently. The school also promoted the dissemination of modern dance, extending its reach and span as it moved into universities and theatres throughout the United States and beyond. Each of these areas of influence overlap and coincide so that writing about one area necessitates writing about the other. This speaks to the substantial effects the school achieved over a span of just nine years.

Shelly says early in this book "no two went back where they came from with an identical sense of accomplishment but, for certain, none went back unaffected by so intense and kaleidoscopic an experience." As with any successful summer camp, people developed close friends and came away with new knowledge including heightened self-understanding. But because Bennington was about a new American art form — modern dance — it went much, much farther in its impact on individuals. The excitement of being in at the beginning of a new movement, of meeting and associating with these great choreographers, is very clear, instilling a passion that helped drive the modern dance movement. Modern dance was a "cause." It inspired a zealous commitment. Those who came to Bennington mostly left feeling deeply a part of this movement, and believing that the changes in the field of dance were revolutionizing the art form — that *they* were revolutionizing the art form. It was a catalyst for the expansion of modern dance across the United States with an electric and contagious energy.

Faculty and students made connections they would benefit from for

279

years to come in their professional careers and personal lives. Faculty and students made connections they would benefit from for years to come in their professional careers and personal lives. For teachers who were studying at the school, making connections with professional dancers and choreographers allowed them to learn about professionalism generally and specifically about modern dance as being taught and developed in New York. They could then share this with their students, and/or bring an artist out to teach their students. For the artists, it was a financial boon and an opportunity to promote themselves and modern dance, and to form important artistic alliances and friendships. Helen Alkire noted that she became friends with the choreographer Anna Sokolow whom she would bring out as guest artist to Ohio State University in following years. Jeanne Beaman and Anna Halprin both speak about the close friendship they developed with each other as students, a friendship which has lasted to this day. Sophie Maslow recalls getting to know dancers in other companies, which did not happen so much in New York where they lived and worked separately. This led to the formation of the Dudley-Maslow-Bales trio whose directors came out of both the Graham and the Humphrey-Weidman Companies. In addition, the professional choreographers met and worked with students whom they would employ as dancers in their companies. Perhaps the best known of these is Merce Cunningham who joined the Graham Company after being at the Bennington School of the Dance, but there are others such as Sybil Shearer and Joseph Gifford who joined the Humphrey-Weidman Company after and as a result of their summers at Bennington.

The largest population of students at the Bennington School of the Dance was teachers (primarily of physical education) up until 1940. One reason for this was that the Bennington School of the Dance was one of the few places to go to study modern dance in the form that was being developed in the New York professional dance scene, and secondly, that teachers were fervent about learning it. One could go to this idyllic Vermont setting and study three styles of modern dance in one summer. The physical education teachers also had salaries and therefore the ability to pay for this training when many could not (during the Great Depression), and they needed to do professional development in their field as well. Modern dance seemed to fit seamlessly into physical education curricula for women particularly. Because women were attending colleges more and more in the 1930s, courses especially designed for them were needed. (In this time period, women and men mostly took physical education courses separately.)

The physical education teachers at the Bennington School of the Dance often had little or very poor dance training because professional quality dance training was not widely available across the country. When one looks at the photos of all of the students with their faces intent on what they are doing, their persistence and courage is quite moving. It can be so difficult to learn something new, especially when one has advanced training and degrees in a different, but related field, and is used to being afforded great respect. What daring they had to put on the ill-fitting leotards and dance around the fields to be photographed and filmed, as they were learning. And what bravery to continually subject themselves to Louis Horst's wickedly honest, barbed comments. That they came year after year — there were always many repeaters — indicates that they were receiving what they considered to be important professional development. When they returned home, many encouraged their friends and students to go to Bennington in following years.

There were concerns among the faculty and professional company members, however, about the "smorgasbord" of modern dance that the physical education teachers were learning at the Bennington School of the Dance. These modern dance techniques took years of study to perform properly. What the teachers were teaching when, after six weeks of a variety of classes, they would go back across the United States and begin to transmit this new knowledge to their students, was probably quite limited. But the overall sentiment was that learning something about modern dance was better than learning nothing about it. Many teachers came back year after year to learn more, and some took semesters off to study in New York. As they taught their students, modern dance came to be "known" across the United States and abroad.

Many students recalled that the work in choreography classes with Louis Horst was particularly meaningful, even if very difficult. As Norman Lloyd made note of, it was a new idea that dance composition could be taught. And this was important because when the teachers went back home to their schools and universities, they would often be in charge of choreographing productions. Not only did Horst's class give them information on new ways to do that from a personal standpoint, it also gave them information they needed to teach dance composition as a course. Form

Martha Hill at left, directing her students at the Bennington School of the Dance, 1937 (photograph by Edith Vail, courtesy Suzanne Brewer).

and structure were important elements of Horst's classes, and these ideas were added to the already existing, more free form idea of self-expression in creating dances.

As several of the interviewees quoted in the "Recollections and Anecdotes" section of this book note, there were two schools of thought on the nature and focus for dance education at the university level, one led primarily by Margaret H'Doubler and one led primarily by Martha Hill. H'Doubler's teaching methods focused on self-expression and body mechanics while Hill's focused on foundations of technique and modern dance vocabulary with a continual push to tie the professional field of modern dance to the university. Interestingly, H'Doubler gave a demonstration lesson at the Bennington School of the Dance in 1934, but she did not return to teach in subsequent years.

The curriculum at the Bennington School of the Dance quickly evolved into separate tracks so that there was a program for the student looking toward a professional career and a second program for those at a less advanced level, many of them teachers in physical education. The courses were primarily the same, however the levels were different. For both, the class work had a performance focus, in that the courses centered on technique and composition with showcases of student choreography and demonstrations of technique. The curriculum was, particularly toward the later years, very typical of what one may find in a university dance program today: ballet, modern, tap, choreography, music for dancers, repertory workshops, dance history, even Labanotation in some years. In 1951, Hill became the founding director of the Juilliard Dance Department (later Division) where she would use largely the same curriculum with quite a few of the same faculty from the Bennington School of the Dance. She would also put into place informal monthly workshop performances that would showcase student work, much like at Bennington. Many of the attendees at Bennington went on to direct dance programs or departments across the United States and were undoubtedly influenced by the curriculum at the Bennington School of the Dance in creating their own. Although the Bennington School of the Dance was certainly not the only catalyst for the expansion of dance as a field of study at the university level, it very much supported this development.

Hill states that at the Bennington School of the Dance "we were a community of artists working together and trying to do the best thing for the arts and, incidentally, for themselves; and maybe first of all for themselves but then secondarily for the art — whichever way."[4] That Hill speaks of the "artist" and "the arts" almost as one thought indicates her focus on the professional field. However, she was certainly aware of the benefits for all aspects of dance as she was working to build educational and professional ties. Hill was known for stating that dance in education and dance in performance are not separate fields, but one in the same — deeply connected.

The implications and outreaching benefits of having professional choreographers at Bennington College was enormous. To start, the summer dance school put Bennington College "on the map" as Bessie Schönberg recalled.[5] Martha Hill remembered that President Leigh of Bennington College loved to tell the story that when he was traveling in Europe and introduced himself, people would say, "That's that American college where they do so much with dance."[6] Bennington College had its own dance curriculum during the academic year from the founding of the college, and it continues to this day. The dance program benefited by the publicity surrounding the Bennington School of the Dance, and Bennington College is very aware of the college's importance in the lexicons of dance history.

Hill indicated that she created the Bennington School of the Dance for Martha Graham. That may have been part of her original intent, but only because Graham was the choreographer she knew best, having danced with Graham's company. Hill described her relationship with Humphrey and Weidman as follows: "I knew them professionally, but I didn't know them intimately, as I grew to know them. But they didn't know me so they didn't know how much they could trust me either. Because, why, if I were in Martha's company, why wouldn't I, if a question would come up, toss the coin so that it would benefit Martha more than it would benefit them? You see, that would be natural in their mind."[7]

As Hill grew to know the other choreographers, largely through the Bennington School of the Dance, she became very close to each of them professionally and as friends. Hanya Holm became the director of the summer dance program at Colorado College on the recommendation of Hill to the president of Colorado College, Thurston Davies, who would become Hill's husband in 1952. Later, Holm taught at Juilliard in the years just before Hill's retirement in 1985 from running the Juilliard Dance Division. Doris Humphrey was on faculty from the beginning of the Juilliard Dance Division in 1951 until her death in 1958.

The professional choreographers benefited from the Bennington School of the Dance in many ways. First, they had employment for the summer, with food and housing provided for themselves and often their company members. Hill explains how this made life so much easier because if one wanted to call an extra rehearsal or cancel or extend a rehearsal, everyone was on site in close proximity. There was no added hassle of trying to get word to their dancers and then of the dancers dealing with transportation and juggling other commitments. As well, the Bennington School of the Dance produced choreography with costumes, set, and music provided. The choreographers could then head into a New York season with new choreography that had been "tried out" in Vermont. In addition, the physical education teachers (who came from all 48 states that existed at that time) got to know the choreographers and would bring them out to their schools to provide longer and sustained touring and teaching possibilities. This would benefit modern dance for decades, and continues to this day.

As revealed by Gertrude Shurr in the "Recollections and Anecdotes" section of this book, the Bennington School of the Dance was, in addition, an impetus behind the choreographers codifying their techniques. Because they gave demonstrations in front of the other choreographers/master teachers, they worked to develop sequences for these demonstration that exemplified their ideas, and these sequences would then be adopted into their classes if they had not already been. They were often teaching beginning classes to experienced teachers of physical education, which also pushed them to clarify, explain, and codify.

The ties that developed between dance in education and professional dance (particularly modern) were fundamental in establishing what we know today in both areas of the dance field. To have professional dancers and choreographers teaching and choreographing on college students is seen as the standard today. That modern dance is the primary focus of most college level dance programs (even ones that offer ballet) also relates back to the beginnings of dance moving into the university, which was primarily through the physical education departments where modern dance was being introduced. And many of those professors who were introducing dance studied at the Bennington School of the Dance. As Hill states in Chapter 1, Bennington nurtured the roots of modern dance.

The School also supported the development of American music by commissioning new scores and using established scores by American composers. In this era there was a large focus on European composers, at least in terms of what symphony orchestras and opera companies were performing. The American modern dance field was wide open: new, fresh, and looking for inspiration and support from the American music field. Musician and composer Louis Horst influenced generations of modern dancers, many at Bennington, through his dance composition courses. Composers such as Ray Green and Norman Lloyd maintained long-term connections to the dance field.

Designer Arch Lauterer introduced ground-breaking ideas in terms of design that Alwin Nikolais mentioned specifically as being a great influence but that undoubtedly affected other students at the Bennington School of the Dance as well. Lauterer had expansive ideas about how best to present dance, using innovation to make even a small space "dance-friendly." He presented original ideas in terms of lighting dance as well.

Although the Bennington School of the Dance is frequently men-

Martha Hill (left), Ben Belitt, and Bessie Schönberg at the Bennington School of the Dance at Mills College, 1939 (photograph by Ralph Jester, courtesy the Juilliard School, by permission of Lois Jester).

tioned in dance history texts, it is often hardly more than a footnote. The extent of its influence on a broad expanse of the dance field (and related fields) is undeniable, a powerful and distinct legacy.

Final Words

As a student at Juilliard in the late 1980s, Martha Hill was my teacher for a course called Senior Seminar. One of my strongest memories of Hill is her talking about dance and dancers in a very personal manner. What to me had been names and events from a history book, to her were personal friends and experiences. Her stories made history very immediate and inspired me on my current path of exploring personal experience and personal voice in dance — to recognize the humanness in the great artist and their followers in an effort to understand their contributions in a multidimensional manner.

The recollected memories from the Bennington School of the Dance speak volumes about the early days of the modern dance movement. As staff member Mary Shaw Schlivek recalls: "The whole field of modern dance was coming into being at that time, and everyone felt it. The atmosphere of the Bennington School of the Dance was absolutely vibrant. All of us were having so much fun."[8] And they worked very, very hard. It was a fortuitous time and place where passions ran high, and commitment was intensely strong in spite of the financial constraints related to the era of the Great Depression. Martha Hill and Mary Josephine Shelly brought people together to study and create, to learn and grow in a climate of freedom and deep artistic stimulation. Despite multitudes of problems, they kept at it summer after summer for nine years. The lists of works premiered (see appendix) and students who went on to forge their own important paths in schools, universities, and dance companies are numerous, and the effects profound and far-reaching.

The school began with a thought from President Leigh that the plant of Bennington College should be used during the summer, and that thought developed into a school that ignited the American modern dance movement, one of the few distinctly American art forms. It is a reminder that one or two or three people can start a project that will affect the course of history, for the Bennington School of the Dance certainly did this, despite its humble beginnings in a small, quiet Vermont town during the Great Depression.

Appendix A

Timeline of Dance Premieres and Other Historic Events

[Originally developed by Martha Hill with some later editing and additions.]

1935

- *Panorama*
  Choreographed by Martha Graham
  Music by Norman Lloyd
  Set design by Arch Lauterer
  Mobiles by Alexander Calder
- *New Dance*
  Choreographed by Doris Humphrey and Charles Weidman
  Music by Wallingford Riegger
  Costumes by Pauline Lawrence
- *Sinister Resonance*
  Choreographed by Tina Flade
  Music by Henry Cowell

1936

- *With My Red Fires*
  Choreography by Doris Humphrey
  Music by Wallingford Riegger
  Costumes by Pauline Lawrence
- *Quest*
  Choreography by Charles Weidman
  Music by Norman Lloyd
- Also in 1936, it is of special significance, in describing the free style and policy of Bennington, to note that Ballet Caravan, the first touring company of what is now the New York City Ballet, gave its performances at Bennington and presented demonstrations to the community that summer.

289

1937

- *Immediate Tragedy*
  Choreography by Martha Graham
  Music by Henry Cowell
- *Opening Dance*
  Choreography by Martha Graham
  Music by Norman Lloyd
- *Trend*
  Choreography by Hanya Holm
  Music by Wallingford Riegger and Edgard Varèse

The Bennington Fellows Concert included new works by Esther Junger, Louise Kloepper, and José Limón:

- *Dance to the People*
  Choreographed by Esther Junger
  Music by Jerome Moross
- *Ravage*
  Choreographed by Esther Junger
  Music by Harvey Pollins
- *Festive Rites*
  Choreographed by Esther Junger
  Music by Morris Mamorsky
- *Danza de la Muerte*
  Choreographed by José Limón
  Music by Henry Clark and Norman Lloyd
- *Opus for Three and Props*
  Choreographed by Esther Junger and José Limón
  Music by Dmitri Shostakovitch
- *Façade-Esposizione Italiana*
  Choreographed by Anna Sokolow
  Music by Alex North

1938

- *American Document*
  Choreographed by Martha Graham
  Music by Ray Green
- *Dance of Work and Play*
  Choreography by Hanya Holm
  Music by Norman Lloyd

- *Dance Sonata*
  Choreography by Hanya Holm
  Music by Harrison Kerr
- *Passacaglia and Fugue in C Minor*
  (Also called *Passacaglia in C Minor*)
  Choreography by Doris Humphrey
  Music by J.S. Bach
  Costumes by Pauline Lawrence
- *Opus 51*
  Choreography by Charles Weidman
  Music by Vivian Fine

The Bennington Fellows Concert included new works by Eleanor King, Anna Sokolow, and Marian Van Tuyl:

- *Ode to Freedom*
  Choreographed by Eleanor King
  Music by John Colman
  Voices and Percussion arranged by Norman Lloyd
- "Bonja Song" from *American Folk Suite*
  Choreographed by Eleanor King
  Music arranged by Esther Williamson
- *Earth Saga*
  Choreographed by Louise Kloepper
  Music by Esther Williamson
- *Romantic Theme*
  Choreographed by Louise Kloepper
  Music by Harvey Pollins
- *Statement of Dissent*
  Choreographed by Louise Kloepper
  Music by Gregory Tucker
- *Out of One Happening*
  Choreographed by Marian Van Tuyl
  Music by Gregory Tucker

1939

(at Mills College)

Lecture demonstrations by the artists of the faculty and informal presentation of new works by José Limón, Ethel Butler:

- *Ceremonial Dance*
  Choreographed by Ethel Butler
  Music by Ralph Gilbert
- *The Spirit of the Land Moves in the Blood*
  Choreographed by Ethel Butler
  Music by Carlos Chavez
- *Danzas Mexicanas*
  Choreographed by José Limón
  Music by Lionel Nowak

1940

(The Bennington School of the Dance became the Bennington School of the Arts.)

- *El Penitente*
  Choreography by Martha Graham
  Music by Louis Horst
  Set Design by Arch Lauterer
  Costumes by Edythe Gilfond
- *Letter to the World*
  Choreography by Martha Graham
  Text by Emily Dickinson
  Music by Hunter Johnson
  Set Design by Arch Lauterer
  Costumes by Edythe Gilfond
- *Insubstantial Pageant—A Dance of Experience*
  Choreographed by Erick Hawkins
  Music by Lehman Engel
- *Liberty Tree*
  Choreographed by Erick Hawkins
  Music by Ralph Gilbert
- *Yankee Bluebritches—A Vermont Fantasy*
  Choreography by Erick Hawkins
  Music by Hunter Johnson

1941

- *Punch and the Judy*
  Choreography by Martha Graham

Music by Robert McBride
Set design by Arch Lauterer

- *Decade*
  Choreography by Doris Humphrey and Charles Weidman
  Musical arranger, director and pianist, Lionel Nowak
  Music by Aaron Copland
- *In Time of Armament*
  Choreography by Erick Hawkins
  Music Hunter Johnson

(Pearl Harbor — December 7, 1941)

1942

- *Seeds of Brightness*
  Choreographed by Jean Erdman and Merce Cunningham
  Music by Norman Lloyd
- *Credo in Us*
  Choreographed by Jean Erdman and Merce Cunningham
  Music by John Cage
- *Renaissance Testimonials*
  Choreographed by Merce Cunningham
  Music by Maxwell Powers
- *The Transformations of Medusa*
  Choreographed by Jean Erdman
  Music by Louis Horst
- *Ad Lib*
  Choreographed by Jean Erdman and Merce Cunningham
  Music by Gregory Tucker

Appendix B

Students, Faculty/Staff and Audiences, 1934 to 1942

Developed from Mary Josephine Shelly's reports of 1940 and 1941. The 1942 figures are from the advance bulletin of 1942 and Kriegsman's book Modern Dance in America: The Bennington Years. (There are few statistics available for 1942.)

	1934	*1935*	*1936*	*1937*	*1938*	*1939*	*1940*	*1941*	*1942*
# of students	103	132	148	147	150	170	110*	126**	70†
Age range	15–49 av. 27	16–50 av. 26	15–48 av. 26	16–44 av. 26	16–41 av. 25	16–48 av. 26	16–47 av. 24	15–44 av. 22	
male students	0	2	11	4	8	5	32	17	
# of states	26	27	29	31	34	29	27	28	
East	59%	57%	55%	41%	40%	16%	60%	60%	
Midwest	27%	28%	32%	38%	27%	24%	20%	20%	
South	8%	8%	7%	12%	20%	5%	15%	15%	
Far West	5%	6%	6%	8%	11%	50%	5%	4%	
% students classified as teachers	66%	58%	66%	66%	65%	70%	32% (Dance 38%)	38% (Dance 42%)	
# of faculty and staff	23	33	36	40	52	28	65	59	24†
Audience numbers at public perf. at College Theatre and Armory	437	1000†	2500†	2000†	3800†	1000 (demonstrations only)	Dance 1,212 Drama 1,065 Music 680	Dance 2,273 Drama: no figures for this year Music 510	

*Dance 75, drama 15, music 13, design 7. **Dance 90, drama 14, music 17, design 5.
†Approximate.

294

Appendix C

Biographies of Contributors of Recollections

(Whose biographies do not appear in other parts of the book)

Ben **Belitt** (1911–2003) was born in New York City and received his undergraduate and masters degrees from the University of Virginia. He began teaching at Bennington College in 1938, and stayed there until retirement. Belitt wrote several books of poetry and essays and also translated other writers' works. A great friend to modern dance, he was influential in dancers using text as accompaniment and inspiration for their choreography.

Ethel **Butler** (1913–1996) studied with Martha Graham at the Neighborhood Playhouse, then joined the Martha Graham Dance Company in 1933. She was at the Bennington School of the Dance in 1935 as a company member for Martha Graham, then in 1938–1942 as a company member and assistant teacher or teacher of Graham technique. In the mid 1940s, after leaving the Graham Company, she began teaching and choreographing in Washington D.C., first at Howard University and the Georgetown Day School, then from 1946 to 1978 in Bethesda, Maryland, at her own studio. She was a founder of The Performing Arts Guild in Washington, D.C. Her students include Paul Taylor and Dan Wagoner.

Marian Van Tuyl **Campbell** (1907–1987) was born in Wascousta, Michigan, and received her bachelor's degree in education from the University of Michigan in 1928. She taught dance at the University of Chicago from 1928 to 1938, during which time she spent summers as a student at the Bennington School of the Dance from 1934 to 1937, and a fellow in 1938. In 1938, Campbell also became the founding director of the Dance Department at Mills College where she would remain until 1970, with intermittent leaves from 1947 to 1950 and from 1956 to 1963. She had her own dance company that toured extensively in the 1940s primarily through the North-west and Southwest. In addition to editing and publishing *Impulse, an Annual of Contemporary Dance,* she edited two books: *Modern Dance Forms in Relation to Other Arts* and *An Anthology of Impulse.* Campbell was also a founder of the Congress on Research in Dance.

Hermine Sauthoff **Davidson** (1910–2007) was born in Madison, Wisconsin, and was one of the first graduates of the dance program in the Physical Education Department at the University of Wisconsin under the direction of Margaret H'Doubler. She taught in the Physical Education Departments of Ohio State University as well as New York University from which she earned her master's degree under Martha Hill. She had additional dance studies at the Martha Graham Studio and attended the Bennington School of the Dance in 1935. During World War II, she served in the American Red Cross, and after the war worked as a supervisor of elementary and high school physical education and organizer of women's sports and adult recreation programs for the Madison, Wisconsin School District. She was an avid square dancer and caller.

Jean **Erdman** (1916–) first studied dance in Hawaii, learning ancient hula, tap, and Isadora Duncan dance. She attended Sarah Lawrence College where she met her husband Joseph Campbell, the noted scholar, and also first encountered Martha Graham. She was a member of the Martha Graham Dance Company from 1938 to 1942, during which time she would originate many roles. A student at the Bennington School of the Dance in 1937, she would return as a member of the Martha Graham Dance Company from 1940 to 1942. She left the Graham Company in 1942, after which she choreographed extensively, amassing more than fifty dances and total-theatre works.

Vivian **Fine** (1913–2000) was a composer and pianist. Born in Chicago, at age 5 she was awarded a scholarship to the Chicago Musical College. She was a student of Djane Lavoie-Herz and Ruth Crawford, who would introduce her to Imre Weisshaus, Dane Rudhyar, and Henry Cowell, all of whom became her supporters. She composed over 140 works during the course of her career. In the dance world, she was an accompanist for Doris Humphrey, Charles Weidman Gluck Sanders, and Maria-Theresa Duncan. She played for performances at the Bennington School of Dance in 1934 and 1935, and was there all summer in 1938 when she composed the music for Charles Weidman's *Opus 51.*

Eve **Gentry** (1909–1994), birth name Henrietta Greenhood, grew up in San Bernadino, California. Martha Graham saw her perform in Los Angeles and offered her a scholarship in New York City. Gentry would go on to dance with Hanya Holm's dance company from 1936 to 1942, later establishing her own company, Eve Gentry Dancers. She attended the Bennington School of the Dance in 1937, 1938, and 1940 as a member of Hanya's Holm's company, and taught Holm technique in 1942. Gentry was a founder of the Dance Notation Bureau and an original faculty member at New York City's High School of Performing Arts. She studied with Joseph Pilates, teaching "contrology" at the Pilates Studio in New York. Gentry later taught the Pilates method at New York University and in New Mexico where she established the Institute for the Pilates Method of Physical Conditioning.

Martha **Graham** (1894–1991) was born in Pennsylvania, but moved with her family to California at age 10. She began studying at the Denishawn School in 1916, joining the company in 1919. It was at Denishawn that she met Louis Horst who became a major influence on her development as an artist and choreographer. She left Denishawn in 1923, to pursue her own visions — her first solo concert was in 1926. Graham was at the Bennnington School of the Dance every year from 1934 to 42, premiering experimental and important work such as *American Document*. She was a major force in the dance world most of her adult life, grooming countless other artists (Merce Cunningham and Paul Taylor to name but two) and making enormous contributions to modern dance repertoire such as *Appalachian Spring, Diversion of Angels*, and *Night Journey*. She received the Presidential Medal of Freedom in 1976.

Nancy McKnight **Hauser** (1909–1990) was born in Great Neck, New York. She studied with Hanya Holm, Louise Revere Morris, Doris Humphrey, and Charles Weidman from 1926 to 1936, and danced with the Hanya Holm Dance Company from 1932 to 1936. She was an assistant to Hanya Holm at the Bennington School of the Dance from 1934 to 1936 and also assisted Tina Flade in 1935. She taught at numerous colleges and universities including Carleton College, Macalester College, and the University of Minnesota. She ran her own dance company, Nancy Hauser Dance Company, from 1968 to 1990 in Minneapolis and taught numerous students at the Nancy Hauser Dance School, including Ralph Lemon and Sara Pearson.

Hanya **Holm** (1893–1992) was born in Germany, birth name — Johanna Eckert. She studied at the Institute of Emile Jacques-Dalcroze as a young adult, and then at age 28 began studying with Mary Wigman. She was soon a dancer and teacher for Wigman, and in 1931, when Wigman was asked to start a school in the United States, she sent Holm. The school originally carried Wigman's name, but later was called the Hanya Holm Studio. She contributed greatly to the establishment of modern dance in the United States, and was also an enormously successful Broadway choreographer of such shows as *My Fair Lady* and *Kiss Me Kate*. Well-known students include Mary Anthony, Don Redlich, and Alwin Nikolais. One of the principal four choreographers and teachers at the Bennington School of the Dance, Holm was on faculty 1934 and 1936–1940, after which she began teaching summer dance sessions at Colorado College.

Doris **Humphrey** (1895–1958) was born in Oak Park, Illinois, and grew up in Chicago. She showed talent early on in her childhood dance classes, and began teaching as a teenager. In 1917, she traveled to California to study at the Denishawn School. Before long, she joined the teaching staff and the company. Along with Charles Weidman and Pauline Lawrence whom she had met at Denishawn, Humphrey left to follow a new vision in 1928. With her partner Weidman, she became a major leader in establishing the new form of modern dance through her acclaimed choreography as well as her expert teaching. Humphrey was a member of the Juilliard dance faculty from 1951 until her death in 1958 and authored the essential dance composition treatise *The Art of Making Dances*. One of the principal four choreographers and teachers at the Bennington School of the Dance, Humphrey was on faculty 1934–1940.

Eleanor **Lauer** (1915–1986) grew up in Iowa. Pursuing her undergraduate degree at the University of Chicago, she majored in English, but also studied dance with Marian Van Tuyl. She was a member of Van Tuyl's dance company in the 1930s and 1940s, and was a student at the Bennington School of the Dance in 1937 and 1938 performing in Van Tuyl's dances. She went to Mills in 1938 to work on her master's degree and received the first MA degree offered in dance from Mills in 1940 at which time she joined the dance faculty. She later chaired the Dance Department from 1950 until her retirement in 1981. A founding member of the California Dance Educators Association in 1972, she received an award from

CDE in 1983. Well-known students include Molissa Fenley and Trisha Brown.

Eugene **Loring** (1911–1982) was born in Milwaukee, Wisconsin, birth name — Le Roy Kerpestein. As a child, he studied gymnastics, piano, and drama. He moved to New York in 1934 and began studying at George Balanchine and Lincoln Kirstein's School of American Ballet. He danced with Balanchine's first company, American Ballet, and then Ballet Caravan in 1936. Ballet Caravan performed at the Bennington School of the Dance in 1936 and 1937. In 1938, Loring choreographed his well-known ballet *Billy the Kid*, and he joined Ballet Theatre in 1939. In addition to choreographing ballets, he also choreographed for Broadway shows and for film. In 1965, he took the position of chair of the Department of Dance at the University of California at Irvine, and would remain until his retirement in 1981.

Sophie **Maslow** (1911–2006) was an American choreographer, modern dancer, and teacher. As a founding member of the New Dance Group, she helped to define and establish it as a performance entity dedicated to using dance to make social and political statements. She choreographed and performed extensively with the Dudley-Maslow-Bales Trio. Maslow's works set to folk music, such as *Folksay* and *Dust Bowl Ballads* were especially popular. She was at the Bennington School of the Dance and School of the Arts as a member of Martha Graham's dance company in 1935, 1938, 1940, and 1942, and in 1948 she performed and was a faculty member at the first Connecticut College School of the Dance/American Dance Festival.

Ruth Lovell **Murray** (1900–1991) was born in Detroit, Michigan. She attended the Detroit Normal School, majoring in physical education, and received a credential to teach elementary school. At the Detroit Normal School, she learned the [Louis] Chaliff method of dancing that combined "ethnic" dance with ballet positions. She received her bachelor's and master's degrees from Teachers College in New York City, and also studied at the Humphrey-Weidman school. She attended the New York University summer camp where Martha Hill was teaching in 1933, and was at the Bennington School of the Dance in 1934 and 1937. Murray authored the book *Dance in Elementary Education: A Program for Boys and Girls* and taught at the Detroit Teachers College (which became Wayne State University) for 46 years, starting in 1928.

Alwin **Nikolais** (1910–1993) was first a musician before becoming a dancer and choreographer. Born in Connecticut, he studied piano and organ, and one of his first jobs was playing the organ for silent movies. After seeing a performance by Mary Wigman, he became very intrigued by modern dance, and attended the Bennington School of the Dance from 1937 to 1939. His first fully produced work was *Eight Column Line* in 1940, the start of a career in which he would become known for emphasizing all aspects of theatre in his work. In 1948, he was appointed the director of Henry Street Settlement Playhouse which became a home for his dance company. He worked closely with Murray Louis, and the two would lead the company to international acclaim and success.

Lionel **Nowak** (1911–1995) was an American composer and pianist. He was born in Ohio and studied at the Cleveland Institute of Music from 1929 to 1936. He interviewed at Bennington in summer of 1938 for the position of musical director of the Humphrey-Weidman Company, a position he would hold until 1942. He was at the Bennington School of the Dance in that position in 1939, 1940 and 1941. He wrote the score for José Limón's *Danzas Mexicanas,* which premiered at the Bennington School of the Dance (held at Mills College) in 1939. Nowak was a faculty member at Bennington College from 1948 to 1993.

Claudia Moore **Read** (1913–2002), born in Concord, North Carolina, was a 1934 graduate of the North Carolina College for Women, now the University of North Carolina at Greensboro. Her dance teacher was Minna Lauter, and Read joined the Dance Club under Lauter's direction. After graduating, she applied to the University of Nebraska to teach modern dance and was hired, but realized she needed to learn more about modern dance, so she went to the Bennington School of the Dance in the summer of 1934. She returned to Bennington in 1938 to be in the *Passacaglia* Workshop and then again in 1939. She moved to New York where she danced at the Humphrey-Weidman studio and was an understudy for the Humphrey-Weidman Company. When the Humphrey-Weidman Company went on tour, she would teach the classes and keep the studio running. In 1940, she taught the Weidman technique classes at the Bennington School of the Dance, and she assisted Doris Humphrey in 1941. Read received her masters degree from New York University in 1942. In addition to teaching at the University of Nebraska and University of Colorado among other universities, Read helped establish a dance major at the University of Mary Washington where she was on faculty from 1945 to 1975.

Helen Priest **Rogers** (1913–1999) was born in Ogdensburg, New York. She attended St. Lawrence University for two years, then finished her education (bachelor's and master's) at Columbia's New College where Mary Josephine Shelly was head of the Physical Education Department. She was a student at the Bennington School of the Dance in 1934, 1935, 1938, and 1939, and was a member of Graham's auxiliary company in 1935 and 1938. In 1940, she was part teacher and part student because she taught a dance notation course. Rogers was one of the founders of the Dance Notation Bureau in 1940. In addition to her interests in notation, Rogers oversaw the filming of 75 productions for the Connecticut College School of the Dance/American Dance Festival as well as making early films at the Bennington School of the Dance. She held positions at various colleges and was the director of the Dance Program at Mt. Holyoke College from 1953 to 1975.

Mary Shaw **Schlivek** (1915–) was born in Pittsfield, Massachusetts. She entered Bennington College in 1933 and graduated in 1937. In the summers of 1934–1938, she worked at the Bennington School of the Dance as a waitress in the dining room, doing office work, and as head usher. She also took some of the dance classes. From 1937 to 1939, Shaw attended the University of Arizona where she completed a Master of Arts degree in literature. She later worked as a secretary to the Literature Division at Bennington College. Shaw married the photographer and writer Louis B. Schlivek in 1948.

Gertrude **Shurr** (1903–1992) was born in Riga, Latvia, and immigrated to the United States as a child. She studied at Denishawn and danced with the Denishawn Company from 1925 to 1927, after which she joined the newly formed Humphrey-Weidman Company. Shurr left the Humphrey-Weidman Company and joined the Martha Graham Dance Company in 1930 and also began teaching at Graham's school. Shurr assisted Martha Graham in technique classes at the Bennington School of the Dance in 1935, and returned to Bennington in 1938 as a member of Graham's company. She left the Graham Company to join May O'Donnell's company in 1938. O'Donnell and Shurr opened a dance studio where they taught such notable dance figures as Robert Joffrey and Gerald Arpino.

In the 1940s, Shurr received her bachelor's degree from San Francisco State College and her master's degree from the University of Oregon. She taught at New York City's High School of Performing Arts for more than twenty years and co-authored the book *Modern Dance: Techniques and Teaching*.

Anna **Sokolow** (1910–2000) was born in Hartford, Connecticut, but grew up in New York City. In her teens, she studied dance at the Neighborhood Playhouse where her teachers included Blanche Talmud, Bird Larsen, Louis Horst, and Martha Graham. Sokolow joined Graham's company in 1929, remaining until 1937. By 1931, Sokolow had already begun to choreograph and present solos often for union and political organizations, and established her first company, Dance Group of the Theatre Union, in 1933. Two of Sokolow's best known choreographic works are *Rooms* (1955) and *Dreams* (1961). Sokolow taught and choreographed extensively in both Mexico and Israel. In New York City, she taught at The Actor's Studio for several years and was a dance and drama faculty member of Juilliard for more than thirty years (starting in 1957), deeply influencing generations of young dancers and actors. She was at the Bennington School of the Dance in 1935, 1936, and 1937, the year she was a fellow.

Dorothy Bird **Villard** (1912–1996) was born on Vancouver Island, where she studied dance as a child with Nelle Thacker of the Cornish School in Seattle, Washington. One summer, Bird traveled to the Cornish School to study dance, and there met Martha Graham. She danced with the Martha Graham Dance Company from 1930 to 1937, and was with Graham at the Bennington School of the Dance from 1934 to 1937, assisting her in technique classes in the later years. Bird went on to perform in numerous Broadway shows, working with such choreographers as George Balanchine, Jerome Robbins, and Helen Tamiris. After retiring from performing, she taught on Long Island for many years. She co-wrote the book *Bird's Eye View: Dancing with Martha Graham and on Broadway*.

Charles **Weidman** (1901–1975) was one of the foremost pioneers of American modern dance. Born in Lincoln, Nebraska, he received a scholarship to the Denishawn School at age 19, soon joining the company. In 1928, he and Doris Humphrey left Denishawn, to follow their own visions. They worked closely together as dance partners with a combined company until 1945 when Humphrey retired from dancing, after which Weidman continued to teach, perform, and choreograph on his own. Two of his most enduring dances are *Lynchtown* and *Brahms Waltzes*. His immeasurable contribution to the dance world was recognized in 1970 by the National Dance Association, which honored him with the Heritage Award. One of the principal four choreographers and teachers at the Bennington School of the Dance, Weidman was present each summer except 1940 and 1942.

Theodora **Wiesner** (1908–1992) was born in Rice Lake, Wisconsin. She was a physical education major at the University of Wisconsin in Madison which is where she discovered dance. After graduating, she did graduate work in dance and physical education at New York University, starting in 1930. She was at the summer graduate camp at Lake Sebago in 1933 where Martha Hill was teaching dance, and took over teaching dance at the camp in 1934. Prior to World War II, she taught at the University of Pennsylvania and the University of Chicago and attended the Bennington School of the Dance in 1935, 1937, 1938, 1939, 1941, and 1942. During the war, she served as a lieutenant commander in the Navy Women's Reserve and as director of emplacement for the Waves in San Diego. She was the director of the Connecticut College School of the Dance/American Dance Festival from 1963 to 1968 and directed the Dance Program at Brooklyn College from 1950 to 1975.

Charles Humphrey **Woodford** (1933–) was the youngest member of the group of Humphrey-Weidman Company principals who combined resources to share an apartment in Greenwich Village during the Great Depression. The household included his mother Doris Humphrey, his father Chief Mate Charles Francis Woodford, Charles Weidman, Pauline Lawrence, and José Limón. He was at Bennington during the sessions of 1936–1938 and at Mills College in 1939. His story is the remembrance of a young child. After serving in the U.S. Navy as a commissioned officer, he joined the publishing firm, Harper & Brothers, as editor, later becoming senior editor at Dodd, Mead & Company. In 1976, he started his own company, Princeton Book Company, Publishers, specializing in dance books and dance DVDs He received an award from American Association for Health, Physical Education, Recreation, and Dance for meritorious service to those professions in 2011. As editor-in-chief, his wife Connie works closely with him, and they both keep in close touch with their grown children.

David **Zellmer** (1918–2004) graduated from the University of Wisconsin in 1940. He studied some dance at the university and began writing about dance. He received a scholarship to attend the Bennington School of the Arts for the summer of 1940 and returned in both the summers of 1941 and 1942. Martha Graham "discovered" him at Bennington, and he danced with her company, originating roles in both *Letter to the World* and *Every Soul is a Circus*. Zellmer joined the Air Force in fall of 1942 and flew B-24 bombers in the South Pacific. After leaving the Air Force, he returned to the Graham Company for a brief period. He later joined the staff of CBS News in New York and worked as a newswriter, editor, producer, and administrative manager for the next 19 years. After his retirement, he wrote the book *The Spectator* about his year in the Air Force in the South Pacific.

Chapter Notes

Chapter 1

1. Reminiscences of Alwin Nikolais (Nov. 7, 1979), p. 4, in the Columbia Center for Oral History Collection (hereafter CCOHC).
2. Martha Hill, "Bennington: An Historic Milepost," 1–15.
3. The quote Hill references is from William Shakespeare's *Julius Caesar.* Brutus says, "There is a tide in the affairs of men. Which, taken at the flood, leads on to fortune." Act 4, Scene 3, lines 218–224.
4. John Martin, *America Dancing,* 175–176.
5. These are the dates that Martha Graham, Doris Humphrey, and Charles Weidman left Denishawn.
6. Margaret Lloyd, *The Borzoi Book of Modern Dance,* 321.

Chapter 2

1. Reminiscences of Martha Hill (March 21 and March 29, 1979), p. 83, in the CCOHC.
2. Reminiscences of Martha Hill (March 21 and March 29, 1979), p. 80, in the CCOHC.
3. Reminiscences of Martha Hill (March 21 and March 29, 1979), p. 79, in the CCOHC.
4. Mary Josephine Shelly, "Bennington and the Dance in America, or The Dance and Bennington (The Improbable Made Real or Turning Point)," c1970s.

Chapter 3

1. Reminiscences of Ruth Lovell Murray (Jan 20 and Feb. 14, 1979), p. 42–43, in the CCOHC.
2. Interview of Eva Desca Garnet by Elizabeth McPherson, Dec. 7, 2011.
3. Reminiscences of Claudia Moore Read (September 29, 1979), p. 30, in the CCOHC.
4. Mary Josephine Shelly, "Bennington and the Dance in America, or The Dance and Bennington (The Improbable Made Real or Turning Point)" c1970s.
5. Bennington College Bulletin, Vol. 2, No. 3: The Bennington School of the Dance at Bennington College, Summer 1934, 6.
6. Sybil Shearer, *Without Wings the Way Is Steep: The Autobiography of Sybil Shearer,* 13–22.
7. Marion Streng was a professor at Barnard College, and Marian Knighton (Bryan) was a professor of at Sarah Lawrence College (founder of dance program).

Chapter 4

1. Reminiscences of Martha Hill (March 21 and March 29, 1979), p. 89, in the CCOHC.
2. Mary Josephine Shelly, "Bennington and the Dance in America, or The Dance and Bennington (The Improbable Made Real or Turning Point)," c1970s.
3. Bennington College Bulletin: The Bennington School of the Dance at Bennington College, Summer 1935: 9.

4. Bennington College Bulletin: The Bennington School of the Dance at Bennington College, Summer 1935: 9.

5. Martha Graham and the Workshop Group Program, Bennington School of the Dance, 14–15 August 1935.

6. Ruth Lloyd, Writings on the Bennington School of the Dance, 1977 and 1981.

7. Warwick was one of only two or three African American attendees of the Bennington School of the Dance. She graduated from Spelman College in 1935, and then taught dance as a faculty member there. She attended the Bennington School of the Dance from 1935 to 1938.

8. Sali Ann Kriegsman notes that there were no students registered for this course. *Modern Dance in America: The Bennington Years*, 233.

Chapter 5

1. Reminiscences of Eugene Loring (September 18, 1979), p. 1, in the CCOHC.

2. Reminiscences of Eugene Loring (September 18, 1979), p. 3, in the CCOHC.

3. Mary Josephine Shelly, "Bennington and the Dance in America, or The Dance and Bennington (The Improbable Made Real or Turning Point)," c1970s.

4. Program. Doris Humphrey and Charles Weidman with their concert groups and students of the workshop of the school. Bennington School of the Dance. August 12 and 15, 1936.

5. Interview of May O'Donnell by Dawn Lille on September 9, 1999.

6. Marion Streng was a professor at Barnard College.

Chapter 6

1. Reminiscences of Anna Sokolow (November 27, 1978, and January 20, 1979), p. 46, in the CCOHC.

2. Mary Josephine Shelly, "Bennington and the Dance in America, or The Dance and Bennington (The Improbable Made Real or Turning Point)," 1970s.

3. Narrative developed from interview of Helen Alkire by Elizabeth McPherson, July 13, 2008.

Chapter 7

1. Reminiscences of Ethel Butler (April 21, 1979), p. 94, in the CCOHC.

2. Mary Josephine Shelly, "Bennington and the Dance in America, or The Dance and Bennington (The Improbable Made Real or Turning Point)," c1970s.

3. Narrative developed from interview of Jeanne Hays Beaman by Elizabeth McPherson, January 28, 2011.

4. Charlotte Moton (married name Kennedy and then Hubbard) was one of only two or three African American students at the Bennington School of the Dance. She graduated from the Sargent School of Physical Education in 1934, then was an instructor at the Hampton Institute working with Charles Williams. She attended the Bennington School of Dance in 1938.

5. Bennington College Bulletin: The Bennington School of the Dance at Bennington College, Summer 1938: 1.

Chapter 8

1. José Limón, *José Limón: An Unfinished Memoir*, 1999, 90.

2. Reminiscences of Ruth and Norman Lloyd (January 23, 1979), p. 81, Vol. I in the CCOHC.

3. Mary Josephine Shelly, "Bennington and the Dance in America, or The Dance and Bennington (The Improbable Made Real or Turning Point)," 1970s.

4. Narrative developed from interview via telephone of Anna Halprin by Elizabeth McPherson, June 23, 2009.

Chapter 9

1. Reminiscences of Ruth and Norman Lloyd (January 23, 1979), p. 89, Vol. I in the CCOHC.
2. Mary Josephine Shelly, Bennington College, Reports of Officers, 1939–1940, Vol. VIII, No. 3.
3. The *New York Times* Rotogravure Picture Section, August 11, 1940, 2.
4. *PM's Weekly* (PM Sunday Edition), August 18, 1940, 61–63.
5. Narrative based on interview by email correspondence of Ann Hutchinson Guest by Elizabeth McPherson, August 25 and September 8, 2008 as well as by telephone July 16, 2011.

Chapter 10

1. Reminiscences of Ruth and Norman Lloyd (January 23, 1979), p. 77, Vol. I in the CCOHC.
2. Mary Josephine Shelly, Bennington College, Reports of Officers, 1940–1941, Vol. IX, No. 3.
3. Narrative developed from interview by telephone of Joseph Gifford by Elizabeth McPherson, July 14, 2008.
4. John Martin, "The Dance: A Major Work; Martha Graham's 'Letter to the World' a Vivid Study of Emily Dickinson," The *New York Times*, January 26, 1941: X2.
5. These ideas stated somewhat differently are found in: John Martin, *Introduction to the Dance*, 251–263.

Chapter 11

1. Reminiscences of Martha Hill (March 21 and March 29, 1979), p. 96, in the CCOHC.
2. Letter from Doris Humphrey to Eva Desca Garnet, February 1942.
3. John Martin, Excerpt from "Dance: Bennington: Report on the First War Summer at Vermont Center — Current Bills," The *New York Times*, August 23,

1942, X2. "From the *New York Times*, August 21, 1942, © 1942 The *New York Times*. All rights reserved. Used by permission and protected by the Copyright Laws of the United States. The printing, copying, redistribution, or retransmission of this Content without express written permission is prohibited."
4. No official final report has been found for the year 1942. This figure is from Kriegsman, Sali Ann. *Modern Dance in America: The Bennington Years*, 119.

Chapter 12

1. Horst, Louis; José Limón; Pauline Limón; Norman Lloyd; Ruth Lloyd; Bessie Schönberg. Group Discussion on the Bennington School of the Dance, 1959.

Chapter 13

1. David Zellmer, *The Spectator: A World War II Bomber Pilot's Journal of the Artist as Warrior*, 1999, 92.
2. Reminiscences of Alwin Nikolais (Nov. 7, 1979), p. 3, in the CCOHC.
3. Reminiscences of Helen Priest Rogers (May 13, 1979), p. 4, in the CCOHC.
4. Reminiscences of Helen Priest Rogers (May 13, 1979), p. 14, in the CCOHC.
5. Reminiscences of Theodora Wiesner (June 27, 1980), p. 30, in the CCOHC.
6. Reminiscences of Theodora Wiesner (June 27, 1980), p. 32, in the CCOHC.
7. Reminiscences of Ruth and Norman Lloyd (January 23, 1979), pp. 18–19, Vol. 1 in the CCOHC.
8. Reminiscences of Ruth Lovell Murray (January 29 and February 14, 1979), p. 55, in the CCOHC.
9. Reminiscences of Ruth Lovell Murray (January 29 and February 14, 1979), p. 55, in the CCOHC.
10. Reminiscences of Ruth Lovell Murray (January 29 and February 14, 1979), p. 55, in the CCOHC.

11. Reminiscences of Hermine Sauthoff Davidson (September 26, 1979), pp. 37–38, in the CCOHC.

12. Dorothy Bird, *Bird's Eye View: Dancing with Martha Graham and on Broadway*, 104.

13. Audiotaped Interview of Charles Weidman by Billy Nichols, 1965.

14. Reminiscences of Vivian Fine (December 10, 1978), p. 34, in the CCOHC.

15. Reminiscences of Vivian Fine (December 10, 1978), p. 36, in the CCOHC.

16. Reminiscences of Martha Hill (March 21 and March 29, 1979), p. 99, in the CCOHC.

17. Reminiscences of Theordora Wiesner (June 27, 1980), p. 49, in the CCOHC.

18. Reminiscences of Hermine Sauthoff Davidson (September 26, 1979), p. 6, in the CCOHC.

19. Reminiscences of Eleanor Lauer (September 23, 1979), p. 64, in the CCOHC.

20. Reminiscences of Gertrude Shurr (May 14, 1979), pp. 7–8, in the CCOHC.

21. Reminiscences of Dorothy Bird Villard (July 25, 1979), p. 20, in the CCOHC.

22. Reminiscences of Dorothy Bird Villard (July 25, 1979), p. 18, in the CCOHC.

23. Reminiscences of Dorothy Bird Villard (July 25, 1979), p. 19, in the CCOHC.

24. Audiotaped Interview of Holm by Billy Nichols 1965.

25. Reminiscences of Ethel Butler (April 21, 1979), pp. 14–15, in the CCOHC.

26. Reminiscences of Theordora Wiesner (June 27, 1980), p. 26, in the CCOHC.

27. Reminiscences of Sophie Maslow (November 29, 1978, and February 3, 1979), pp.108–109, in the CCOHC.

28. Doris Humphrey, "Martha Hill," *Bennington College Alumnae Quarterly*, 1952: 11.

29. Transcription of Interview of Schönberg by Rose Ann Thom, 1976–77: 126.

30. Reminiscences of Hermine Sauthoff Davidson (September 26, 1979), p. 36, in the CCOHC.

31. Reminiscences of Claudia Moore Read (September 29, 1979), pp. 25–26, in the CCOHC.

32. Reminiscences of Claudia Moore Read (September 29, 1979), p. 26, in the CCOHC.

33. Reminiscences of Claudia Moore Read (September 29, 1979), p. 42, in the CCOHC.

34. Reminiscences of Nancy McKnight Hauser (September 29, 1979), p. 34, in the CCOHC.

35. Reminiscences of Eve Gentry (Henrietta Greenhood) (September 21, 1979), p. 67, in the CCOHC.

36. Reminiscences of Eve Gentry (Henrietta Greenhood) (September 21, 1979), pp. 71–72, in the CCOHC.

37. Reminiscences of Alwin Nikolais (November 7, 1979), p. 5, in the CCOHC.

38. Reminiscences of Alwin Nikolais (November 7, 1979), p. 7, in the CCOHC.

39. Reminiscences of Marian Van Tuyl Campbell (May 10–11, 1979), p. 38, in the CCOHC.

40. Reminiscences of Helen Knight (September 19, 1979), p. 23 in the CCOHC.

41. Reminiscences of Claudia Moore Read (September 29, 1979), p. 21, in the CCOHC.

42. Reminiscences of Claudia Moore Read (September 29, 1979), pp. 22–23, in the CCOHC.

43. Reminiscences of Claudia Moore Read (September 29, 1979), p. 23, in the CCOHC.

44. Interview of Mary Shaw Schlivek by Elizabeth McPherson, September 22, 2011.

45. Reminiscences of Eleanor Lauer (September 23, 1979), p. 34 in the CCOHC.

46. Reminiscences of Eleanor Lauer (September 23, 1979), p. 35 in the CCOHC.

47. Reminiscences of Eleanor Lauer (September 23, 1979), p. 36 in the CCOHC.

48. Reminiscences of Alwin Nikolais (November 7, 1979), pp. 9–10, in the CCOHC.

49. Reminiscences of Alwin Nikolais (November 7, 1979), pp. 9–10, in the CCOHC.

50. Reminiscences of Ruth and Norman Lloyd (January 23, 1979), pp. 38–39, Vol. I in the CCOHC.

51. Reminiscences of Otto Luening (January 23 and February 5, 1979), p. 49, in the CCOHC.

52. Woodford, Unpublished writings on the Bennington School of the Dance, 2011.

53. Transcript of Interview of Bessie Schönberg by Rose Ann Thom 1976–1977: 142.

54. Reminiscences of Helen Priest Rogers (May 13, 1979), p. 25, in the CCOHC.

55. Reminiscences of Lionel Nowak (December 10, 1978), pp. 26–27, in the CCOHC.

56. Audiotaped Interview of Charles Weidman by Billy Nichols, 1965.

57. Martha Graham, *Blood Memory*, 1991: 162–163.

58. Reminiscences of Ben Belitt (February 17, 1979), p. 6, in the CCOHC.

59. Reminiscences of Eugene Loring (September 18, 1979), p. 54, in the CCOHC.

60. Reminiscences of Jean Erdman (July 16, 1979), p. 72, in the CCOHC.

61. Reminiscences of Sophie Maslow (November 29, 1978 and February 3, 1979), pp. 54–55, in the CCOHC.

62. Reminiscences of Eleanor Lauer (September 23, 1979), p. 61, in the CCOHC.

63. Reminiscences of Gertrude Shurr (May 14, 1979), pp. 4–5, in the CCOHC.

64. Reminiscences of Gertrude Shurr (May 14, 1979), pp. 5–6, in the CCOHC.

65. Reminiscences of Martha Hill (March 21 and March 29, 1979), pp. 89–90, in the CCOHC.

66. Reminiscences of Martha Hill (March 21 and March 29, 1979), p. 94, in the CCOHC.

67. Reminiscences of Martha Hill (March 21 and March 29, 1979), p. 115–116, in the CCOHC.

68. Reminiscences of Martha Hill (March 21 and March 29, 1979), p. 119, in the CCOHC.

69. Martha Hill Video Project, Hong Kong Academy of Performing Arts, 1990.

70. Reminiscences of Alwin Nikolais (Nov. 7, 1979), pp. 1–2, in the CCOHC.

71. Reminiscences of Alwin Nikolais (Nov. 7, 1979), p. 4, in the CCOHC.

Epilogue

1. John Martin, "Martha Graham and Troupe Introduce New Work by Hawkins at Dance Fete Finale," The *New York Times*, August 23, 1948, 14.

2. New York University Bulletin, Vol. XLIX, No. 50, Nov. 14, 1949, 48.

3. Transcript of Interview of Theodora Wiesner by Lesley Farlow, March 8, 1979: 31.

4. Reminiscences of Martha Hill (March 21 and March 29, 1979), p. 94, in the CCOHC.

5. Horst, Louis; José Limón; Pauline Limón; Norman Lloyd; Ruth Lloyd; Bessie Schönberg. Group Discussion on the Bennington School of the Dance, 1959.

6. Reminiscences of Martha Hill (March 21 and March 29, 1979), p. 85, in the CCOHC.

7. Reminiscences of Martha Hill (March 21 and March 29, 1979), p. 78, in the CCOHC.

8. Interview of Mary Shaw Schlivek by Elizabeth McPherson, September 22, 2011.

Bibliography

Alkire, Helen. Narrative developed from interview of Helen Alkire by Elizabeth McPherson on July 13, 2008. Interview was transcribed and edited by Elizabeth McPherson and approved by Alkire.

American Ballet Theatre website. www.abt.org.

American Dance Festival website. *www.americandancefestival.org.*

Anderson, Jack. *The American Dance Festival.* Durham, NC: Duke University Press, 1987.

Bartos, Martha Voice. Reminiscences of Martha Voice Bartos (April 4, 1979) in the Columbia Center for Oral History Collection (hereafter CCOHC).

Battle Creek Normal School of Physical Education Bulletin, 1922–1923. Personal collection of Elizabeth McPherson.

Beaman, Jeanne Hays. Narrative developed from interview by telephone of Jeanne Hays Beaman by Elizabeth McPherson, January 28, 2011. Interview was transcribed and edited by Elizabeth McPherson and approved by Beaman.

Belitt, Ben. Reminiscences of Ben Bellit (February 17, 1979) in the CCOHC.

Bennington College Bulletin, Vol. 2, No. 3: The Bennington School of the Dance at Bennington College, Summer 1934. February 1934.

Bennington College Bulletin, Vol. 3, No. 3: The Bennington School of the Dance at Bennington College, Summer 1935. February 1935.

Bennington College Bulletin, Vol. 4, No. 3: The Bennington School of the Dance at Bennington College, Summer 1936. February 1936.

Bennington College Bulletin, Vol. 5, No. 3: The Bennington School of the Dance at Bennington College, Summer 1937. February 1937.

Bennington College Bulletin, Vol. 6, No. 3: The Bennington School of the Dance at Bennington College, Summer 1938. February 1938.

Bennington College Bulletin, Vol. 7, No. 3: The Bennington School of the Dance at Mills College, Summer 1939. February 1939.

Bennington College Bulletin, Vol. 8, No. 3: The Bennington School of the Arts at Bennington, College, Summer 1940. March 1940.

Bennington College Bulletin, Vol. 9, No. 3: The Bennington School of the Arts at Bennington College, Summer 1941. March 1941.

Bennington College Bulletin, Vol. 10, No. 3: Summer Session, 1942. March 1942.

Bird, Dorothy, and Joyce Greenberg. *Bird's Eye View: Dancing with Martha Graham and on Broadway.* Pittsburgh: University of Pittsburgh Press, 1997. Reprinted by permission of the University Press of Pittsburgh. (See also Villard, Dorothy Bird.)

Brennan, Mary Alice (author); John M. Wilson and Thomas Hagood (eds.). *Margaret H'Doubler: The Legacy of America's Dance Education Pioneer.* Youngstown, New York: Cambria Press, 2007.

Brockway, Thomas. "Dance at Bennington

1932–41." *Quadrille.* Vol. 12, No. 1. Spring 1978, pp. 25–37.

Brockway, Thomas. *Bennington College: In the Beginning.* Bennington, VT: Bennington College Press, 1981.

Butler, Ethel. Reminiscences of Ethel Butler (April 21, 1979) in the CCOHC.

Campbell, Marian Van Tuyl. Reminiscences of Marian Van Tuyl Campbell (May 10–11, 1979) in the CCOHC.

Davidson, Hermine Sauthoff. Reminiscences of Hermine Sauthoff Davidson (September 26, 1979) in the CCOHC.

De Mille, Agnes. *Martha: The Life and Work of Martha Graham.* New York: Random House, 1991.

Einert, Margaret. "Bennington ... July ... 1938: Focal Point of the American Modern Dance." *The Dancing Times.* July 1938, pp. 645–648.

Erdman, Jean. Reminiscences of Jean Erdman (July 16, 1979) in the CCOHC.

Fine, Vivian. Reminiscences of Vivian Fine (December 10, 1978) in the CCOHC.

Garnet, Eva Desca. Interview by telephone of Eva Desca Garnet by Elizabeth McPherson, December 7, 2011. Interview was transcribed and edited by Elizabeth McPherson and approved by Desca.

Gentry, Eve (Henrietta Greenhood). Reminiscences of Eve Gentry (Henrietta Greenhood) (September 21, 1979) in the CCOHC.

Gifford, Joseph. Narrative developed from interview by telephone of Joseph Gifford by Elizabeth McPherson, July 14, 2008. Interview was transcribed and edited by Elizabeth McPherson and approved by Gifford.

Gitelman, Claudia. *Dancing with Principle: Hanya Holm in Colorado, 1941–1983.* Boulder: University Press of Colorado, 2001.

Graham, Martha. *Blood Memory.* New York: Doubleday, 1991.

Gruen, John. *People Who Dance.* Pennington, NJ : Princeton Book Co., 1988.

Guest, Ann Hutchinson. Narrative based on interview by email correspondence of Ann Hutchinson Guest by Elizabeth McPherson, August 25 and September 8, 2008 as well as by telephone July 16, 2011. Interviews were transcribed and edited by Elizabeth McPherson and approved by Guest.

Halprin, Anna. Narrative developed from interview by telephone of Anna Halprin by Elizabeth McPherson, June 23, 2009. Interview was transcribed and edited by Elizabeth McPherson and approved by Halprin.

Hauser, Nancy McKnight. Reminiscences of Nancy McKnight Hauser (September 29, 1979) in the CCOHC.

Hill, Martha. "Bennington: An Historic Milepost." Unpublished paper presented at American Dance Symposium, August 1968.

Hill, Martha. Reminiscences of Martha Hill (March 21 and March 29, 1979) in the CCOHC.

Hill, Martha, and Mary Josephine Shelly. The Bennington College Report of Officers 1933–1934, Vol. II, No. 3: First Annual Report of the Bennington School of the Dance, July 7–August 18. October 1934.

Hill, Martha, and Mary Josephine Shelly. The Bennington College Report of Officers 1934–1935, Vol. III, No. 3: Second Annual Report of the Bennington School of the Dance, July 5–August 17. August 1935.

Hill, Martha, and Mary Josephine Shelly. The Bennington College Report of Officers 1935–1936, Vol. IV, No. 3: Third Annual Report of the Bennington School of the Dance, July 3–August 15. August 1936.

Hill, Martha, and Mary Josephine Shelly. The Bennington College Report of Officers 1936–1937, Vol. V, No. 3: Fourth Annual Report of the Bennington School of the Dance, July 2–August 14. August 1937.

Hill, Martha, and Mary Josephine Shelly. The Bennington College Report of Officers 1937–1938, Vol. VI, No. 3:

Fifth Annual Report of the Bennington School of the Dance, July 2–August 13. August 1938.

Hill, Martha, and Mary Josephine Shelly. The Bennington College Report of Officers 1938–1939, Vol. VII, No. 3: Sixth Annual Report of the Bennington School of the Dance, July 1–August 11. August 1939.

Holm, Hanya. Audiotape. Interview of Hanya Holm by Billy Nichols for The National Education Network — "Four Pioneers." New York Public Radio, c1965. Dance Collection, New York Public Library for the Performing Arts. Used by permission of WNET 13.

Horst, Louis; José Limón; Pauline Limón; Norman Lloyd; Ruth Lloyd; Bessie Schönberg. Group Discussion on the Bennington School of the Dance, 1959. Held at Connecticut College. Moderators Jeanne Schlottman and Martin Masters.

Humphrey, Doris. Letter from Humphrey to Eva Desca, February 1942. From the Princeton Book Company Publishers website: http://www.dancehorizons.com/grapx/dhletter1942.pdf. Accessed December 7, 2011.

Humphrey, Doris. Quoted in "Martha Hill," Bennington College Alumnae Quarterly, 1952, 11.

Johnson, Hazel. Reminiscences of Hazel Johnson (July 30 and August 1, 1979) in the CCOHC.

Knight, Helen. Reminiscences of Helen Knight (September 19, 1979) in the CCOHC.

Kriegsman, Sali Ann. Modern Dance in America: The Bennington Years. Boston: G.K. Hall and Co., 1981.

Lancos, Jonette. Reclaiming Charles Weidman (1901–1975): An American Dancer's Life and Legacy. Lewiston, NY: Edwin Mellen, 2007.

Lauer, Eleanor. Reminiscences of Eleanor Lauer (September 23, 1979) in the CCOHC.

Limón, José. José Limón: An Unfinished Memoir. Lynn Garafola (ed.). Hanover, NH: University Press of New England, 1999.

The Limón Foundation website: www.limón.org.

Lloyd, Margaret. The Borzoi Book of Modern Dance. Brooklyn, NY: Dance Horizons, 1949. Reprint, 1974.

Lloyd, Ruth, and Norman Lloyd. Reminiscences of Ruth and Norman Lloyd (January 23, 1979) in the CCOHC.

Lloyd, Ruth. Writings on Bennington School of the Dance. 1977 and 1981. Unpublished. Used courtesy of Alex and David Lloyd.

Loring, Eugene. Reminiscences of Eugene Loring (September 18, 1979) in the CCOHC.

Luening, Otto. Reminiscences of Otto Luening (January 23 and February 5, 1979) in the CCOHC.

"Martha Hill." Bennington College Alumnae Quarterly, Vol. 3, No. 2. 1952, pp. 10–11.

Martin, John. America Dancing. Brooklyn, NY: Dance Horizons, 1936. Reprint, 1968, 175–176.

Martin, John. "The Dance: A Major Work; Martha Graham's 'Letter to the World' a Vivid Study of Emily Dickinson." The New York Times, January 26, 1941, X2.

Martin, John. "Dance: Bennington: Report on the First War Summer at Vermont Center — Current Bills." The New York Times, August 23, 1942, X2.

Martin, John. Introduction to the Dance. Brooklyn, NY: Dance Horizons, 1939. Reprint 1965.

Martin, John. "Martha Graham and Troupe Introduce New Work by Hawkins at Dance Fete Finale," The New York Times, August 23, 1948, p. 14.

Maslow, Sophie. Reminiscences of Sophie Maslow (November 29, 1978, and February 3, 1979) in the CCOHC.

McDonagh, Don. Martha Graham: A Biography. New York: Praeger Publishers, 1973.

McNally, Tom. Interview with Tom Mc-

Nally by Elizabeth McPherson at the 92nd Street Y, New York City. April 15, 2011.

McPherson, Elizabeth. *The Contributions of Martha Hill to American Dance and Dance Education* (1900–1995). Lewiston, NY: Edwin Mellen, 2008.

Murray, Ruth Lovell. Reminiscences of Ruth Lovell Murray (January 29 and February 14, 1979) in the CCOHC.

Nikolais, Alwin. Reminiscences of Alwin Nikolais (November 7, 1979) in the CCOHC.

Noble, Cynthia Nazzaro. *Bessie Schönberg, Pioneer Dance Educator and Choreographic Mentor.* Lewiston, New York: Edwin Mellen, 2005.

Nowak, Lionel. Reminiscences of Lionel Nowak (December 10, 1978) in the CCOHC.

O'Donnell, May. Interview of May O'Donnell by Dawn Lille on September 9, 1999 in New York City. Personal collection of Elizabeth McPherson.

Read, Claudia Moore. Reminiscences of Claudia Moore Read (September 29, 1979) in the CCOHC.

Rogers, Helen Priest. Reminiscences of Helen Priest Rogers (May 13, 1979) in the CCOHC.

Schlivek, Mary Shaw. Reminiscences of Mary Shaw Schlivek (April 4, 1979) in the CCOHC.

Schlivek, Mary Shaw. Interview by phone with Elizabeth McPherson, September 22, 2011.

Schönberg, Bessie. Transcript. Interview by Rose Ann Thom. 1976–1977. Oral History Project, New York Public Library for the Performing Arts.

Shearer, Sybil. *Without Wings the Way Is Steep: The Autobiography of Sybil Shearer.* 1st ed. Vol. 1. Northbrook, IL: Morrison-Shearer Foundation, 2006.

Shelly, Mary Josephine. "Bennington and the Dance in America, or The Dance and Bennington (The Improbable Made Real or Turning Point)." Unpublished Manuscript. c1970s.

Shelly, Mary Josephine. Bennington College, Reports of Officers, 1939–1940, Vol. VIII, No. 3, (Seventh in series of reports on the Summer Session), First Annual Report of the Bennington School of the Arts at Bennington College, Bennington, Vermont, June 29 through August 17, Summer 1940.

Shelly, Mary Josephine. Bennington College, Reports of Officers, 1940–1941, Vol. IX, No. 3 (Eighth in series of reports on the summer session), Second Annual Report of the Bennington School of the Arts at Bennington College, Bennington, Vermont, July 5 through August 17, Summer 1941.

Shurr, Gertrude. Reminiscences of Gertrude Shurr (May 14, 1979) in the CCOHC.

Siegel, Marcia. *Days on Earth: The Dance of Doris Humphrey.* New Haven, CT: Yale University Press, 1987.

Soares, Janet. *Louis Horst: Musician in a Dancer's World.* Durham, NC: Duke University Press, 1992.

Sokolow, Anna. Reminiscences of Anna Sokolow (November 27, 1978, and January 20, 1979) in the CCOHC.

Sorell, Walter. *Hanya Holm: The Biography of an Artist.* Middletown, CT: Wesleyan University Press, 1969.

Stapp, Philip. Reminiscences of Philip Stapp (October 26, 1979) in the CCOHC.

Van Tuyl, Marian. (See Campbell, Marian Van Tuyl.)

Villard, Dorothy Bird. Reminiscences of Dorothy Bird Villard (July 25, 1979) in the CCOHC. (See also Bird, Dorothy.)

Weidman, Charles. Audiotape. Interview of Charles Weidman by Billy Nichols for The National Education Network — "Four Pioneers." New York Public Radio, c1965. Dance Collection, New York Public Library for the Performing Arts. Used by permission of WNET 13.

Wiesner, Theodora. Reminiscences of Theodora Wiesner (June 27, 1980) in the CCOHC.

Wiesner, Theodora. Transcript. Interview of Wiesner by Lesley Farlow. March 8, 1979. Dance Collection, New York Public Library for the Performing Arts.

Woodford, Charles Humphrey. Unpublished writings on the Bennington School of the Dance, 2011.

Zellmer, David. *The Spectator: A World War II Bomber Pilot's Journal of the Artist as Warrior*. Westport, CT: Praeger Publishers, 1999. Reproduced with permission of ABC-CLIO, Santa Barbara, CA.

Zera, Hortense Lieberthal. Narrative developed from interview of Hortense Lieberthal Zera by Elizabeth McPherson in New York City on July 6, 2008. Interview was transcribed and edited by McPherson and approved by Zera.

Index

Page numbers in **_bold italics_** indicate illustrations.

315

Index

Index